Power Up Your Life
Accessing the Twelve Powers to Achieve Health, Happiness, Abundance, and Inner Peace

Bil Holton, Ph.D. **Cher Holton, Ph.D.**
Paul Hasselbeck, D.D.S.

(adapted and expanded version of *PowerUP: The Twelve Powers Revisited as Accelerated Abilities* by Paul Hasselbeck & Cher Holton)

Prosperity Publishing House

Copyright ©2014 Bil Holton and Cher Holton

All rights reserved.

Reproduction or translation of any part of this work beyond that permitted by Section 107 or 108 of the 1976 United States Copyright Act without the permission of the copyright owner is unlawful. Requests for permission or further information should be addressed to the authors, c/o Prosperity Publishing House, 1405 Autumn Ridge Drive, Durham, NC 27712.

This publication is designed to provide accurate and authoritative information in regard to the subject matter covered. It is sold with the understanding that the publisher is not engaged in rendering legal, accounting, or other professional service. If legal advice or other expert assistance is required, the services of a competent professional person should be sought. *From a Declaration of Principles jointly adopted by a Committee of the American Bar Association and a Committee of Publishers.*

Prosperity Publishing House
Durham, NC

Library of Congress Cataloging-in-Publication Data

Holton, Bil
Power Up Your Life: Accessing the Twelve Powers to achieve health, happiness. abundance, and inner peace / Bil Holton, Cher Holton, and Paul Hasselbeck
    p. cm.
    Includes bibliographical references.

ISBN 978-1-893095-84-7

1. Self Help   2. Positive Psychology   3. Spiritual
II. Title

Library of Congress Control Number: 2013912359

Printed in the United States of America

10 9 8 7 6 5 4 3 2 1

*To all who are brave enough
to claim their Twelve Powers
and use them to master the art of living ...
as they walk the spiritual path
on practical feet.*

There is an extraordinary you at your core. All you have to do is get the ordinary you out of the way by claiming your Twelve Powers at the highest, most elevated level of consciousness. (Bil & Cher Holton)

Table of Contents

Introduction 1
   How the Twelve Powers Operate 4
   How to Read This Guide 6
   Putting It Into Practice 8

FAITH 11
   Putting It Into Practice 22

STRENGTH 27
   Putting It Into Practice 38

LOVE 41
   Putting It Into Practice 52

IMAGINATION 55
   Putting It Into Practice 65

POWER 69
   Putting It Into Practice 82

UNDERSTANDING 85
   Putting It Into Practice 93

WISDOM 97
   Putting It Into Practice 111

WILL 115
   Putting It Into Practice 127

ORDER 131
   Putting It Into Practice 141

RELEASE 143
   Putting It Into Practice 155

ZEAL 159
   Putting It Into Practice 170

LIFE 173
   Putting It Into Practice 182

Save Time by Learning From Our Case Example ... *185*
   The Case Example 185

Appendices 191
    Appendix 1: Historical Background
        on the Twelve Powers 193
    Appendix 2: Additional Commentaries 194
        The Colors Associated with the Powers 194
        Body Locations Associated with the Powers 194

Summary Chart of the Twelve Powers 196

Index 197
Photo/Artwork Credits 203
About the Authors 205
Ordering and Contact Information 207

Introduction

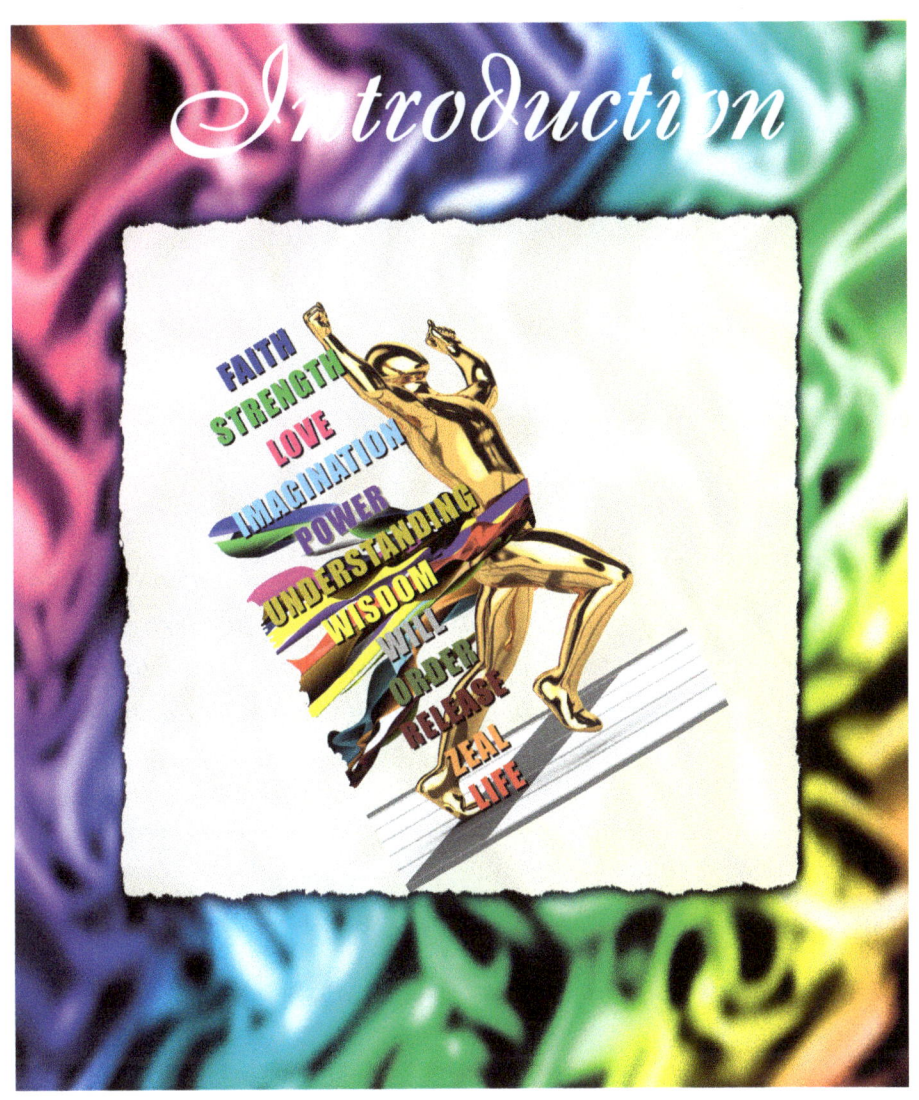

*Whatever you do, or dream you can, begin it!
Boldness has genius, power, and magic in it. (Goethe)*

Within each person there is a new world waiting discovery, a world in which there are capabilities of unlimited strength, perfect knowing, radiant life, and other latent powers beyond our greatest present capacity to conceive.
~ Winifred Wilkinson Hausmann
Your God-Given Potential

Imagine being able to live life more fully, more consciously, more masterfully. Imagine expressing your extraordinary nature in every situation you experience. Imagine being the best person you can be! This guide is designed to give you powerful tools for doing just that—tools that allow you to transform your life.

This book is all about a concept called the Twelve Powers, which are core abilities within each of us that can be called upon to help us handle every life situation from our highest, most elevated level of consciousness. Originally made popular by Unity co-founder Charles Fillmore in his book, *The Twelve Powers of Man*, first published in 1930, the Twelve Powers include:

- FAITH
- STRENGTH
- LOVE
- IMAGINATION
- POWER
- UNDERSTANDING
- WISDOM
- WILL
- ORDER
- RELEASE
- ZEAL
- LIFE

Each Power has a specific purpose, location in the body, and color associated with it. For the purposes of this guide, we will be looking at each Power individually, even though they work together as One. If you think about a medical student who is studying the human body, the student will have classes that focus individually on different areas such as the heart and circulatory system, the skeletal system, our cell structure, the brain, etc. But in the actual practice of medicine, all these areas are closely linked, and a physician must be able to recognize the impact each has on the other. In a similar way, each of our Twelve Powers has a focused role to play, while together they work in concert to support one another as we master the art of living.

This book is an expanded and updated adaptation of the 2010 book, *PowerUP: Revisiting the Twelve Powers as Accelerated Abilities*, by Paul Hasselbeck and Cher Holton. It more fully develops the information describing each Power, and complements it with the sciences of Positive Psychology (founded by Martin Seligman); neuroscience; quantum physics; sociology; positivity; and neurotheology. We believe including scientific research adds depth and credibility to the Twelve Powers, and creates an easy-to-understand guide for the practical application and use of these Twelve Powers to experience abundance, health, inner peace, and joy.

When it comes to human beings, scientists tell us there are two causal forces that work together to help us adapt to the natural world. The implications of neuroplasticity combined with quantum physics cast new light on the question of humankind's place, and role, in nature. At its core, the new physics combined with neuroscience suggests that the natural world evolves through an interplay between two causal processes. The first includes the physical processes we are all familiar with: electricity streaming, gravity pulling. The second includes the contents of our consciousness, including volition. The importance of this second process cannot be overstated, for it allows human thoughts to make a difference in the evolution of physical events (*Schwartz, J.M. and S. Begley, The Mind and the Brain, New York: Harper Perennial, 2002, pg.20*). The activities in this guide are designed to help you actively call on your Twelve Powers in order to use them at your highest, most elevated level of consciousness.

A Quick Peek at the Sciences We Include

Throughout this book, we will be citing various quotes, research findings, and relevant supporting data drawn from a variety of scientific fields. We felt it might be helpful to give you a quick peek at the three major sciences we've included, to help you feel comfortable with them.

Positive Psychology is a recent branch of psychology whose purpose was summed up by Martin Seligman and Mihaly Csikszentmihalyi: "We believe that a psychology of positive human functioning will arise, which achieves a scientific understanding and effective interventions to build thriving individuals, families, and communities." Positive psychologists seek "to find and nurture genius and talent," and "to make normal life more fulfilling," and not simply to treat mental illness *(Martin Seligman and Mihaly Csikszentmihalyi, (2000). "Positive Psychology: An Introduction". American Psychologist 55 (1): 5–141; William Compton, (2005). An Introduction to Positive Psychology. Wadsworth Publishing, pp. 1–22).*

Our study of the current research in Positive Psychology supports our belief that we can, indeed, create our reality by applying the spiritual principles we know. Throughout this guide, we quote various research findings and thoughts expressed by scientists in this field, to help clarify the incredible impact the Twelve Powers can have on our lives.

Neuroscience is the scientific study of the nervous system. Traditionally, neuroscience was seen as a branch of biology; however, it is an interdisciplinary science which collaborates with other fields such as chemistry, biology, engineering, linguistics, mathematics, medicine, computer science, philosophy, physics, and psychology. There is an incredible amount of research that directly applies to the brain, nervous system, and behavior that directly impact the effects of using our Twelve Powers.

Neurotheology is exactly what its name implies: a study of the symbiotic relationship of science and religion. According to Andrew Newberg, in his book *Principles of Neurotheology*, anyone engaging in neurotheology must be open to the perspectives of both science and religion. He continues by saying, "...a crucial element of neurotheology, which really should be true for all academic fields, is a passion for inquiry." Through neurotheological research, Dr. Newberg actually scanned the brains of praying nuns, chanting Sikhs, and meditating Buddhists, studying the relationship between the brain and religions experience. By comparing this with the same brains in a state of rest, he is able to demonstrate the physiological impact of our spiritual practices.

> Positive psychology began as a new area of psychology in 1998 when Martin Seligman, considered the father of the modern positive psychology movement, chose it as the theme for his term as president of the American Psychological Association, though the term originates with Maslow, in his 1954 book *Motivation and Personality*, and there have been indications that psychologists since the 1950s have been increasingly focused on promoting mental health rather than merely treating illness *(Carey Goldberg, (March 10, 2006, Harvard's crowded course to happiness; Secker J (1998). "Current conceptualizations of mental health and mental health promotion". 13. Health Education Research. p. 58.; Dianne Hales (2010). "An Invitation to Health, Brief: Psychological Well-Being" (2010–2011 ed.). Wadsworth Cengage Learning. p. 26).*

How the Twelve Powers Operate

It is our assertion that a person is always using their Twelve Powers, either consciously or subconsciously. Our intention with this guide is to encourage you to begin making conscious choices about how and when you use your Twelve Powers, rather than simply allowing them to function on a default setting. Our aim is to simplify and clarify each of the Powers, creating easily understood and practical ways to apply them in our everyday lives.

It is important to realize that our Twelve Powers do not care how they are used. They are simply spiritual abilities that come from what neuroscientists refer to as the Deeper Self. Psychologists call this "Self" the Authentic Self or Core Self. We call it the Extraordinary You. The Powers are available regardless of who the person is or what the intent might be. According to the latest research in the neurosciences, Dr. Andrew Newberg asserts, "Beneath the mind's perception of thoughts, memories, emotions, and beneath the subjective awareness we think of as the self, there is a Deeper Self, a state of pure awareness that sees beyond the limits of subject and object, and rests in a universe where all things are one" *(Newberg, Andrew, in Born to Believe, Free Press, New York, 2006).*

A good analogy from our physical world is the idea of a table. The idea of a table does not care how it is used. It does not care how much money a person makes, what job the person has, or even what belief system the person practices. It simply is. Each person who uses the idea of a table decides what kind of a table is built in terms of shape, size, color, function, etc.

From a perspective of natural laws, the Law of Gravity is another example. The Law of Gravity works, whether someone is performing an incredible acrobatic feat, dunking a basketball, slipping on a patch of ice, or jumping off a building. There is no judgment on the part of Gravity; it simply does what it does. But the more we understand it, the better we can use it in our favor.

In a similar way, we can choose to use our Spiritual Powers to experience the good, the bad, or the ugly. The choice is always ours. It is much like humor. We could think of humor as the capability to be funny. Each of us determines how we use humor according to our own level of consciousness. Humor does not come with one preset and predetermined way in which it must be used. It simply is. The use of humor is up to the person making the joke and then it is interpreted by the listener. It can be used to uplift, or it can be used to put people down and demean them. We can use it in the highest, most uplifting ways, or we can choose to use it in mean-spirited and hurtful ways. The choice is always ours!

As an aside to the subject of humor, neurotheology admits the crucial importance of humor in understanding the human mind and its ability to deal with an ever changing and confusing world. In fact, "it may be humankind's greatest legacy to be able to look upon an incredibly short lifespan, often filled with anxiety, fears, loss, suffering, and death and still find some way of laughing at ourselves and at the very world which causes us so much angst" (*Newberg, Andrew, Principles of Neurotheology, Burlington, Vermont: Ashgate Publishing, pg. 21*).

As you grow in your understanding of each of your Powers, you will discover the amazing impact they can have on your life. You get to choose how to use them. for example, one of our Powers is IMAGINATION, which can be used to fuel our fear or feed our dreams. Think about how empowering it is to be able to choose which direction you channel your IMAGINATION.

How to Read This Guide

Each chapter of this guide is structured to help you, the reader, understand a particular Power from several points of view. To help with clarity in reading this material, we will always refer to the Power's name in capital letters, so it is clear when we are talking about the Power versus using the same word in a different context.

In addition to describing each Power and sharing examples of how it can be used, we will also explore the impact of a Power when it is either underdeveloped or egocentric. A person exhibiting what we call an "underdeveloped Power" is someone who allows the Power to operate by default. This person fails to call on the Power to effectively handle a situation, and as a result, often experiences consequences that are

Introduction

less than desirable. For example, a person with underdeveloped ORDER might have a very messy home or office. While feeling frustrated about the disorder, he/she does not do anything to correct the situation, and may even feel overwhelmed and helpless with it.

On the other hand, when a Power becomes egocentric in expression, it manifests in an overpowering manner and does not come from the highest, most elevated level of consciousness. When that happens, the resulting consequences are less than desirable. For example, a person with egocentric ORDER might be obsessive compulsive about orderliness in their home or office, and become ridiculously critical if one paper is moved out of place.

Obviously, the goal is to learn how to use each Power from the most elevated level of consciousness, for the highest and best outcomes in your life.

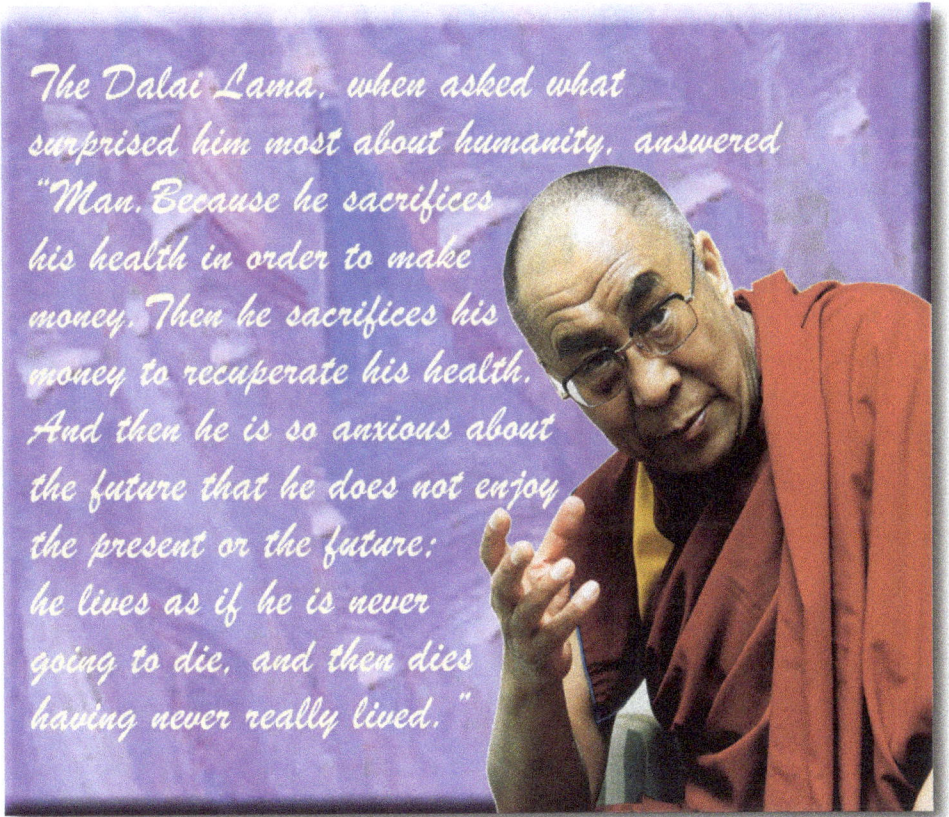

The Dalai Lama, when asked what surprised him most about humanity, answered "Man. Because he sacrifices his health in order to make money. Then he sacrifices his money to recuperate his health. And then he is so anxious about the future that he does not enjoy the present or the future; he lives as if he is never going to die, and then dies having never really lived."

Here's what's really interesting. Even when we use the Powers consciously, they can be used from several levels, which we will explore in detail for each Power. As you read through the four levels we will be addressing, notice that within each level you always have the option of choosing to use the Power in a positive, more effective way, or in a debilitating, less effective way. As we've said a few times already (and you'll hear it often throughout this guide), the choice is always yours!

Here are the four levels we will explore for each Power, as we move through this guide:

- **We can use the Powers from an unconscious level**, based on a cause in subconscious mind which consists of beliefs that are not in our moment-to-moment awareness. This includes choices we make without thinking, when we are operating from an emotional "default" position. If someone asked us why we did something, we probably could not even explain our reasoning. Our embedded theology (the theology of our childhood and other mainstream theological systems we have studied) can create many subconscious beliefs, as can traditions and experiences from our families of origin.

  From a neurological perspective, images of our Deeper Self are unavoidable, but from many theological perspectives, there is no true image of that Deeper Self. Thus, if you cling to your childhood perceptions, you will limit your perception of the nature of your Deeper Self. This is the drawback to any belief system that insists upon a literal image of the Deeper Self. If you limit your vision, you will probably feel threatened by those who have more expanded visions of their Deeper Self *(Andrew Newberg in Born to Believe, Free Press, New York, 2006, pg.104)*.

- **We can use the Powers consciously from our senses,** based on something in physicality we are gleaning through our sight, sound, scent, touch, and/or taste. We may take a free dance class, and because of that experience, decide to pursue dance as an avocation (or decide to never don dance shoes again)! The taste of a certain food may cause us to develop an addiction to it; hearing a certain news broadcast may stimulate us to text in a donation for a worthy cause.

- **We can choose to use the Powers consciously from our human personality,** which psychologists call our ordinary self. This "self" is dependent on thoughts, feelings, attitudes, and/or beliefs held in ordinary consciousness. An example, from a less empowering consciousness, would be a belief in a fear we allow to imprison us.

- **From the highest level of consciousness we can muster, we can choose to use these Powers consciously from our True Identity, or Authentic Self,** based upon Divine Ideas, Laws, and Principles. We employ the Powers in order to more fully express our innate Divine Nature, to be the best person, the most extraordinary us we can be.

Introduction

Putting It Into Practice

The final section of each chapter is devoted to practical ways to apply the Powers in everyday life. As you progress through this intentional study of the Twelve Powers, we encourage you to integrate the powers into your life in a deliberate, conscious way. To do this, we invite you to **choose one specific area in your current experience that you want to create, enhance, or change.** It could be a habit, a skill, a financial issue, a goal to achieve, etc. The key is you will be focusing on this specific item throughout this intentional process, tracking your improvement as you learn how to appropriately apply each new Power. So be sure to choose something really important to you and that you have primary control over! Here are a few specific examples, to give you an idea of what you might select:

- Achieve an ideal body weight/image;
- Create a flow of prosperity (or even more specifically, pay your bills and have enough money for fun things);
- Eliminate a habit such as smoking, nail biting, or dependence on pain medication;
- Learn a new skill, such as dancing or playing the piano;
- Travel more;
- Obtain the right job;
- Go for the Gold! Be the best YOU you can be!

You get the idea! The list of possibilities is endless. So invest some time right now, before you dive into the contents of this book, and decide what you would like to work on during your Power Up experience. Remember—everything begins and ends with mind or consciousness. Do you want to stop something in your life? Use your mind/consciousness. Do you want to start something in your life? Use your mind/consciousness. Once you have decided, capture it in the box on the next page:

The specific area I want to focus on throughout my intentional study of the Twelve Powers is:

_____

_____

_____

I am ready to "Power Up" my Powers and master the art of living!

It is the application of the Powers in your everyday life that deepens your understanding of them. The more you consciously use them, the more practical they become! As you progress through this guide, we know that you will transform your life. It is our hope that you will continue to revisit this book, choosing different aspects of your life to focus on. You can also revisit the material as you grow in your spiritual awareness, because you will discover different 'aha's' even though you are reading the same material.

If you are ready to experience change at the deepest core of your being, you are in the right place with the right book in your hands! Let's begin our journey in exploring the Twelve Powers to master the art of living, as we walk the spiritual path on practical feet!

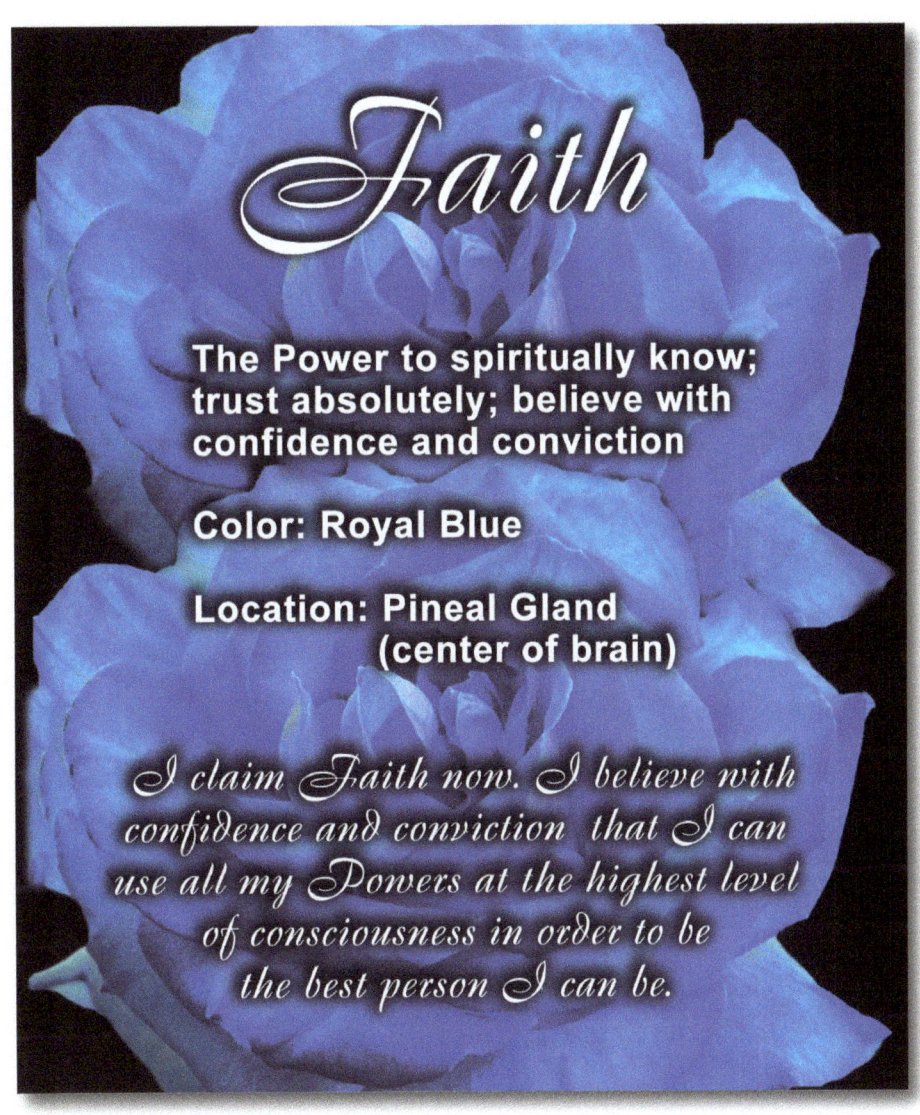

Sometimes your only transportation is a leap of faith.
(Margaret Shepherd)

If faith and reason are both (spiritual) gifts, then they should play complementary, not conflicting, roles in our struggle to understand the world around us.
~ Kenneth R. Miller,
Finding Darwin's God

FAITH

Overview

- Location: At the pineal gland, center of the brain. The pineal gland is sometimes called the master gland. FAITH is located here because FAITH is our ability to believe, and our beliefs determine how we think, feel, and act in any given situation.
- Color: Royal Blue

FAITH is the Power to spiritually know; trust absolutely; believe with confidence and conviction.

From ordinary consciousness: The ability to spiritually know, trust absolutely, believe with confidence and conviction based on our senses, thoughts, feelings, and beliefs. We use FAITH to believe in the law of the land or to believe our fears are real. (When we were kids, we might have believed in a boogeyman under the bed!)

- *Underdeveloped FAITH* results in distrust, doubt, misgiving, skepticism, suspicion, and simply an overall inability to believe anything. It may manifest in a person with an overall inability to believe anything. S/he is always questioning everything anyone else says or does, and often lives in fear, regardless of how much data to the contrary is presented.
    The human brain has the propensity to reject any belief that is not in accord with one's own view. However each person also has the biological power to interrupt detrimental, derogatory beliefs and generate new ideas. These ideas can alter the neural circuitry that governs how we behave and what we believe *(Andrew Newberg in Born to Believe, Free Press, New York, 2006, pg. 9).*
- *Egocentric FAITH* results in being narrow minded, dogmatic, or doctrinaire. These are the folks who walk around with the attitude that says, "My mind is made up! Don't confuse me with the facts!"

From elevated consciousness: The ability to spiritually know, trust absolutely, believe with confidence and conviction based on Ideas, Truths, Principles, and Laws that are Divine in nature. We use FAITH to be the best person, the most spiritual, the most trusting person we can be, regardless of outer appearances.

If we planted an apple seed, can you believe we would actually get an apple tree? If we squeezed an orange, can you believe we'd actually get orange juice?

If we visualize an abundant flow of prosperity flowing from our innate awareness of an aspect of our connection with Divine Substance, can you believe we would actually see a manifestation of prosperity? Ah, that one is a little tougher, isn't it?

Why is it so easy to believe, without doubt, that apple seeds produce apple trees, and oranges produce orange juice—but so difficult to believe we can claim Divine Substance to manifest everything we ever need in terms of our supply? Maybe it has something to do with what we have actually seen and experienced, versus what we have been told, but haven't actually experienced.

This truly is the foundation of FAITH! In John 20:29, Jesus said to Thomas, "…because you have seen me, you have believed; blessed are they who have not seen, and yet have believed."

According to neurotheology, beliefs are usually considered to be based on some data even though the full data set is not available. This is distinct from faith which is generally regarded as being based on very little, if any, physical evidence, and it is strongly adhered to as the basis of a particular belief system *(Andrew Newberg, Principles of Neurotheology, Burlington, Vermont: Ashgate Publishing, pg. 69).*

Believing even when we have not seen: that's FAITH. But it is really important to recognize that FAITH is a powerful essence which we can develop and grow. We get critical of ourselves when it appears we don't have the faith we think we should, and we beat ourselves up. But look at how you handle other growth areas in your life.

If you decide to learn to play the piano, do you sit down and expect to play Mozart perfectly on your first sitting? If you decide to take up golf or tennis, do you expect to walk in and hit the perfect drive or land the perfect serve on your first lesson? If you decide to take up ballroom dancing, do you expect to go out on the dance floor and do a professional-level routine your first day out? Of course not! Whenever we begin a new skill or hobby, we realize there is a learning curve, and we go in expecting—and allowing—ourselves to be bad before we get good! We know we will go through a period of seeing our ability grow, as we willingly put in the time to practice and learn. And we also discover that with each thing we learn, there is another level to tackle. No matter how old you are or how skilled you become, there's always more to learn. Even professionals work with coaches, as they continue to refine and perfect their skills, always pushing the envelop and discovering new and better ways to do things in their chosen field.

Here's an interesting research tidbit that relates to this. Older adults are frequently told in order to keep their mind sharp, they need to stimulate it with activities such as crossword puzzles and reading. But activities done repeatedly become second nature, demanding less attention than new skills do. The result: a brain that gets fewer attention workouts, and thus fewer chances to keep its acetylcholine (a neurotransmitter responsible for focus and paying attention to new experiences) system turned up. And because of the centrality of attention to neuroplasticity, a brain that cannot pay attention is a brain that cannot tap into the power of neuroplasticity *(Sharon Begley, Train Your Mind, Change Your Brain, New York: Ballantine Books, 2007, pg.249)*.

So how does this relate to the development of our FAITH faculty? It's the same process. First of all, you need to know *you never have no FAITH!* In other words, you *always* have FAITH! FAITH is one of the Divine Powers inherent within us. It is *our* responsibility to quicken or strengthen it. So we are really being incorrect when we say, "I lost my FAITH or I don't have any FAITH." You cannot lose your FAITH—you might just have forgotten how to call upon it. The comforting knowledge is that your FAITH is always there, just waiting to be developed.

The FAITH Condo

Emilie Cady, in her masterpiece *Lessons In Truth*, talks about the different levels of FAITH. From her work, we have created a continuum of FAITH, which helps us identify where we are in a certain situation—and also helps us recognize the Truth of where we can be. We use the metaphor of a condo to illustrate how the levels build on one another. Here's how the "Faith Condo" works:

We begin with *Hope, which can pull a person out of the basement of despair. Hope* takes a lot of flack in spiritual circles as a kind of cop out, but we want to go on record saying hope is an important element on our spiritual journey, because hope provides the stimulus to keep people moving forward when otherwise they may give up. It's kind of like our training wheels! And when we don't have a really strongly developed FAITH, *Hope* is the light at the end of the tunnel that keeps our journey going in the right direction! You hear people say things like, "Don't give them false hope." We personally believe there is no such thing as false hope. There are lies and wishful thinking, but if there is hope, it is real and powerful and affirming.

Research supports the idea that believing we are better than we actually are turns out to be neurologically enhancing. It gives us confidence and hope in the most difficult situations; without it, we are more likely to give up. Having a positivity bias helps us to sustain hope, and the part of the brain most activated is the anterior cingulate, a key center for generating compassion *(Brassen, S., Gamer, M., Buchel, C.,*

"Anterior cingulate activation is related to a positivity bias and emotional stability in successful aging," Biological Psychiatry; 2011 July 15; 70 (2): 131-37).

So why don't we just want to operate at the *Hope* level all the time? When we work from a basis of *Hope*, we tend to live in a fearful state, concerned that we may or may not receive. And in the *Hope* state, we fall into the habit of seeing our affirmations, dream boards, and visualizations as magic bullets. If we don't say it just right, or create it perfectly, we won't manifest the result. But it's a start, and we've all been there (and at different times in different situations, we may even revisit!)

We want to move up the FAITH Condo, moving into *Blind FAITH*. *Blind FAITH* is where we move forward, instinctively feeling that wherever we are, God is, and all is well. There is light at the end of the tunnel, and we don't know how or why, but we just believe things will work out. This *Blind FAITH* is higher than *Hope* on our continuum, because it is based on Truth, but we may find a need to reassure ourselves often that it will work; it may be hit and miss, and we may question it often when we don't see the results we expect as quickly as we expect them. But the important thing is that we persist, and continue to hold strong to the Truth we believe and use the tools, even if we aren't sure why. *Blind FAITH* feels kind of like magic—but it is only magic until we know how it is done!

As we grow and learn, we are able to move to the highest level of FAITH— *Understanding FAITH*. This is where we know and understand there are Spiritual Laws as immutable as physical laws seem to be. They both may sometimes appear unpredictable—but only because they are not totally understood.

> Using advanced supercomputers and programming, we simulate the complex interplay of gravity, radiation, and magnetic fields that constitutes the life of stars like the sun. Our goal is to better understand how stars are born, grow old, and die. Fundamentally, we start with the known laws of physics and take them wherever they lead us. The implicit understanding is that nature's rules are eternal, unbreakable, and all-controlling. As Albert Einstein once said, learning to read the laws of physics is like reading the mind of God. Such thinking has animated much of the enterprise of physics ever since Isaac Newton formulated his laws of universal gravitation in 1687: one set of laws for both the heavens and the earth. The idea took full root a century ago, when Einstein developed his general theory of relativity. If we work hard enough, he suggested, we will eventually find the elegant and simple rules that undergird the entire universe. Physicists have taken it as an article of faith that the bedrock laws are there to be discovered, if only we are clever enough in looking for them. The dogged pursuit of that ultimate truth has led to many great discoveries, but recently it has begun to seem like a promise unkept *(Frank, A., "Is the Search for Immutable Laws of Nature a Wild-Goose Chase?" Discover Magazine, April 2010).*

Once we realize that Spiritual Laws operate the same way, we move into that powerful level of *Understanding FAITH*, where we can be just as certain that when we apply Spiritual Laws, we are assured of the results that will follow. And that brings us to one other similarity between our apple seed and our orange analogies: you have to do something to get the desired result. To quote Emilie Cady, as she shared in *Lessons In Truth:*

> One of the unerring truths in the universe ... is that the supply of every good always awaits the demand. Another truth is that the demand must be made before the supply can come forth. [You could have a bank account filled with money, but the only way to access it is to request a withdrawal.] To recognize these two statements of Truth and to affirm them are the whole secret of Understanding Faith—Faith based on principle! [p. 77]

When we operate from *Understanding FAITH*, we can say, "We have the funds and resources necessary to move forward with this project" with as much conviction as we say, "We squeeze this orange and get orange juice!"

A Practical Look at FAITH

FAITH is an innate ability, the vehicle through which each of us believes, intuits, and perceives. Conviction is based on what we believe.

Let's begin by taking a practical look at FAITH in our everyday lives. There is FAITH based on an appropriate interpretation of our senses, thoughts, and feelings:

- We have FAITH based on true information we have been told, learned, and experienced, like having FAITH that a particular set of ingredients, measured, combined, and prepared in a certain way, will produce an incredibly delicious cake that's been a family recipe for generations!

- We have FAITH we can accomplish certain tasks based on our experience. For example, most of us have ridden a bike or driven a car before, and have FAITH we can do it again.

- We have FAITH we can learn new things based upon our past experience of successfully mastering something new.

We also have FAITH that is based on an *erroneous* interpretation or understanding of our senses, thoughts, and feelings:

- There was a person who saw rats squeezing through some very small holes in a fence. Based on his interpretation of that experience, he believed rats had no bones. FAITH in this belief was so strong, no discussion of the fact that a rat is a mammal with an internal skeleton would deter him from this belief.

- Children and adults see scary movies and then, when there is a strange sound in the house, they believe something awful is going to happen.
- Children believe in boogeymen under the bed or in the closet. No matter how much an adult tries to change this belief, a child holds on to it as a means of protection. Consider this illustration: *A young boy lived where there was a detached garage far from the house. Every evening he would put his bike away in the dark garage. Every evening he was fearful when he put the bike away because he believed, had FAITH, that there was someone in the garage who was going to grab him. The boy held on to this belief, and as an adult is still afraid of the dark, even after years and years of putting that bike away with nothing happening. In spite of all the evidence indicating there was nothing to fear, he still held on to the belief.*

FAITH can also show up as prejudices and stereotypes based on the interpretation of information gathered from our senses, thoughts, and feelings.
- A person can have FAITH in one particular car manufacturer or political party, simply based on what was learned from his/her family.

In each of these cases, there is conviction based on where a person places his or her FAITH.

> The term "belief" first appeared in English when it was adapted from the gothic word "galuabjan," which meant, literally, "to hold dear" *(Andrew Newberg, Principles of Neurotheology, Burlington, Vermont: Ashgate Publishing, pg. 35).*

FAITH can also be cultivated from a higher state of consciousness. Again, there can be the simple *Blind FAITH* in God, or a Higher Power, that is somehow working everything out for good despite our clumsy human actions and interventions. Or, there can be an *Understanding FAITH*, based on the knowledge and experience of Ideas, Truths, Principles, and Laws that are Divine in nature.

Astronomer Alan Battenwhich shared a great example of this idea in the *Quarterly Journal of the Royal Astronomical Society,* describing British Astrophysicist Sir Arthur Eddington's spiritual orientation: "He (Eddington) was trying to reconcile, or even unite, the two most important things in his life: the excitement of scientific research and the profundity of his own mystical experience. In each realm alike, he saw himself as a seeker led by an 'Inner Light' *(referenced in Bernard Haisch's book, The Purpose-Guided Universe, Franklin Lakes, N.J.; New Page Books, 2010, pg. 99).*

- In *Blind FAITH*, a person simply trusts that everything is working out for good. There is a kind of abdication of responsibility because the belief is that God or some other external power will somehow intervene. For example, if a person really wants something, and in the moment decides not to buy it, s/he might say something like, "It will be mine if it is meant to be." This expresses the belief of having FAITH in a God or Universe or outside Higher Power that decides whether he/she gets it.
- In *Understanding FAITH*, a person takes more personal responsibility for the understanding and application of Divine Ideas, Truths, Principles, and Laws that are Divine in Nature. This person sees what is wanted and consciously uses the Divine Laws and Principles in order to have it.

FAITH From the Four Levels of Consciousness

Let's look at FAITH in another way. FAITH (along with all the other Powers) can be expressed from four different levels of consciousness:

1. **Unconscious FAITH:** based on a cause in subconscious mind which consists of beliefs that are not in our moment to moment awareness. A person may know the beliefs exist, and simply forget about them during daily activities. For instance, when driving, many women have a habit of stretching out their right arm across the seat when there is a need to stop quickly. It comes from the unconscious belief that the driver had to protect the child from crashing into the windshield (a 'throwback belief' to a time before we had seatbelts and laws about children riding in the front seat).

2. **Conscious FAITH from our senses:** based on something in physicality we are gleaning through our sight, sound, scent, touch, and/or taste. An example would be a man who takes a class in scuba diving, and experiences the way the safety equipment works. He then trusts the equipment and is able to scuba dive confidently.

3. **Conscious FAITH from our human personality:** based on thoughts, feelings, attitudes, and/or beliefs held in ordinary consciousness. A woman has FAITH in the strength of her relationship with her spouse, and experiences no doubts when her spouse needs to travel for business.

4. **Conscious FAITH from our True Identity, or Authentic Self:** based on Divine Ideas, Laws, and Principles. We have FAITH in the Spiritual Principles and use them to be the best person we can be.

So often you hear the phrase "Fake it till you make it." We prefer to say, "FAITH it till you make it!" Have faith that the world of Divine Ideas is one thought away.

Have faith in the 'still small voice'—and the world of Divine Ideas will be opened to you.

Become one with that Deeper Self, the Extraordinary You within you—and the world of Divine Ideas will be opened to you.

Go to Headquarters (that inner sanctuary where you connect with your Authentic Self)—and the world of Divine Ideas will be opened to you.

In his book entitled, appropriately enough, *In the Flow of Life*, Eric Butterworth says: "The great truth taught by the mystics of all ages is our whole existence flows inexorably from a Universal process which is always from within-out … The eternal flow of life is present within us … All we need to do is have faith in that relationship with our Source."

Your inner peace and happiness won't come from Wall Street. Wall Street is not your Source. Your security won't come from government promises. The government is not your Source. Your ultimate happiness won't come from infomercials which tell you their product brings lasting happiness. Advertisers are not your Source.

You are immersed in this guide because you want spiritual answers to human questions. You want answers that work. Answers that will bring joy, and peace, and happiness, and prosperity.

There is only one answer: Have FAITH in your innate divinity. Have FAITH in your connection with your Authentic Self. There is no other way. Go to your Extraordinary Self within, not the egocentric world without.

Raise your consciousness by lowering your material attachments. Go inside. Live from the inside-out.

The truth is FAITH works when we work the Truth principles we know are real.

FAITH works when we close our outer eyes and go to Headquarters.

FAITH works not because someone says it works. It works because it is the rock, the foundation, the internal scaffolding of your spiritual and human beingness. It is the ultimate expression of your belief in your oneness with Spirit.

FAITH is your open sesame to the life you want to build for yourself.

But there's one thing we positively, absolutely understand about the power of FAITH. It's an inside-out process. We know that thoughts underwrite our reality. The power of the universe is localized in our consciousness. **We believe in the power of mind over molecules.**

It is our consciousness which alchemizes thoughts. Our thoughts alchemize beliefs. Our beliefs produce world views. Our world views predispose us to certain kinds of intentions. Our intentions produce choices, and our choices lead to the actions that define our lives. So, we encourage you to remain FAITH-full.

Most people seek external proof *before* they step out on faith. Here's the secret about FAITH-full-ness: People usually don't act contrary to their faith. They act contrary to their profession of faith.

In Buddhist philosophy FAITH is called the "seed" without which no spiritual effort can begin. FAITH includes not only conviction, but also imagination and the will to succeed.

In Sanskrit, the word for FAITH is *shraddha*, which is akin to *cor*, "the heart," in Latin. FAITH is more a quality of the heart than of the mind. It is the knowing of the heart that transcends the intellect.

It is FAITH that grows into intuition, and then flowers into self-realization. This FAITH or *shraddha* is described by Radhakrishnan as not so much the "acceptance of a belief, but the concentration of all of our spiritual powers on an inner knowing."

In the Bhagavad-Gita, Krishna deals with the subject of FAITH in great detail. In the 17th Discourse he tells Arjuna that everyone's FAITH is in accordance with their *svabhava*, their own nature and disposition.

Like the bird that knows when and where to migrate, each of us possesses a spiritual homing instinct. Our souls ceaselessly yearn for FAITH-lifts and a connection to a higher power.

There is a FAITH center within us at a cellular level. That's what Charles Fillmore called it. We believe this FAITH center is our Deeper Self, the Extraordinary Us, our Divine Nature.

Now that you have a better idea of the Power of FAITH, we invite you to practice strengthening it in your own life experience, using the following *Putting It Into Practice* exercises for FAITH.

FAITH:
Putting It Into Practice!

FAITH—Activity One:

Complete the following sentences quickly, without giving a lot of thought to it:

Growing up, I was taught _____

When it comes to goal setting, I realize _____

The last time I affirmed success, _____

I feel like prayer is _____

When things do not go the way I expect, I _____

If I could have a "re-do" in some area of my life, _____
_____

The word "impossible" _____

Now that you have completed the sentences, read back through your responses, and identify underlying beliefs you have that affect the way you make life choices. Over the next week, become aware of how your beliefs are impacting your experience. In your journal, it might look like this:

Experience	Underlying Belief
I got upset when a store clerk was rude to me.	I always get treated badly by service people.
I was depressed because my favorite jeans were tight.	I'm never going to get into shape. I'm fat!
When I didn't get selected to give the presentation for the Executive Briefing, I took it personally.	I am unworthy. I don't deserve anything good. They wanted someone who looks more professional.

As you read through your "beliefs," apply this question: What would this belief look like if it came from my highest and best spiritual perspective? Then practice using that new, revised belief and notice any outward changes in your experience. Your journal might continue:

Revised Belief from highest spiritual perspective	New Experience
Everyone is Divine, including me. I deserve to be treated with respect, & I treat others with respect and love.	Clerk apologized and actually gave me a value-added!
I am beautiful ... I am Divine ...and I deserve to be fit and healthy.	I changed my diet and lost 5 pounds in two weeks! Jenny told me I looked radiant! Wow! I feel radiant!
I am worthy! I deserve the best.	I realized I needed to improve my skills in presentation. It is not personal.

FAITH—Activity Two:

As you think about the specific area you want to work on throughout this development process, **brainstorm a list of your beliefs related to this issue, up until now.** For example, if your area was wanting to learn to dance, beliefs up till now might include: I believe I am way too old to take dance lessons now; I've always been so clumsy; I am not flexible enough to be a dancer; I just don't have the body of a dancer. As you think about your selected area, **what specific beliefs do you need to develop?** Create specific denials and affirmations to support the revised beliefs. (Let's take a moment to clarify denials and affirmations, so we are all approaching it from the same viewpoint! Denials are not an attempt to deny the reality of an event in our lives, or even a feeling we might be having; rather, they are used to deny or release the power we have given an idea, thought, belief, or attitude. Every denial is followed by an affirmation, which is simply a statement of a Spiritual Truth as it relates to us. Affirmations are stated in the first person, and are stated in a positive way.)

For example:

I give no power to age affecting my ability to achieve my goals. I affirm my FAITH in infinite possibilities as I move forward and dance!

Repeat the denials and affirmations you have created five times (yes, five times!) each morning, and five times before retiring for the day. Throughout the day, become consciously aware of any doubts that surface related to your ability to achieve your chosen issue, and immediately upon becoming aware of a doubt, stop! In that moment, repeat your denial and affirmation five times (out loud, if possible ~ depending on where you are)!

Example: Healthy Eating

Throughout this guide, we will have a specific example to help you understand how to complete the activity related to your selected area of improvement. For the purposes of the guide, we will imagine that someone selected the goal of Healthy Eating as the area to improve. We will use Healthy Eating to demonstrate how to work with each Power's "Putting It Into Action" activity. Here is the example for FAITH, Activity Two:

Belief I have had up till now: I have believed I am a carbo-holic, and cannot handle any type of diet that requires a restriction on carb-related foods.

Belief I need to develop: I have FAITH in my ability to choose how much of any one food I eat, and I can manage to keep a healthy amount of carbohydrates in my diet.

Denial: I give no power to the need for excessive carbohydrates in my diet.
My new affirmation: I am in charge of what I eat, and I choose foods that are healthy, energizing, and delicious!

FAITH Affirmation:

*I claim FAITH now. I believe with confidence and conviction that I can use
all my Powers at the highest level of consciousness
to be the best person I can be.*

If you have faith as small as a mustard seed, you can say to this mulberry tree, 'Be uprooted and planted in the sea,' and it will obey you.

~ Jesus
Luke 17:6

Quotes to Inspire FAITH

Faith means living with uncertainty—feeling your way through life, letting your heart guide you like a lantern in the dark. (Dan Millman)

Have faith in the power of your mind to penetrate and release the energy that is pent up in the atoms of your body, and you will be astounded at the response. Paralyzed functions anywhere in the body can be restored to action by one's speaking to the spiritual intelligence and life within them. (Charles Fillmore)

Faith is that quality within us which enables us to look past appearances of lack, limitation, or difficulty, to take hold of the Divine Idea and believe in it even though we do not see any evidence of it except in our mind. Through faith, we know with an inner knowing the Truth that has not yet expressed in our manifest world. (Winnifred Wilkinson Hausmann)

Faith is like radar that sees through the fog, the reality of things at a distance that the human eye cannot see. (Corrie Ten Boom)

My own experience has led me to the knowledge that the fullest life is impossible without an immovable belief in a living law, in obedience to which the whole universe moves. A (person) without that faith is like a drop thrown out of the ocean which is bound to perish. (Mahatma Gandhi)

Faith doesn't influence God "out there" to send riches to fill our needs "down here." Faith is the spiritual capacity by which we may form and shape this ever-present basic element of spiritual substance. Certainly all things are possible, not because God makes an exception for you by reason of your plea, but because your faith is the key to the kingdom of the power within you to apply the laws that transcend human limitations. (Eric Butterworth)

As increasing numbers of people lose faith in the institutions of state and church alike, they often find themselves adrift in a spiritual wasteland. This is the mythic desert space, which, contrary to popular opinion, does not alienate people from God and from meaning, but awakens a renewed sense of the sacred, often setting the seeker on a lifelong journey of spiritual exploration. (Mairmuid O'Murchu)

There can be no great courage where there is no confidence or assurance, and half the battle is in the conviction that we can do what we undertake. (Orison Swett Marden)

*Strength is the capacity to break a Hershey bar into four pieces with your bare hands—
and then eat just one of the pieces.*
(Judith Viorst, Love & Guilt & The Meaning Of Life, Etc.)

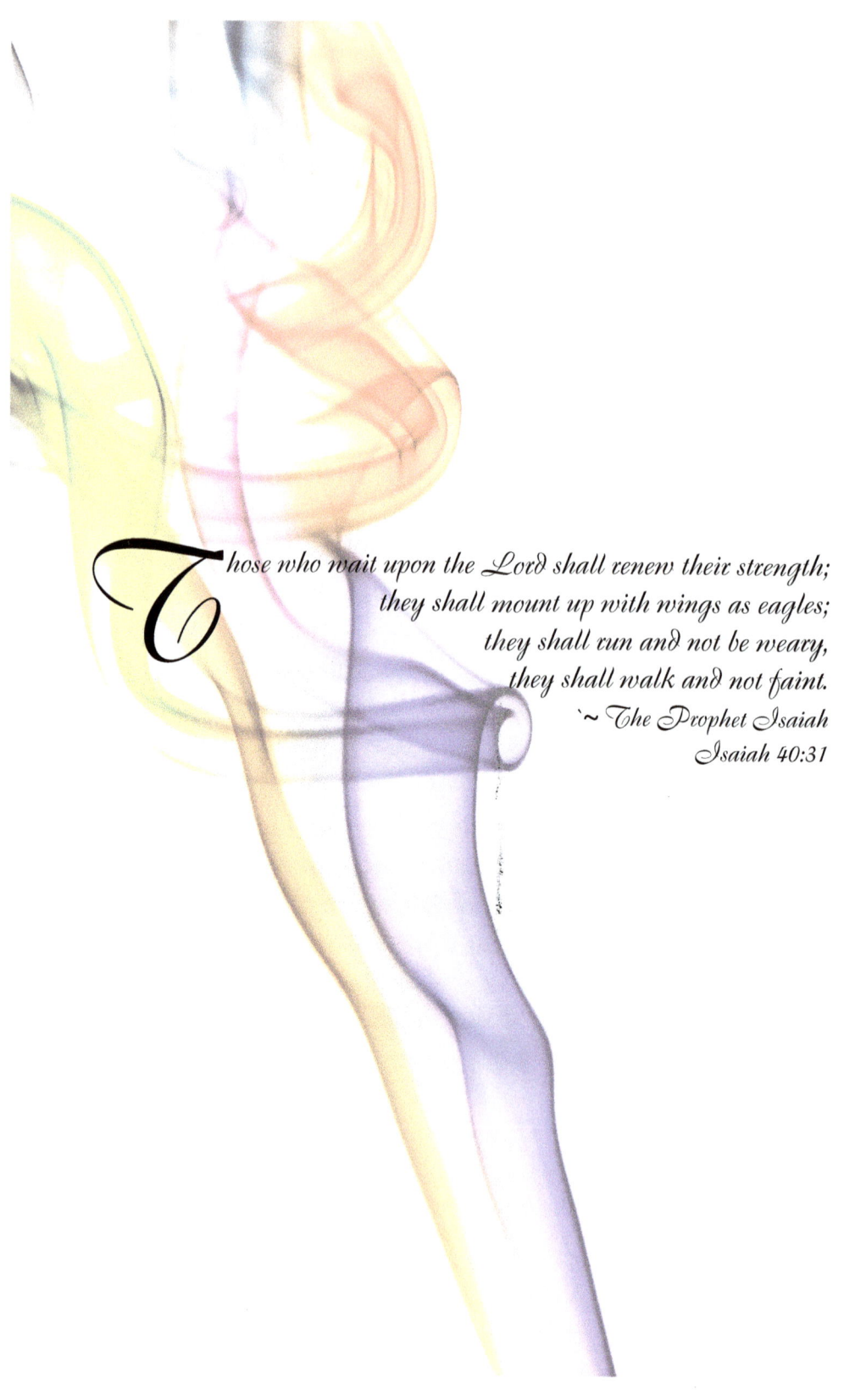

*Those who wait upon the Lord shall renew their strength;
they shall mount up with wings as eagles;
they shall run and not be weary,
they shall walk and not faint.
~ The Prophet Isaiah
Isaiah 40:31*

STRENGTH

Overview

- Location: Small of the Back
- Color: Spring Green
- Linked with FAITH

STRENGTH is the Power to be resilient; endure; persist; stay the course; persevere; and be mentally tough.

From ordinary consciousness: The ability to be resilient; endure; persist; stay the course; persevere; and be mentally tough based on our senses, thoughts, feelings and beliefs. We use STRENGTH to stick to a diet or a workout program. We can also use STRENGTH to be stubborn with a "don't confuse me with the facts" attitude.

- *Underdeveloped STRENGTH* shows up as the inability to stick with a project or a goal. A person with underdeveloped STRENGTH may flit from unfinished project to unfinished project.

- *Egocentric STRENGTH* shows up as being stubborn, unduly forceful or perhaps obsessive compulsive. For example, a person with egocentric STRENGTH might forge ahead with a plan, even though everyone else realizes the futility of it.

From elevated consciousness: The ability to be resilient; endure; persist; stay the course; persevere; and be mentally tough based on Ideas, Truths, Principles, and Laws that are Divine in nature. We use STRENGTH to be persistent in being the best person we can be.

A recent research study shared that when the researchers peered into the heart of perseverance—tracking heart rate, blood pressure, and constriction of blood vessels before, during, and after the public speaking task—they saw that even though these physiological measures spiked similarly high for all personality styles, they came down faster for those with the most 'stay the course' personality traits. Within seconds, their hearts calmed. By contrast, the hearts of the others remained perturbed. These findings tell us people with 'stay the course' personality styles are emotionally responsive. They are not disconnected, head-in-the-sand, unflappable robots. They are emotionally moved like the rest of us. But they are quick to move, to let go *(Tugade, M., and B. Fredrickson, 2004, "Resilient individuals use positive emotions to bounce back from negative emotional experiences," Journal of Personality and Social Psychology 86: 320-333).*

Have you ever gone to an amusement park and spied a ride you really wanted to go on? It looked so exciting, and yet, there was a level of fear that kept you from riding it. Then perhaps you began to have a conversation with yourself! Your intellect began by telling you, "Look, it's only a ride! It's got to be safe. Look at all those people coming off the ride laughing and having fun." Then you start feeling queasy and nervous, and your internal dialogue switches to, "STOP! DANGER! WHAT ARE YOU THINKING? You are going to get hurt or maybe even die if you go on that ride."

In a sense, you are carrying conflicting beliefs: one says it is safe and fun, while the other says it is not safe and you will surely get hurt. Finally you make the decision to get on the ride, and you get in line. As you wind through the line, you are still having the internal dialogue, increasingly using your Power of STRENGTH. You use STRENGTH to stay the course … maybe even endure ... with the decision to take the ride no matter how loud and stringent that "voice" for the belief that it is dangerous screams in your head. Finally, you use your strength to step onto the ride—and off you go on a fun-filled experience. And the cool part is that when you get off the ride, the first thing you'll say is, "Wow! I want to do that again!"

Of course, the story could go the other way, and you choose to use STRENGTH to stubbornly refuse to be convinced to ride ... in which case, you always wonder what it would have been like to experience the thrill.

Using your STRENGTH to stubbornly cling to old beliefs without exploring new ideas, or to give up easily regardless of the prize at the end of the task, can lead to problems. People who have a low level of perseverance succumb to what Daniel Goleman calls 'emotional hijacking.' What happens is that small stresses pile up over time and cause many people to lose control. As a result, their decision-making skills, productivity, and effectiveness plummet *(Goleman, D., Working With Emotional Intelligence, Bantam, New York, 1998, pg. 77)*.

> The baseline resting state of our brain activates a 'default network' which tracks our environment and body for possible threats. This threat awareness is often accompanied by a background feeling of anxiety that keeps us vigilant *(M.E. Raichle, A.M. MacLeod, A.Z. Snyder, W.J. Powers, D.A. Gusnard, and G.L. Shumlan, "A default mode of brain function," Proceedings of the National Academy of Sciences, 2001; 98: 676-682).*

Let's explore another example of our STRENGTH. Imagine you are in a position of authority with employees. You become aware of some behavior or performance that is not up to speed. You know you need to say something to this person, but are reluctant. Perhaps you are afraid the person will not like you anymore. You have a strong need to be liked, and yet, you know it is the right thing to do to speak up. Sometimes doing the right thing is not necessarily the easiest thing to do! After dealing with an internal struggle, you give yourself a good talking to, and pump up your STRENGTH to do what you must do, despite "the egocentric voice" that says you need to be liked.

> A study by Tali Sharot and colleagues from New York University asked participants to recall past events as well as imagine future ones based upon on-screen cues (such as winning an award or getting a hug). They were then asked to describe their thoughts—how strong, emotional, and positive each thought was, and whether or not the positiveness was experienced first-hand. The results clearly demonstrated a rosier picture. Participants rated upcoming events more positively than they did happy past events—things they had actually experienced. Interestingly, participants viewed future events from a first-hand perspective if they were positive, but from an outsider's perspective if negative. Isn't that amazing! Now, here's the neuroscience of optimism: As thoughts of happy future events flooded their minds, two brain structures were strongly activated. The rostral anterior cingulated cortex (RACC) and the right amygdala areas were lit up. The RACC, it seems, works hand-in-hand with our emotional center, the amygdala, to actually downplay negative emotions, helping us to stay more positive in the face of negative situations *(Sharot T, Riccardi AM, Raio CM, and Phelps EA (2007). Neural mechanisms mediating optimism bias. Nature, 450 (7166), 102-5).*

STRENGTH and FAITH are connected. The more we really believe in something, the easier it is to support or sustain. It is harder to stand up for something we are lukewarm about, and nearly impossible when we do not really care at all.

Our practice of STRENGTH shows in our brain. Psychologist Richard Davidson explored the differences in people who can stay the course in the face of crises and stress versus others who are easily debilitated. He found that in people who persevere, the prefrontal cortex rapidly wins over the limbic system. And in the easily disturbed group, the amygdala (sometimes called the 'seat of our fear') takes over *(Davidson, R., ed. (July 15, 2000). Anxiety, Depression, and Emotion. Oxford University Press. New York, 2,000, pp. 306).*

Another time we experience difficulty standing firm comes when we have conflicting beliefs. We feel strongly both ways! In these cases, we must decide which belief we want to support, and then reinforce it by using our STRENGTH, which impacts our thoughts, feelings and actions. As we do so, that belief will increasingly become the prominent one.

STRENGTH is that innate ability by which we are able to be resilient; endure; persist; stay the course; persevere; and be mentally tough. A person can use brute physical strength to accomplish something like removing a stuck lid on a jar. In the same way, there is a deeply embedded Power of STRENGTH we call on to plow through a difficult project or handle a major emotional hit like the loss of a loved one.

Individuals who have developed their STRENGTH possess a resilience and endurance that brings them through difficulties, emerging even better than before. Here's an example from research: From 1975 to 1986, psychologist Salvatore Maddi tracked 450 employees at Illinois Bell Telephone before, during, and after the breakup of AT&T. Illinois Bell almost halved its work force in one year. Job descriptions and chains of command changed regularly. Even so, one-third of the people excelled, maintaining their performance, morale, and health. However, two-thirds fell apart, suffering problems such as anxiety, depression, and high blood pressure. Maddi found that those who excelled (the "hardy") shared the following characteristics. They:
- stayed involved rather than feeling isolated;
- tried to influence outcomes rather than lapsing into helplessness; and
- chose to learn from their experience rather than feeling threatened by it. Instead of blaming themselves or bosses for their firing, they recognized that the layoffs were due to forces beyond the control of anyone in the company.

"Seeing that in a broader perspective makes it less terrible. Less personal," Maddi reported. "They were good at giving and receiving help and encouragement, neither too passive to be effective nor too assertive to be sensitive" *(Salvatore Maddi and Deborah M. Khoshaba, Resilience at Work, AMACOM, N.Y. 2005).*

> Julia Cameron, author of the best-seller *Artist's Way*, talks about STRENGTH in terms of how to move past a debilitating loss. She says, "I learned, when hit by loss, to ask the right question: "What next?" instead of "Why me?" *(Julia Cameron, Artist's Way, p.136.)*

As with each of our Powers, STRENGTH can be used in a variety of ways, some of which are more ineffective than others.

A person with **underdeveloped STRENGTH** gives up easily or has difficulty sticking to a goal. This person finds excuses to rationalize their inability to follow through with commitments, and blames others for their problems. They have trouble completing a project, a desire to exercise or eat healthily, or fulfill a commitment.

On the other hand, individuals with **egocentric STRENGTH** end up being ridiculously obstinate about giving up, even when it is obvious that their approach is not working. They might also use STRENGTH to support a resistance to part with "stuff" or release a negative habit or belief. They are persistent to a fault, and have a reputation of approaching life from a "my way or the highway" point of view. In this regard, STRENGTH is coupled with an underdeveloped Power of RELEASE, whereby STRENGTH is used to support the inability to let go of something that is no longer serving the person's highest and best goals.

A Practical Look at STRENGTH

The more people work themselves up into a worried tizzy in anticipation of possible negativity, the slower they are to appreciate they have in fact dodged a bullet, so to speak. For people with resilient personality styles, less worry means faster relief *(Waugh, C., T. Wager, et al, 2008, "The neural correlates of trait resilience when anticipating and recovering from threats," Social Cognitive and Affective Neuroscience 3: 322- 332)*. We've discussed some extreme examples of unbalanced STRENGTH, so now let's take a look at how we can effectively use STRENGTH in our everyday lives—in our ordinary thoughts, feelings, and actions as we discern, interpret, and perceive situations:

- Imagine someone you respect (a person in authority or maybe even one of your parents) says you are irresponsible. You think, "That is not true." You put feeling into your belief that the statement is not true. You use STRENGTH to speak up for yourself, in spite of what that person may think or do. You might respond, "Actually, that is not true, and I refuse to accept that label. I am a responsible person. I get up every morning, get to work on time, finish my projects on time, and take care of my own needs and the needs of my loved ones." Or you may even choose to use STRENGTH to go deeper and inquire for more information by saying, "It's interesting you say that. I never thought of myself as irresponsible. Would you mind giving me a few examples where I have come across that way in your perception?"

- A person shopping in a store is attracted to a beautiful, ornate wooden bird cage. As the person examines the cage more closely, s/he notices (through the senses of touch and sight) that the cage is fragile. Suddenly a piece breaks off. You probably can relate to his/her first response, which might be to look around to see if anyone noticed, quickly put the cage back on the shelf, and get as far from that cage as possible! But imagine that this person also has a strong belief in doing the right thing. By using STRENGTH to overcome the child-like reaction, this person then tells a sales person what happened.

We also can use STRENGTH in adverse ways based on beliefs derived from an erroneous interpretation or understanding of our thoughts, feelings, and what we are discerning, interpreting and perceiving through our senses. For example:

- A man who is relatively new to an organization may be very quiet in team meetings, and be hesitant in offering up new ideas. Even though this individual is encouraged and told that mistakes are welcomed as a way to learn more, he remains silent, which leads others to feel he is not a team player. Later you learn that he was fired from a former job because of a creative idea that did not go well. You discover he was told mistakes were okay and welcomed, but the experience turned out to be different. Based on that, this employee is clinging with STRENGTH to the belief that creative ideas will be punished. Hence, he remains silent rather than risk losing another job.

- Remember the old Frank Sinatra song, "I Did It My Way?" While it made a great #1 hit on the music charts, in the real world a person who must do everything his or her own way is erroneously using STRENGTH. Imagine working with a colleague to finish a joint project. No matter how good your ideas are, your colleague simply has to have it his or her way. Unless one of you gives in, the project will never be completed! Of course, there are times when it is important to do things your way. But it is also important to be open to new ideas or different viewpoints. It means knowing how to employ your STRENGTH appropriately.

In each of these examples, STRENGTH is engaged based on some belief held in sense consciousness. When we become aware of how we are already using STRENGTH in our everyday lives, it becomes easier to know how to consciously apply STRENGTH at ever higher levels of consciousness. As in the other applications of STRENGTH, there is always a belief which supports that STRENGTH.

For example, we can use STRENGTH to express our exceptional qualities, even if that decision puts us at risk. Or, if the price seems too high, we can use it to be as diplomatic as we can be. Whatever the case, there must first be a belief that we can use STRENGTH at its optimal level to handle all of life's challenges.

Some people—either genetically or intuitively—seem to understand the realities of life better than most people. We call those people resilient because they persevere. They are the ones who smile in the face of adversity, reframe bad events as opportunities, and adopt a wait-and-see attitude about future threats. This doesn't mean they never feel bad. They bleed like everyone else. Yet because they also find ways to cultivate good feelings—even in the midst of crises—their bad feelings don't last as long. They rebound (*Fredrickson, B., The How of Happiness, Three Rivers Press, New York, 2009, pg. 119*).

As we use our STRENGTH to reinforce our positive beliefs, it becomes easier and easier to believe our goal of being the very best we can be is possible. Ultimately, we

STRENGTH

are able to achieve it! As we go about the day, we use STRENGTH to stay the course and persevere in being our most Extraordinary Self. In the face of challenges or temptation to act from our personality or ego, we use STRENGTH, buttressed from FAITH, to continue being the best person we can be.

Strength From the Four Levels of Consciousness

Let's look at STRENGTH in another way. STRENGTH (along with all the other Powers) can be expressed from four different levels of consciousness:

1. **Unconscious STRENGTH:** based on a cause in subconscious mind which consists of beliefs that are not in our moment to moment awareness. You might be strong, steadfast or even "bullheaded" without realizing it or really knowing why, because it is being fueled from some unconscious or subconscious belief.

2. **Conscious STRENGTH from our senses:** based on something in physicality we are gleaning through our sight, sound, scent, touch, and/or taste. A person slips and takes a pretty bad fall on the ice. From that point on, this individual is steadfast about being very careful around icy sidewalks.

3. **Conscious STRENGTH from our human personality:** based on thoughts, feelings, attitudes, and/or beliefs held in ordinary consciousness. Because a woman *believes* she can become a doctor, she stays on track to *become* a doctor, no matter what distractions or seeming obstacles come along.

4. **Conscious STRENGTH from our True Identity, or Authentic Self:** based upon Divine Ideas, Laws, and Principles. This is when we are not deterred, no matter what, from staying the course to be the best, the most exceptional, the most heroic we can be. We use STRENGTH to overcome whatever temptations come along.

You may have heard the following story about a very special reunion, but it worth reading again. It's a good story to illustrate the Power of STRENGTH.

A young minister was invited to serve an old church in Brooklyn, with the task of revitalizing a once vibrant church that had declined.

He and his wife arrived in early September and were very excited about the new ministry. But when they saw the church they were very disappointed. The building was run down and needed a great deal of work.

This couple had a huge repair job ahead of them. They set a goal: to have everything reasonably ready by the church's 95th anniversary!

The couple worked hard, repairing pews, patching holes, and painting the plaster walls. On November 21st they were ahead of schedule and almost finished when the city was hit with a snowstorm that lasted two days.

On November 24th when the minister arrived at the church and opened the door to the sanctuary, his heart sank. The roof had leaked and a large area of plaster about 6 feet by 8 feet had fallen from the wall behind the altar and onto the floor.

The minister called his wife and told her he had a few more things to take care of before he came home. He cleaned up the mess, but wondered how the ugly hole would affect the anniversary service.

On his walk home he noticed that a local business was having a charity flea market. One of the items he saw was a beautiful, handmade, ivory colored tablecloth with an exquisite winged globe embroidered in its center. He realized it was just big enough to cover the hole in the sanctuary wall, and its winged globe symbolism added the perfect touch.

He bought it—and on his way back to the church to hang it over the gaping hole in the wall, he noticed that it had started to snow again. He met an older woman who had just missed her bus. She looked cold, so he invited her into the warm church to wait for the next bus.

She sat in a pew in the back of the sanctuary while the minister carried the ladder from the basement and started to fasten the tablecloth to the wall. He was very pleased with how well it covered the hole in the wall and how beautiful it looked as well.

It was then that he noticed the woman walking down the aisle of the church toward him. Her face was as white as a sheet. "Reverend," she asked, "Where did you get that tablecloth?"

He explained about the flea market. Then she asked him to look in the lower right-hand corner to see if he could find the initials WEG.

They were there! They were her initials!

She had made the tablecloth 35 years earlier, in Iraq. She explained that before Saddam Hussein, she and her husband had lived in Bagdad. But when Saddam came they decided to leave. She was captured and sent to prison and when she was released in 2004, she was told that her husband had died.

The minister offered her the tablecloth, but she refused and said that she wanted the church to keep it. The minister insisted on driving her home, and she graciously accepted.

The 95th Anniversary service was wonderful. The church was almost filled to capacity and the music and the energy were terrific. At the end of the service the minister and his wife greeted everyone at the door, thanked them for coming, and wished them a joyous holiday. When they returned to the quiet sanctuary, they noticed an older man sitting in one of the pews, staring at the front of the church.

The man asked where they had gotten the tablecloth because it was identical to one his wife had made.

"How could there be two tablecloths so much alike?" he asked. "This has to be the one she made! Look! There are her initials stitched in the corner!"

He explained that he and his wife had tried to flee Iraq, and that he had arranged for his wife to leave first. He was arrested and sent to prison and never saw her again. He had been told that she had died.

"I never remarried," he said, "because I still feel close to her. They took her physical body away, but they couldn't take the love we felt for each other away. I kept hoping I would see her again. And, in a way I have. I have reunited with her tablecloth."

The minister and his wife looked at each other and said in unison, "Isn't this a wonderful life?" Then the minister turned to the older man and asked him if they could take him for a short drive. They drove him to the apartment where the young minister had taken the elderly woman just the evening before. The couple helped the man climb the three flights of stairs and rang the doorbell.

Then they watched one of the greatest reunions they could ever imagine. Husband and wife embracing, kissing, weeping together. Celebrating their reunion ... the strength of their relationship ... their ability to endure the hardships they had been through ... their phenomenal resilience as they silently hung onto the hope of ever seeing one another again.

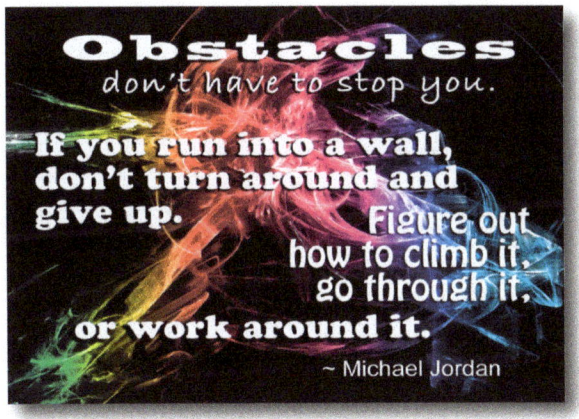

Research in Positive Psychology supports this human quality of sustained, hopeful resilience: Resilience is not just something we find inside ourselves or in our environment. It is something we find midway between the two, because our individual development is always linked to our social development. Resilience reconciles the two parts of the divided ego, until we can at last speak of ourselves as a totality. Resilience is the positive capacity of people to cope with stress and adversity. It is a sweater knitted from developmental, emotional, and social strands of wool. That is why it is more helpful to describe the history of a resilient personality. We can then try to understand how it dodges the strokes of fate and still contrives to use solid supports in order to knit itself *(Cyrulnik, Boris, Resilience: How Your Inner Strength Can Set You Free From the Past, Tarcher, New York, 2011).*

The American Psychological Association suggests ten ways to build mental toughness, which are to:

(1) maintain good relationships with close family members, friends and others;
(2) avoid seeing crises or stressful events as unbearable problems;
(3) accept circumstances that cannot be changed;
(4) develop realistic goals and move towards them;
(5) take decisive actions in adverse situations;
(6) look for opportunities of self-discovery after a struggle with loss;
(7) develop self-confidence;
(8) keep a long-term perspective and consider the stressful event in a broader context;
(9) maintain a hopeful outlook, expecting good things and visualizing what is wished;
(10) take care of one's mind and body, exercising regularly, paying attention to one's own needs and feelings.

(Ozbay, F; Fitterling, H; Charney, D; Southwick, S (2008). "Social support and resilience to stress across the life span: A neurobiologic framework". Current psychiatry reports 10 (4): 304–10).

STRENGTH:
Putting It Into Practice

STRENGTH—Activity One:

Part 1:

Think back to a situation in your past that feels incomplete: a lost opportunity; a decision you wish you could change; an activity or responsibility you left unfinished; etc.

- What were the reasons for the lack of completion?
- As you think back on the situation, what kind of internal conversation did you have with yourself?
- How were you using the power of STRENGTH to sabotage your own success?
- What were the pay-offs to you to leave things incomplete or unsatisfactory?

Part 2:

Now, think back to a situation in your past where you were successful in achieving a goal: completing a course of study; learning a new skill; finishing a project; sealing a business deal; etc.

- What roadblocks did you encounter along the way, and how did you move through them?
- What kept you on track, inspired and motivated to see the situation through to a successful completion?
- How did you use the Power of STRENGTH to stay the course and achieve success?

As you revisit these two life experiences, think about how you handled things differently. What lessons and tools can you identify that can help you more effectively use STRENGTH to be successful? Can you identify the beliefs that were supporting your use of STRENGTH in both situations?

STRENGTH—Activity Two:

As you think about the specific area you are working on throughout this course, brainstorm a list of potential barriers that could sabotage your success. Next to each one, identify STRENGTH tools that can help you stay the course.

Example: Healthy Eating

Potential Barrier	STRENGTH Tools
My mother bakes my favorite dessert, and I don't want to hurt her feelings, so I eat it.	Set boundaries with mother ahead of time ("I know you love to fix my favorite dessert, but I am really trying to stick to my new eating plan, and I'd really appreciate your help.")
	Claim I'm not hungry, and take some home with me for later (and don't eat it!)
	Take only a small piece, and plan my other eating around it.

STRENGTH Affirmation:

I claim STRENGTH now. Regardless of the circumstances, I stay the course so I can be the best, the most spiritually mature person I can be.

Quotes to Inspire STRENGTH

Never let the thought of weakness enter your consciousness, but always ignore the suggestion and affirm yourself to be a tower of strength, within and without. (Charles Fillmore)

How often—even before we began—have we declared a task "impossible"... and how often have we construed a picture of ourselves as being inadequate?... A great deal depends upon the thought patterns we choose and on the persistence with which we affirm them. (Piero Ferrucci)

Everything in us responds to our spiritual strength. (Martha Smock)

Your demonstration of results will be in proportion to the strength and thoroughness of your desire and of your persistence. (Ernest Wilson)

With all our strength we need to love peace and to practice it. This takes strength because we often have a tendency to slip a bit. With our strength we need to love Truth, and to learn it, and to express it. (Donald Curtis)

Nothing so uplifts, nothing so frees us from care and worry, nothing so brings the thought of victory as being established in that sustaining strength which cannot know weakness. To have the strength that makes life seem effortless, nonresistant, is to have the inward joy that no one can take away. (Cora Fillmore)

You cannot have a successful and permanent extension of mental, psychological, and spiritual strength without working toward an enhancement of physiological capacity. (Jean Houston)

To remain indifferent to the challenges we face is indefensible. If the goal is noble, whether or not it is realized within our lifetime is largely irrelevant. What we must do therefore is to strive and persevere and never give up. (Dalai Lama)

If we do not believe within ourselves this deeply rooted feeling that there is something higher than ourselves, we shall never find the strength to evolve into something higher. (Rudolf Steiner)

Life is not easy for any of us. But what of that? We must have perseverance and above all confidence in ourselves. We must believe that we are gifted for something and that this thing must be attained. (Marie Curie)

To love what you do and feel that it matters -- how can anything be more fun?
(Katharine Graham)

As we awaken, we are infused with an even greater
sense of love, eventually with a love
that needs no object. It simply is.
We love, like the rose that gives its perfume,
because that is our nature.
In loving, we experience a warm,
abundant, connecting, expansive energy.
Love has been called the "cosmic glue"—
the force that holds the universe together.
~ Diane Mariechild

LOVE

Overview

- Location: Back of the Heart
- Color: Pink
- Linked with WISDOM and UNDERSTANDING

LOVE is the Power to harmonize; unify; unconditionally attract; feel affection.

From ordinary consciousness: The ability to feel affection for, desire, attract oneself to, harmonize, and unify based on our senses, thoughts, feelings, and beliefs. We can use LOVE to be loving or lustful. Through our desire we can use LOVE to bring good or bad into our lives based on what we are focused upon.

- *Underdeveloped LOVE* results in a person who has a limited ability to feel affection or positive regard for another person. It can also result in a person who has difficulty handling conflict.

- *Egocentric LOVE* results in a person who "loves indiscriminately" or inappropriately. It may also show up as a kind of fatal attraction, neediness, lust, or an inability to compromise when necessary.

From elevated consciousness: The ability to feel affection for, desire, attract oneself to, harmonize, and unify based on Ideas, Truths, Principles and Laws that are Divine in nature. We use LOVE to desire our Divine Nature so that we harmonize everything in our life to be the best, most accomplished, most collaborative person we can be.

Think about the incredible number of ways we use the word "LOVE"—as diverse as "I love my soul mate" to "I love that new song" to "I love chocolate-chip cookie dough ice cream!" It is the same word, but obviously has different intents.

Perhaps one of the most famous phrases from the Bible comes from 1 John 4:8, which simply says "God is love." In fact, the same scripture informs us that those who abide in love abide in God and God abides in them. And at the same time, we must realize that God, Divine Mind, is so much more than love. LOVE is simply one aspect among many.

When we speak of the Power of LOVE, we can really define it as three potential aspects:

- *Emotion*: the ability to feel affection for, or desire something;
- *Attraction*: the ability to attract ourselves toward something; and
- *Harmony*: the ability to unify or bring agreement and accord to our thoughts or to a situation.

Let's explore these a little more deeply.

The Emotion Aspect of LOVE

The *Emotion*, or feeling side of love (to feel affection for, or desire something) is probably one of the most written about, talked about, and sought after experiences. It is defined as a deep, fervent affection for another person.

This is supported by extensive research, including Mark Davis' findings, which demonstrate that positive emotions such as joy and love broaden a person's available repertoire of cognitions and actions, thus enhancing his/her inner harmony and sense of unity (Mark A. Davis (January 2009). "Understanding the relationship between mood and creativity: A meta-analysis." Organizational Behavior and Human Decision Processes 100 (1): 25–38).

This type of LOVE is associated with a warm affection and high regard for another person, be it parent, partner, child, or friend. While some people may not be too good at expressing love, they still have some understanding of it and want it. While we wax elegantly about the positive aspects of this kind of love, we tend to overlook the more egocentric side, which can show up as lust, abuse, or other distorted forms.

The Attraction Aspect of LOVE

The second aspect of LOVE is the *Attraction* side (the ability to attract ourselves toward something). This is the Ability we use to desire another person or thing. We are sure you can easily see it is not entirely separate from the feeling side. The Attraction or thinking side of LOVE is demonstrated in phrases like, "I love chocolate" or "plants love sunlight." It is the Ability to attract oneself to something that is desired, wanted, needed, or required. When it is said that LOVE is like a mighty magnet, the assumption is that LOVE attracts. In truth, it is like a magnet through which we attract ourselves to what we desire, want, need, or require. Not only is this the Power behind the Law of Attraction; it is also the Power behind the Law of Mind Action, which says "thoughts held in mind produce after their kind." This means the thoughts we are holding in the moment are the thoughts we are desiring or wanting through LOVE, and this same Power will also tend to harmonize and unify our thoughts to match the thoughts we are holding. Certain positive words—like 'peace' and 'love'—may actually have the power to alter the expression of genes throughout the brain and body, turning them on and off in ways that lower physical and emotional stress (Dusek, J.A., Out, H.H., Wohlhueter, A.L., Bhasin, M., Zerbini, L.F., Joseph, M.G., Benson, H., Libermann, T.A., "Genomic counter-stress changes induced by the relaxation response," PLoS One; 2008 July 2; 3 (7): e2576).

Okay—let's take a minute to address the Law of Attraction and the Law of Mind Action so we are all on the same page. The Law of Attraction is often taught to mean we attract people, situations, and things to us. We believe it is more accurate to say we attract ourselves to people, situations, and things. For example, when you decide to buy something like a Mercedes-Benz, you will suddenly begin seeing more of them as you drive around. It is obvious that there is not a Universe (aka God) putting more Mercedes on the road  for you to see; they are not coming to you like a magnet attracts iron filings. No, it is actually your decision and desire you use to attract yourself to the Mercedes. They have been there all along. You are now "sorting" the incoming visual data based on your decision and desire. The ability to desire and attract is fired by LOVE.

This works whether the desire is positive or negative. For example, an alcoholic does not attract a co-dependent partner; rather, the alcoholic attracts himself or herself to the co-dependent person … and vice versa.

Similarly, the Law of Mind Action says thoughts held in mind produce after their own kind. This is frequently believed to mean that every thought we hold in our mind and concentrate on through our thinking and feelings will manifest in the material world. We believe it is much more accurate to say thoughts and feelings held in consciousness create in consciousness. This is dealt with in detail in the great little book by Paul Hasselbeck and Bil Holton, *Get Over It! The Truth About What You Know That Just Ain't So!* As they explain:

> Whenever we make a decision to do something, it happens first at the level of mind. Once it is in the mind, it comes to life at the level of consciousness. At this point we have a powerful choice to make! We decide if and how we are going to go about creating that thought in the real world. And assuming we decide to take it to the outer realm, there are a multitude of forms the thought can take.

So thoughts held in mind can produce after their kind in the outer realm, but they do not always do so. Many of the thoughts we hold seem to have no visible effect. It is up to us whether or not we transform those thoughts into manifestation *(Hasselbeck, Paul, and Bil Holton, Get Over It! The Truth About What You Know That Just Ain't So!, Durham, NC: Prosperity Publishing House, 2008).*

The attraction aspect of LOVE is also associated with what Positive Psychology calls positivity. According to Dr. Barbara Fredrickson, Kenan Distinguished Professor of Psychology and Principal Investigator of the Positive Emotions and Psychophysiology Lab at the University of North Carolina, and a leading scholar within social psychology, affective science, and positive psychology:

Positivity doesn't mean we should follow the axioms *Grin and bear it* or *Don't worry, be happy.* Those are simply superficial wishes. Positivity runs deeper. It consists of the whole range of positive emotions—from appreciation to love, from amusement to joy, from hope to gratitude, and then some. It includes the positive meanings and optimistic attitudes that trigger positive emotions as well as the open minds, tender loving hearts, relaxed limbs, and soft faces they usher in. Your mild and fleeting pleasant states are far more potent than you think *(Fredrickson, Barbara, Positivity, Three Rivers Press, New York, 2009, pg. 6).*

The Harmony Aspect of LOVE

The third aspect of LOVE is *Harmony*—the ability to harmonize or unify, to bring into accord or agreement. A singer harmonizes with another singer; strings on a violin are harmonized with each other. We can create amazing results through using LOVE to harmonize and unify when we bring harmony between conflicting positions, people,

or countries. Most of us have a tendency to view this particular aspect purely from the perspective of either/or: there is either harmony or discord related to the people, places, or situations. However, this is only half the truth. The other half of the truth, as described by researcher Arthur Koestler, is there is harmony and wholeness everywhere. For example, a whole thing within nature is called a holon. It is a whole made of its own parts, yet itself is part of a larger whole. Each holon has two opposite tendencies: a self-assertive desire to preserve its individual autonomy (autopoiesis), and an integrative tendency to function as part of the larger whole. In a biological or social system, each holon must assert its individuality in order to maintain the system's stratified order, but it must also submit to the demands of the whole in order to sustain the viability of the system. A human being, a nation, an ecosystem are all holons (Arthur Koestler, Janus, Hutchinson, London, 1978, pg. 57).

However, while LOVE is neutral in character, it's impact can be either positive or negative, depending on how it is applied. Its use is determined by the consciousness of the individual. We must be wise and realize that we can desire, want, or need people and things that are not really good for us. While it may sound odd, remember, it is our LOVE that powers what we desire in the moment ... the good, the bad and the ugly! It harmonizes everything to match what we are desiring. So unless we set a clear intention to control our Power of LOVE, we may find ourselves harmonizing with inappropriate people, outlandish ideas, or inconsequential things.

Think about it. When we are angry, aren't we, in an odd way, desiring and wanting to be angry in that moment? Don't we then tend to filter and therefore harmonize and unify nearly everything to match that anger? What if we are depressed or feeling sad? Once again, it does sound strange and more than a little odd to say that we want to feel depressed or negative. And yet, this is what we are deciding in the moment. That is not to say there is not a good reason to feel sad, negative, or depressed. We simply want to convey that this is what we are choosing in the moment, even if it springs from a subconscious level.

We can see how this happens when we look at recent neuroscience research looking at the impact of negative information on the brain. The brain typically detects negative information faster than positive information. Fearful faces, for example, are perceived much more rapidly than happy or neutral faces, probably fast-tracked by the amygdala (E. Yang, D. Zald, and R. Blake, "Fearful expressions gain preferential access to awareness during continuous flash suppression," Emotion, 2007; 7: 882-886). Even when researchers make fearful faces invisible to conscious awareness, the amygdala still lights up (Y. Jiang and S. He, "Cortical responses to invisible faces: Dissociating subsystems for facial-information processing," Current Biology, 2006; 16: 2023-2029).

> Open your eyes to kindness and gratitude. Savor goodness when you see it. Visualize your best possible future. Be more social. Go outside. These are the small changes you can make to elevate your positivity any time you want. Together these approaches will unlock more of the six most common positive emotions within you—love, joy, gratitude, serenity, interest, and hope. As they do so, they will open your mindset and put you on a course of resilience and growth *(Fredrickson, B., The How of Happiness, Three Rivers Press, New York, 2009, pg. 198).*

If a person is "desiring or wanting" to feel sad or depressed, then LOVE is also harmonizing and unifying everything else to match the sadness and depression. That's where the phrase "Misery loves company" comes from—and we would actually say, "Misery loves *miserable* company!" So, we each want to be vigilant about what we are desiring, wanting, needing, or requiring in the moment, because LOVE is activated, and it will harmonize and unify to "match" whatever we are desiring, wanting, needing or requiring.

Because of the attracting aspect of LOVE, this Power can also be viewed as the ability to focus and intend. What we desire or want, we tend to focus upon. What we desire, we intend to have. Much has been written about the power of intention and basically it is "an act or instance of determining mentally upon some action or result, the end or object intended" (dictionary.reference.com). It is said that what we focus on increases. What we focus on, intend, or desire is what we are "loving" or love in the moment. While it may seem strange, it is true that when we focus on the "negative" we actually "love" the negative in the moment.

A powerful piece of research tells us that the more we focus on negative words and thoughts, the more damage we can cause in key brain structures that regulate our memory, feelings, sleep patterns, appetite, health, and emotions (Talarovicova, A., Krskova, L., Kiss, A., "Some assessments of the amygdala role in suprahypothalamic neuroendocrine regulation: A Mini-review," Endocrine Regulations, 2007 Nov.; 41 (4): 155-62).

It is by our focus (LOVE) on our negative, sad, or depressed feelings that we attract ourselves to more of the same negativity as well as harmonize and unify our thoughts, matching them with that negative thought. We now tend to see things more and more through this negative focus, which then tends to "outpicture" in the outer/exterior realm.

> We have such a biological need for love, our bodies can literally malfunction without it *(Lewis, T., Amini, F., and R. Lannon, A General Theory of Love, Vintage, New York, 2001).*

You see, we limit our definitions and our experience when we view them in the "good" versus "bad" sense, since in the Absolute there is only "Absolute Good." In so doing, we have missed a very important point that, when we fully realize its import, will re-establish our power and control over our consciousness and our lives. Charles Fillmore wrote that each of the Powers can be used on the personal level instead of the universal level. We think of the words like harmony, harmonizer, love, and desire in a positive sense. Bringing harmony to a situation typically means smoothing things out and making everything better. However, if LOVE is a PRINCIPLE, then LOVE does not care how we use it. LOVE, the great harmonizer, is really a principle that brings two or more things into harmony with each other. It says nothing about what the quality is of the things being harmonized. It says nothing about what that harmony looks or feels like. When we are focusing on the negative, we could say we are loving the negative. So this principle called LOVE simply harmonizes thoughts and feelings to match the negative we are focusing upon. This obviously affects our consciousness in the same way, and there will be a tendency to harmonize the outer with the same negative focus. In fact, our brains have a built-in negativity bias that primes us for the fight-or-flight response *(A. Vaish, T. Grossmann, and A. Woodward, "Not all emotions are created equal: The negativity bias in social-emotional development," Psychological Bulletin, 2008; 134: 383-403).*

It may be relatively easy for us to love one another and for some, less so, to love oneself. However, it is both helpful and refreshing to know that we are forever equipped with LOVE. It is not a matter of obtaining it; it is more a matter of figuring out how to use it … wisely. For this reason, LOVE is often linked with WISDOM which, in turn, is linked with UNDERSTANDING (the Power to know).

It is important to be vigilant about how we are using the principle/thinking side of LOVE and the effect this has on our consciousness. We must become aware, moment to moment, what we are thinking and feeling because, through the Power of LOVE, this is what we will be increasing in consciousness. We must use WISDOM with LOVE so that we choose rightly.

Here's one more scientific tidbit about LOVE: Research has revealed that caring for someone without needing to receive any kind of reward involves seven areas of the brain. However these impulses differ from the activity seen in romantic or sexual love—suggesting unconditional love is actually a separate emotion. When the subjects were asked to evoke feelings of unconditional love, the scans showed seven brain areas that became active; three were similar to those of romantic love. The others were different, suggesting a separate  kind of love (Beauregard, Mario, Courtemanche, J., Paquette, V., and E. St-Pierre, The neuro basis of unconditional love, Psychiatry Research: Neuroimaging Vol. 172, Issue 2, May 15, 2009, 93-98).

LOVE From the Four Levels of Consciousness

Let's look at LOVE from four different levels of consciousness:

1. **Unconscious LOVE:** based on a cause in subconscious mind which consists of beliefs that are not in our moment to moment awareness. Now, this may seem strange; however, these would be desires and wants driven from subconscious/unconscious beliefs. We believe this is what the apostle Paul was referring to when he said, "Instead of doing what I know is right, I do wrong" *(Romans 7:19, Contemporary English Version)*. When it seems an alcoholic is unconsciously attracting himself to a co-dependent, he probably "unconsciously reads" a batch of "signals or behavior cues" that a co-dependent is exhibiting.

2. **Conscious LOVE from our senses:** based on something in physicality we are gleaning through our sight, sound, scent, touch, and/or taste. For example, once having tasted a peppermint mocha latté, we might find ourselves desiring and attracting ourselves to that particular coffee treat. Walking through the mall, our senses inform us of a specialty coffee shop up ahead. Our desire for a peppermint mocha latté kicks in and voilá, we attracted ourselves to the coffee shop.

3. **Conscious LOVE from our human personality:** based on thoughts, feelings, attitudes, and/or beliefs held in ordinary consciousness. For example, this occurs when we are aware of a belief that we want a friend who enjoys the same movies we do. Then we would use LOVE to desire that particular trait as a requirement for someone we choose to spend time with. We would then attract ourselves to a person who likes the same movies we do.

4. **Conscious LOVE from our True Identity, or Authentic Self:** based upon Divine Ideas, Laws, and Principles. This would result in the desire to be our True Identity, our Authentic Self in action. And, as a result, we would attract ourselves to behaviors, attitudes and feelings that we believe would support this True Identity, and help us to be the best person we can be.

> The Harvard Men Study—one of the longest-running psychological studies in psychology—has followed 268 men from their entrance into Harvard in the late 1930's until today. The researchers have been able to identify the life circumstances that distinguish the happiest men who have lived, and continue to live the fullest of lives. George Vaillant, the lead researcher, says the difference is the love that comes out of the relationships in which the men are involved *(Vaillant, G., "Yes, I stand by my words, 'Happiness equals love—full stop.'" Positive Psychology News Daily. Retrieved at positivepsychologynews.com, 2009).*

Our LOVE connection would not be complete without hearing from love experts who share their wisdom on the subject. The following questions, answered by the experts, will clear up a lot of the misconceptions about the nature of love. We should mention that our "experts" are children, age 10 and under! Let's hear what they have to say about LOVE:

What do people do on a first date?
On the first date, they just tell each other lies, and that usually gets them interested in a second date (Mike, 9).

When is it okay to kiss someone?
It's never okay to kiss a boy. Yuck! They always slobber all over you (Kathy, 10).

You've got to be a good kisser. It might make your wife forget that you never take out the trash (Randy, 8).

Is it better to be single or married?
It's better for girls to be single but not for boys. Boys need somebody to clean up after them and pick up their socks (Lynette, 9).

It gives me a headache to think about that stuff. I'm just a kid. I don't need that kind of trouble (Kenny, 7).

Why does love happen between two particular people?
No one is sure why it happens, but I heard it has something to do with how you smell. That's why perfume and deodorant are so popular (Jan, 9).

I think you're supposed to get shot with an arrow or something, but the rest of it isn't supposed to be so painful (Carlos, 8).

Why do lovers hold hands?
They want to make sure their rings don't fall off because they paid good money for them (Dave, 8).

When should you fall in love?
I'm not rushing into love. Fourth grade is hard enough (Regina, 10).

How can you tell if two adults eating dinner at a restaurant are in love?
They just stare at each other and their food gets cold (Brad, 8).

It's love if they order one of those desserts that are on fire. They like to order those because it's how they're both feeling inside (Christine, 6).

There you have it. The experts have spoken. They've just told us how LOVE works. LOVE has universal qualities that even children can understand. And, this universality of LOVE transcends the physical. It is a work-in-progress that is both out of this world and integral to it!

> A 2003 study found that not only does hugging, hand-holding and other positive touch make your heart feel happy but it also protects your heart. People in the study who were physically affectionate had lower blood pressure, less reported stress and fewer markers of heart disease *(Elias, M., "Study: Hugs warm the heart and may protect it," Health and Behavior, March 10, 2003).*

LOVE: Putting It Into Practice

LOVE—Activity One:

A popular Bible verse concerning love comes from Matthew 5:44: "I tell you: Love your enemies and pray for those who persecute you." And in Matthew 22:37-39, Jesus said, "Thou shalt love the Lord thy God with all thy heart, and with all thy soul, and with all thy mind. This is the first and great commandment. And the second is like unto it, Thou shalt love thy neighbor as thyself."

Keeping these powerful verses in mind, identify specific ways you have demonstrated LOVE for each of the statements below:

1. LOVE your neighbor:

2. LOVE yourself:

3. LOVE your enemies:

4. LOVE God:

As you reflect on your responses, see what patterns you can identify. How are you using your LOVE Power ... and what conscious decisions can you make so you can use LOVE from a higher level of consciousness?

LOVE—Activity Two:

As you think about the specific area you are working on throughout this course, make a list of what you have attracted yourself to that is either helping or hindering your success. Become aware of what you focused on that contributed to attracting yourself to those particular things. What can you do differently, to use your Power of LOVE more effectively?

Example: Healthy Eating

Helping Me:

I reconnected with an old friend who had just released a guide entitled, *Healthy Living Cookguide*. She gave me a copy and pointed out some of her favorite recipes. These recipes helped me change my eating habits.

How? I realized all my recipes were based on fatty, "comfort" foods, and that led me to be on the lookout for new recipes. While surfing the web, I attracted myself to a *Healthy Living Cookguide* because I noticed it was written by an old friend. I sent her an email which reconnected us.

Hindering Me:

I find myself at fast food restaurants way too often, tempted by the burger and fries that I love.

How? I am still holding thoughts about how much I miss my burger and fries. My thoughts then generate feeling like a martyr. That harmonizes with the thought and feeling of "poor me, I deserve a special treat. Look out burger and fries, here I come!"

How to use my LOVE Power more effectively: Create some affirmations about deserving a healthy, fit, fully-functioning body. Post pictures of my head pasted on a great body, to reinforce why I want to do this. Maybe I could even create a picture of what the saturated fat contained in an order of burger and fries actually looks like! YUK!

LOVE Affirmation:

*I claim LOVE now. I use LOVE to attract myself to what is highest
and most spiritual, so I can be the best, most loving person I can be.*

Quotes to Inspire LOVE

The source of love is deep in us and we can help others realize a lot of happiness. One word, one action, one thought can reduce another person's suffering and bring that person joy. (Thich Nhat Hanh)

As you let joy and praise become your daily companions, both toward yourself and others, you will find everything in your world taking on new appearances. Peace, love, and harmony will reign supreme in your life. (Myrtle Fillmore)

If I told patients to raise their blood levels of immune globulins or killer T-cells, no one would know how. But if I can teach them to love themselves and others fully, the same changes happen automatically. The truth is: love heals. (Bernie Siegel)

The fruit of love is service, which is compassion in action. Religion has nothing to do with compassion. It is our love for God that is the main thing because we have all been created for the sole purpose to love and be loved. (Mother Teresa)

The conclusion is always the same: love is the most powerful and still the most unknown energy in the world. (Pierre Teilhard de Chardin)

Love, in Divine Mind, is the idea of universal unity. In expression, it is the power that joins and binds together the universe and everything in it. Love is a harmonizing, constructive power. When it is made active in consciousness, it conserves substance and reconstructs, rebuilds, and restores (us) and (our) world. (Charles Fillmore)

Always aim at complete harmony of thought and word and deed. Always aim at purifying your thoughts and everything will be well. (Mahatma Gandhi)

Everybody can be great, because anybody can serve. You only need a heart full of grace, a soul generated by love. (Martin Luther King, Jr.)

We, "as seekers of the Light," are united in an invisible bond of love for all (humankind). We know that good shall be victorious and that nothing can defeat it. (May Rowland)

Love starts when we push aside our ego and make room for someone else. (Rudolf Steiner)

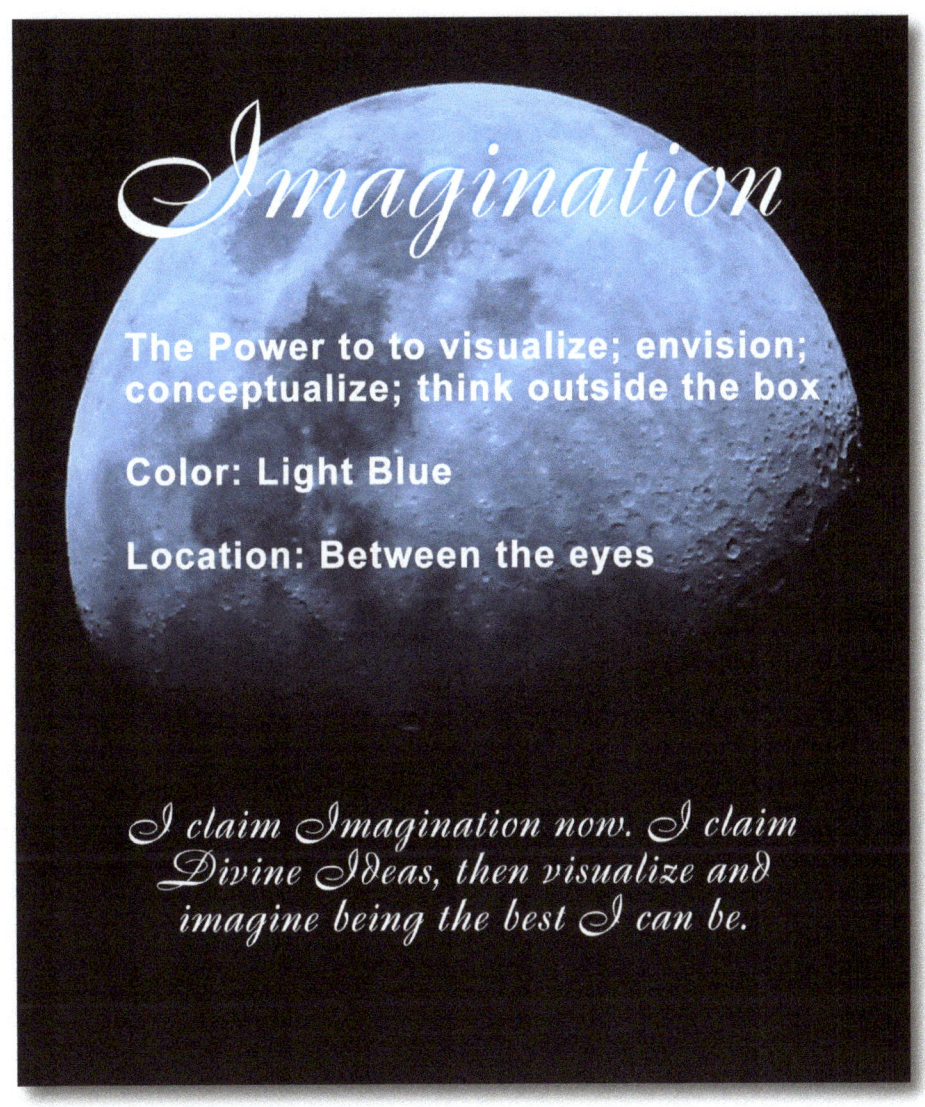

Around here, we don't look backwards for very long. We keep moving forward, opening up new doors and doing new things because we're curious ... and curiosity keeps leading us down new paths.
(Walt Disney)

Imagination is the beginning of creation. First, you imagine what you desire; then you will what you imagine, and finally you create what you will. It begins with imagination.
~ George Bernard Shaw

IMAGINATION

Overview

- Location: Between the eyes
- Color: Light Blue

IMAGINATION is the Power to visualize; envision; conceptualize; think outside the box.

From ordinary consciousness: The ability to visualize; envision; conceptualize, and think outside the box based on our senses, thoughts, feelings, and beliefs. We use IMAGINATION to visualize a beautiful garden or sunset, or to fuel our fear of a tornado or terrorist attack.

- *Underdeveloped IMAGINATION* results in people who demonstrate little ability to visualize or picture anything that is not concrete and visible. They have difficulty conceptualizing an idea. For example, when looking for a new home, people with underdeveloped IMAGINATION would have difficulty visualizing what their furniture would look like in the places they view. Further, they cannot "see beyond" the appearance of the house. They could not visualize how the living room would look without the hot pink carpeting or purple passion paint on the walls, and therefore decide not to buy the house—even though it may be exactly what they need and want in terms of features and function.

- *Egocentric IMAGINATION* results in people who may be excessive daydreamers, who spend so much time daydreaming that little or nothing is accomplished. It can also result in obsessive worrying, even advancing to the point of being delusional. Hypochondriac and doomsday proponents would be good examples of someone with an egocentric IMAGINATION.

From elevated consciousness: The ability to visualize; envision; conceptualize, and think outside the box based on Ideas, Truths, Principles, and Laws that are Divine in nature. We use IMAGINATION to envision ourselves being the best person we can be.

Neuroscientist Dr. Andrew Newberg reports that human beings are not tied to the principles that govern genetic evolution. We are free to reinvent ourselves, and our spirituality. What makes us unique is the extraordinary impermanence of our ideas, and this impermanence is reflected in our brain's extraordinary neuroplasticity *(Andrew Newberg in Born to Believe, Free Press, New York, 2006, pg.104)*. Our IMAGINATION is an incredible Power that helps us soar to new heights.

When you were younger, did you ever lie back on the cool grass with a trusted friend on a hot summer day, enjoying the gentle breeze of summer caressing your face? Did you look up at the clouds and daydream? As you both looked up at the clouds, what  did you see? Did you see more than clouds? Perhaps you saw a face in the clouds, an animal, or even an entire scene. If you had this kind of experience, you were using your Power of IMAGINATION. As you read this, you may have even been experiencing it again right now. If so, you are using your Power of IMAGINATION. Our oldest ancestors looked up at the stars and imagined seeing lions, water bearers, scorpions, and twins. They were using IMAGINATION. Children at Christmas time imagine a jolly old elf delivering Christmas presents, and have no trouble imagining him going to each and every home in a single night, let alone getting down the chimney! They are using their IMAGINATION.

From the perspective of neuroscience, a chief characteristic of an active imagination is thought to be psycho-spatial processing. Psycho-spatial processing is when we conceive of an object, say a cube, in our mind's eye and then, in our mind, move and rotate the cube. It is when we encounter and internalize an object from the external world, creating the mental representation of the thing we're looking at rather than the object itself. Psycho-spatial processing is important, because it's how we pick up on patterns, which are then transferred via the corpus callosum to the left brain, where that information is logically processed and interpreted into familiar functions such as language and mathematics. There's an important point to be taken here: creativity is NOT simply the perceptual and processing capacities of the right hemisphere; it is the combination of perception, processing, transmission, and integration of information from one hemisphere to the other. An active imagination is a neuroplastic (natural adaptive/developmental) process, facilitated by specific brain regions that can be intentionally driven and developed. Creativity is something akin to a skill that can be acquired and optimized by systematically targeting cognitive processes which traverse the corpus callosum—causing the neurons of the left and right hemispheres to fire and wire together, a process known in neuroscience as the Hebbian postulate *(Elevated Labs, Neuroplasticity and Creativity, April 11, 2013).*

One of the great philosophers of all time, Dr. Seuss, described imagination this way, "Think left, think right, think low, think high. Oh, the thinks you can think up if only you try!"

As we thought right and as we thought left, we thought of a quote by Albert Einstein: "Imagination," he says, "is more important than knowledge. Knowledge is limited to all we know and understand while imagination is the preview of coming attractions."

We must live out our imaginations. We are image-makers. We are IMAGINATION machines. And the quality of those images depends on our ability to think right, think left, think high, think low.

One thing is for sure, we can't depend on our eyes when our imagination is out of focus. Our imagination is out of focus when our thinking is out of focus. And our thinking is haywire when our consciousness is hard-wired into worldly attachments.

The word "imagination" has an interesting history. It comes from the word *image*, which comes from the Latin *imago*, which, in turn, was derived from the old Semitic root, *mag*.

The word "magic" comes from similar roots and derives from the Latin *magi,* and the Greek word *magos*, which means wise, learned in the mysteries. Assyrian scholars inform us that the Latin word *imago* comes from an old Akkadian word, *imga*, which means wise, holy, and learned.

Webster's definition of imagination is a bit clinical, and a bit boring. According to Webster imagination is the "ability of forming mental images, sensations and concepts which are not perceived through sight, hearing, or the other outer senses."

Our definition is a bit more, well, imaginative. It takes into consideration the essence, the chutzpa, the ephemeral nature of IMAGINATION (as a Power) itself. Here is a partial definition of imagination from the minds of the Holtons—which we readily admit can be a bit scary. ☺

IMAGINATION, from our perspective, is: "Directed chaos, meticulous nonsense, predictable absurdity, intuitional calisthenics, intellectual spelunking, cognition's pressure-release valve, the Muse's memo, abstraction's punctuality, novelty's field of dreams."

Our feeling is that any definition less exotic will miss the essence of what we mean by 'thinking right, thinking left, thinking high, thinking low.'

IMAGINATION is a great energizer. It is a wonderful catalyst for action. But IMAGINATION, in and of itself, is just a start, a beginning. IMAGINATION must be coupled with our other Powers, as the following story illustrates:

> When she looked ahead, Florence Chadwick saw nothing but a solid wall of dense fog. Her arms felt like rubber. Her body was cold and numb. She ached from head to toe. She had been swimming non-stop for over 15 grueling hours.
>
> She was already the first woman to swim across the English Channel. And now, at age 34, her goal was to become the first woman to swim from Catalina Island to California's golden coast.
>
> On that April morning the ocean was like an ice bath and the fog was so thick that Florence could hardly see the support boats that flanked her. From out of the deep, sharks cruised toward the small boating party that protected her. Occasionally she could hear the crack of a rifle when the sharks got too close. She struggled on, hour after hour in the icy waters.
>
> In one of the boats her mother and trainer shouted words of encouragement. But all Florence could see was the thick menacing fog. With less than a half mile to go, she breathlessly asked to be pulled out of the icy, shark-infested waters.

Still thawing her chilled body three hours later, Florence told a reporter, "If only I could have seen the coast. If only I had known how close I was. I think I could have made it."

So you see, it wasn't the icy waters, the sharks, or the fatigue that defeated Florence that April afternoon. It was her inability to see the outcome. She couldn't imagine how it could have been different than what she was experiencing.

The same thing happens to us. We imagine our success. We image what we want in our mind, and then let the fog of doubt, disbelief, and fear cloud our vision.

Her determination took her back to those icy waters several months later. This time she swam more relaxed and confidently. The fog still blocked her vision, but Florence had her goal pictured clearly in her mind.

She imagined her success and visualized every stroke and kick. Not only did she become the first woman to swim across the Catalina Channel; she eclipsed the men's record by two hours.

IMAGINATION is a powerful gift. It is ours to develop and use. We have the power to imagine what we want. Imagine that! We have the power to imagine what we want! We can use our imagination to change our world and the world around us.

> Creativity requires an incubation period (creative loafing); people need time to soak in a problem and let the ideas bubble up. In fact, it's not so much the deadline that's the problem; it's the distractions that rob people of the time to make that creative breakthrough. People can certainly be creative when they're under the gun, but only when they're able to focus on the work. They must be protected from distractions, and they must know that the work is important and that everyone is committed to it *(Amabile, Teresa, HBS's Teresa Amabile 'tracks creativity in the wild', article by Beth Potier, Harvard Gazette, February 10, 2005).*

IMAGINATION is probably one of the most easily understood Powers. Most of us have heard of the "screen of our minds" where we visualize what we want to create, need, or desire. It is easy to see how we use this Power when we imagine the work we want to do, how we want to decorate our homes, or how a project will turn out. Some of us use the "screen of our minds" to picture how to get from point A to point B. Visionaries use this faculty well, especially if they can move their visions from consciousness to the physical realm.

A young girl may desire to make her own clothes. She daydreams and visualizes herself at the sewing machine making them. As she learns how to sew, she also learns how to make patterns. Soon, using her Ability of IMAGINATION, she starts visualizing clothes of her own design and proceeds to make them.

> Arthur Koestler introduced the concept of bisociation — that creativity arises as a result of the intersection of two quite different frames of reference. This idea was later developed into conceptual blending. In the '90s, various approaches in cognitive science that dealt with metaphor, analogy and structure mapping have been converging, and a new integrative approach to the study of creativity in science, art and humor has emerged under the label conceptual blending *(Koestler, A. (1964). The Act of Creation. London: Pan Books)*.

In his work *Art of Thought,* published in 1926, Graham Wallas presented one of the first models of the creative process. In the Wallas stage model, creative insights and illuminations may be explained by a process consisting of 5 stages:

(i) *preparation* (preparatory work on a problem that focuses the individual's mind on the problem and explores the problem's dimensions);

(ii) *incubation* (where the problem is internalized into the unconscious mind and nothing appears externally to be happening);

(iii) *intimation* (the creative person gets a "feeling" that a solution is on its way),

(iv) *illumination* or insight (where the creative idea bursts forth from its preconscious processing into conscious awareness); and

(v) *verification* (where the idea is consciously verified, elaborated, and then applied) *(Wallas, Graham, Art of Thought. 1926)*.

Like all the Powers, IMAGINATION can be used in positive, uplifting ways (for example, to visualize a new business or solve a sticky problem) or in negative, non-productive ways (such as worrying about the future or imagining people are talking about you behind your back). It is useful to realize that IMAGINATION is what fuels worry. Parents use IMAGINATION to worry about what might happen to their children. People may worry about losing jobs or becoming ill. A child may imagine a monster in the closet or under the bed.

The neurobiology of creativity is a growing field in the neurosciences. Creative innovation requires co-activation and communication between regions of the brain that ordinarily are not strongly connected. Highly creative people who excel at creative innovation have an idiosyncratic knowing that defines their 'creative voice.' They tend to differ from others in three ways:

- they have a high level of specialized knowledge;
- they are capable of divergent thinking mediated by the frontal lobe;
- and they are able to modulate neurotransmitters such as norepinephrine in their frontal lobe.

Thus, the frontal lobe appears to be the part of the cortex that is most important for creativity *(Kenneth M Heilman, MD, Stephen E. Nadeau, MD, and David Q. Beversdorf, MD. "Creative Innovation: Possible Brain Mechanisms" Neurocase (2003).*

IMAGINATION From the Four Levels of Consciousness

Let's take a look at the use of IMAGINATION at the four levels of consciousness we have been exploring:

1. **Unconscious IMAGINATION:** based on a cause in subconscious mind which consists of beliefs that are not in our moment to moment awareness. A person could be holding a subconscious belief that s/he is not intelligent. This person then imagines himself or herself as not intelligent. A painter might have a strong mental impression, totally unaware of the belief fueling it; then the painter begins to put paint to canvas based on what is being visualized in the mind.

   Neuroscience tells us creative drive results from an interaction of the frontal lobes, the temporal lobes, and dopamine from the limbic system. The frontal lobes can be seen as responsible for idea generation, and the temporal lobes for idea editing and evaluation *(Flaherty AW (2005). "Frontotemporal and dopaminergic control of idea generation and creative drive". J Comp Neurol 493 (1): 147–53).* This is all occurring at the unconscious level.

2. **Conscious IMAGINATION from our senses:** based on something in physicality we are gleaning through our sight, sound, scent, touch, and/or taste. This is when we see something we like in the outer world, like granite counter tops at a friend's home, and then visualize them in our own home. Or, when we are shopping for a new home, we visualize our furniture in it.

   One practical consequence of positivity's mind-broadening powers is enhanced creativity. A broad mindset changes the way you think and act in a wider range of circumstances. When you see more, more ideas come to mind, more actions become possible *(Rowe, G., J. Hirsch, and A. Anderson, 2007, "Positive affect increases the breadth of attentional selection," Proceedings of the National Academy of Sciences of the United States of America 104: 383-388)*.

3. **Conscious IMAGINATION from our human personality:** based on thoughts, feelings, attitudes and/or beliefs held in ordinary consciousness. When a person sets an intention to become a writer, he/she begins to imagine and even daydream about creating a best-selling book.

   According to Kenneth Heilman, a neurologist at the University of Florida and the author of *Creativity and the Brain*, creativity not only involves coming up with something new, but also with shutting down the brain's habitual response, or letting go of conventional solutions. There may be, for example, a dampening of norepinephrine, the neurotransmitter that sets off the fight-or-flight alarm. That's why creative connections often occur when people are peaceful and relaxed *(Heilman, K., Matter of Mind: A Neurologist's View of Brain-behavior Relationships, 2007)*.

4. **Conscious IMAGINATION from our True Identity, or Authentic Self:** based upon Divine Ideas, Laws, and Principles. This is when we visualize and conceptualize what it is like to be our Authentic Self, so we can be the best, most imaginative person we can be.

   In studying exceptionally creative people in history, some common traits in lifestyle and environment are often found. Creative people usually had parents who were supportive, but rigid and non-nurturing. Most had an interest in their field at an early age, and most had a highly supportive and skilled mentor in their field of interest. Often the field they chose was relatively uncharted, allowing for their creativity to be expressed more than would be possible in a field with large amounts of  previous information. Most exceptionally creative people devoted almost all of their time and energy into their craft, and after about a decade had a creative breakthrough which made them famous. Their lives were marked with extreme dedication and a cycle of hard-work and breakthroughs as a result of their determination *(Gardner, 1993a, Cited work: Harold Ruegg, Imagination: An Inquiry into the Sources and Conditions That Stimulate Creativity (New York: Harper, 1954)*.

We found a very interesting quote by Albert Einstein about a subject you wouldn't normally associate with a physicist. Einstein had this to say about *optical delusions*: "A human being is part of the whole called the 'Universe.'(We) experience (ourselves) as something separated from the rest—a kind of optical delusion in consciousness. This delusion is a kind of prison for us, restricting us. Our task is to free ourselves from optical delusions."

He is right, of course. Many people are in a prison of sorts. They are incarcerated by optical delusions, as they throttle back their consciousness, and thus their creativity, by holding onto past beliefs and old scripts that keep them mired down in the shadows of rigid convention, religious dogma, and unhealthy assumptions.

Billions of people live in a world of B.S.—Debilitating BS. (By the way, in case you're wondering, B.S. stands for Belief System!) They live in a world of shadows, of 'optical delusions,' as Einstein so aptly put it. They live in a world of separation and duality. A world that gives power to outer appearances instead of inner transformation.

Most people have sold out to the world of form. They have created a world of optical delusions to satisfy their material appetites. They let their IMAGINATION run wild in ineffective, destructive ways.

Plato gave us a brilliant description of the world of optical delusions we've created. He described it in the Cave Allegory in his masterpiece, *The Republic*.

> In the Cave Allegory, Plato imagines a group of people who have lived in a cave all of their lives. They are chained to a wall so they can't see the cave entrance. They can only face the wall.
>
> Behind them is a constant light that illuminates various statues that have been placed behind them. The light's movements cause shadows to flicker around the cave.
>
>
> When the people of the cave see these shadows they think they're seeing life in action. The prisoners imagine that the shadows are reality.
>
> Plato then explains how a philosopher who was a former prisoner is freed from the cave and realizes that the shadows on the wall are not reality at all. He sees that the light outside the cave and the statues which cause the shadows are real but that the shadows themselves are optical delusions.
>
> The philosopher realizes that the shadows in the cave were just effects created by the real objects. He had given power to things that weren't real.
>
> At the end of the allegory, Plato is adamant that it is the philosopher's responsibility to re-enter the cave.
>
> Plato reasons that those who have seen the light have a duty to educate those in the material world so they can spread light to those in darkness.

For us, it is our privilege—not so much of a forced responsibility—but privilege as Unity minsters, to help people move out of the world of shadows, and beyond the world of optical delusions into the light. As a result, we can all master this human experience by realizing that WE ARE THE LIGHT! Imagine that! You are the LIGHT. We are the LIGHT in human form.

We want to assure you that no matter what happens to you here on the human plane, you have the power to move beyond any and all optical delusions by using your IMAGINATION in conjunction with the other Powers. You can use your IMAGINATION for the good of your family, for your own good, and for the good of humankind.

IMAGINATION: Putting It Into Practice

IMAGINATION—Activity One:

Choose *at least three* from the "Baker's Dozen" idea list below, to strengthen your IMAGINATION in a very practical way. Capture your experiences and thoughts in your journal.

1. Pay attention to the world around you, and notice sights, sounds, colors, scents, patterns, textures, etc.
2. Question unquestioned answers.
3. Grab some blank paper, and doodle. Make up stories about your doodling.
4. Travel off beaten paths, and record new experiences.
5. Welcome analogies and metaphors into your life. (For example, my car is like a coffee mug because ...; this tough project is like a clock because ... ; this difficult customer is like a magic marker because ...; etc. You just fill in any object that comes to mind, and let the metaphors roll)!
6. Tear pictures and words out of magazines, and paste them into a collage that reflects your goals and dreams.
7. Go outside and look at the clouds. See how many different images and forms you can see.
8. Let out your wonderfully imaginative child within by playing games, going to the playground, spending time with children playing imaginary games.
9. Develop an unfailing bias for creative loafing.

10. Take 365 'guilt-free' vacations each year. (This means doing something every single day that is fun, different, and exciting. It can be 10 minutes, or the entire day! But every day, build in a mini-vacation!)
11. Schedule a 20-minute meditation time, and sit quietly. You can listen to soft music, light a candle, or use a guided imagery CD. Just allow yourself to visualize whatever comes to mind.
12. Begin capturing your dreams, and reflecting on the messages they bring you.
13. Improve your storytelling ability.

IMAGINATION—Activity Two:

As you think about the specific area you are working on throughout this course, create a vivid image of yourself successfully achieving your goals. What will it look like? How does it feel? What are you doing, saying, thinking? Who are you with? Make your visualization as specific, broad-reaching, and impactful as you possibly can. Once you have a vivid description, record yourself sharing it. Then, listen to this recording at least twice a day, until you can bring the images to your waking consciousness effortlessly.

Example: Healthy Eating

My goal: entertaining friends while still eating in a healthy way.

My visualization: I am filled with such amazing energy, as I sit around my kitchen table with a group of my friends, serving them a magnificent meal I have prepared that is healthy and delicious. The aroma of the rich, fresh vegetables fill the air, and I feel so relaxed because I have time to be with my friends. It was so easy to prepare this incredible meal! Everyone is joyful, and people are complimenting me on how wonderful I look, and how great the food tastes. (You get the idea!!)

IMAGINATION Affirmation:

I claim IMAGINATION now. I claim Divine Ideas, then visualize and imagine being the best person I can be.

Quotes to Inspire IMAGINATION

Your imagination is your preview of life's coming attractions. (Albert Einstein)

If we are picturing good, happy things we are charting a pleasant journey for the future. We can do this by seeing God as Spirit present in every experience and greater than the outer aspect of it. (Lowell Fillmore)

Imagination needs moodling—long, inefficient, happy idling, dawdling and puttering. (Brenda Ueland)

The debt we owe to the play of imagination is incalculable. (Carl Jung)

I like to think of the basic law of prosperity as radiation and attraction: that what you radiate outward in your mental pictures, thoughts, feelings, and affirmations, you attract into your life. (Catherine Ponder)

When the faculties of mind are understood in their threefold relation—spirit, soul, body—it will be found that every form and shape originated in the imagination. It is through the imagination that the formless takes form. (Charles Fillmore)

The simple declaration 'I see' becomes sufficient to trigger the picture-making mechanism of imagination into forming clear mental images so we can claim our good. (Hypatia Hasbrouck)

The genius of vision is to see the possibilities of the present moment, the present environment, the things within our grasp. (Ernest Wilson)

The shaping of the desire is the forming of the mental image. The mental image is the mold that the creative power of mind fills. (Georgiana Tree West)

Cellular activity is not dependent upon us, but cellular form is our responsibility and depends upon the images we hold in mind. (Richard Lynch)

If you create in your mental realm a picture of yourself, radiant, successful, self-disciplined, master of your life and destiny, then you are creating a new you which in the process of time will become objectified in your outward life. (Henry Thomas Hamblin)

Bless a thing and it will bless you. Curse it and it will curse you.
If you bless a situation, it has no power to hurt you,
and even if it is troublesome for a time,
it will gradually fade out if you sincerely bless it.
(Emmet Fox)

The Vedanta recognizes no sin. It only recognizes error. And the greatest error, says the Vedanta, is to say that you are weak, that you are a sinner, a miserable creature, and that you have no power and you cannot do this or that.
~ Swami Vivekananda

POWER

Overview

- Location: The throat, back of tongue, voice box
- Color: Purple

POWER is the Power to claim mastery; command authority of thoughts, feelings, and beliefs; express perogatives and preferences.

From ordinary consciousness: The ability to claim mastery; command authority; express perogatives and preferences based on our senses, thoughts, feelings, and beliefs. We use POWER to master a new concept or idea. We can also use POWER to control our thoughts and feelings. Or, we can use it to be domineering and controlling.

- *Underdeveloped POWER* results in a person who cannot master things easily, and allows the world of appearance to have control over their feelings and actions. This person has no sense of control in his/her life, takes on a "victim" status, and looks outside of him/herself for answers.

- *Egocentric POWER* results in a person who comes across as overly controlling about his or her own life and the lives of others, and is typically very vocal and domineering. This type of individual used POWER as a way to force ideas through and bring about the results they desire. often at the expense of others.

From elevated consciousness: The ability to claim mastery; command authority of thoughts, feelings, and beliefs; express perogatives and preferences based on Ideas, Truths, Principles, and Laws that are Divine in nature. We use POWER to master the Divine Ideas that make it possible for us to be the best, the most proficient person we can be.

The "Power of POWER" always sounds redundant and a bit confusing. In addition, in today's language, the term "power" gets a bad rap. It is usually associated with being "power hungry" or controlling of others in negative ways. In fact, a person who uses POWER from an egocentric orientation is often seen as calculating or domineering. It is also important to emphasize that there are situations where having a great amount of influence and control over others is important and appropriate. A good example would be in raising children, where a family might be thought of as a kind of benevolent dictatorship. Equally, an adult child might have to take control of his or her parent's finances or living arrangements if the parent becomes ill or mentally unstable. Whatever the situation, it is best to have the healthy Powers of WISDOM, LOVE, and UNDERSTANDING working with POWER in order to ensure you are using it in the highest and best capacity.

Since the phrase Power of POWER is redundant and it is certainly open to being misunderstood, it helps to realize the terms "dominion" and "mastery" come closer to the original intention. Further, it is helpful to distinguish between STRENGTH and POWER. STRENGTH, you'll remember, is our ability to hold onto a thought or idea, to stay the course, and to be persistent. POWER is the ability to master, have dominion, or demonstrate a commanding proficiency over those thoughts or ideas. It is easy to see how we employ STRENGTH in order to be persistent and stay the course until we master an idea or concept.

Recent research reinforces the importance of developing and effectively employing our POWER. Researchers have determined that while masters of life are innately ordinary people, they perceive, comprehend and experience life—the world, others, and themselves—differently than most of us do. As a consequence, they interact with the world, others, and themselves differently than most of us do. And, it is the way they interact with life and with themselves that makes them extraordinarily effective in dealing with life while enjoying an exceptionally high quality of life *(Erhard, W., Jensen, M., and J. DiMaggio, "Living With Mastery: Where Life Actually Happens," Harvard Business School Working Paper 11-067, May 31, 2011)*.

It is important to remember that all the POWERS operate at their highest essence when we use them at an elevated level of consciousness. They equally have usefulness in our relative, physical realm, and work together to support one other. While it is true that POWER, as with all of the Powers, can be misused, it is best to put our emphasis on its brighter, more positive side. POWER has a dual function. We use it to master and have dominion over new ideas and concepts ... especially Divine Ideas, Truths, and Principles. However, we also use POWER to control and have dominion over unwanted thoughts, feelings, and beliefs (toxic patterns) which may interfere and impede our ability to master those ideas.

According to neuroscientist Athena Staik, our brain is wired to produce change, as constant in the brain as it is in life. Change involves learning, and all learning generates change in the brain. When you seek to replace a behavior, such as a toxic thinking pattern, your actions produce neurochemical and molecular changes in cells known as neurons. As messengers, neurons communicate by transmitting electrical signals between them, and these signals are activated by the exchange of chemicals in the synapses. Your brain and body are a sophisticated communication network. Your subconscious mind, the mind of your body, manages all of the systemic processes that you do not have to think about—as well as all of your personal requests, wants or commands—both conscious and subconscious. Toxic thinking is self-perpetuating. It not only stimulates the body's reward or learning centers with pseudo feel-good feelings; it also activates the body's fear response, which further increases the likelihood that the defensive behaviors it triggers will be repeated.

Unless you set an intention to make conscious changes more often, change that occurs at subconscious levels tends to be self-perpetuating. In other words, if you do not have the life and relationships you want, you likely do not have the thinking patterns you need to create the optimal emotional states, and thus actions, that would sustain your momentum in the overall direction of your aspirations *(Staik, A., "The Neuroscience of Changing Toxic Thinking Patterns," Neuroscience and Relationships, May 2013).*

> UCLA life scientists have identified for the first time a particular gene's link to optimism, self-esteem and "mastery," the belief that one has control over one's own life. The gene Shelley E. Taylor, a distinguished professor of psychology at UCLA and senior author of the new research, and her colleagues identified is the oxytocin receptor gene (OXTR). Oxytocin is a hormone that increases in response to stress and is associated with good social skills such as empathy and enjoying the company of others *(Saphire-Bernstein, S., Way, B.M., Kim, H.S., Sherman, D.K., & Taylor, S.E. (2011) Oxytocin receptor gene (OXTR) is related to psychological resources. Proceedings of the National Academy of Sciences, 108, 15118-15122).*

Here are a couple of practical examples of the different ways we put POWER to work in our lives:

- Suppose someone wanted to learn Spanish, but had a belief that learning new languages is difficult. That individual could use POWER to have dominion over that erroneous belief, and to master the nuances of Spanish.

- We can choose to use POWER to master being the best person we can be, while also using it to have dominion and control over negativity, toxic situations we face, and the challenging effects of our personality/ego.

Here is one more case in point to illustrate how we use POWER to impact our lives. Every time we speak, we charge our words with energy. The character of that energetic charge is determined by the consciousness of the individual. Just listen to a person speak, and within moments the level of consciousness from which they are coming is obvious, because they are what they repeatedly think. And our repeated thoughts, reinforced by our words, fueled by POWER, can literally affect the wiring of our brain.

There is a great story that illustrates this perfectly. It focuses on a man whose boss had come to his home for dinner. The boss was a surly kind of guy, and spent much of the meal complaining and talking about all the problems he was experiencing. Throughout the meal, the man's 7-year-old son kept staring at the boss. Finally, the boss could not stand it any longer. He turned to the boy and snapped, "Why do you keep staring at me?"

"Well," explained the boy, "my dad said you were a self-made man."

At that, the boss swelled up in pride and bragged, "My young man, that is absolutely right! I am a self-made man!"

"If that's true," said the boy, "then why on earth did you make yourself like that?"

In a recent article from *Psychology Today*, clinical and health psychologist Melanie Greenberg, Ph.D., explains that over long periods, our patterns of thinking become etched into the billions of neurons in our brains, connecting them together in unique, entrenched patterns. When certain brain pathways—connections between different components or ideas—are frequently repeated, the neurons begin to "fire" or transmit information together in a rapid, interconnected sequence. Once the first thought starts, the whole sequence gets activated. Over time, because of the nature of your consciousness, you can begin to change the wiring of your brain so your prefrontal cortex (the executive center, responsible for setting goals, planning and executing them), is more able to influence and shut off your rapidly firing, fear-based amygdala (emotion control center). And, this is exactly what brain imaging studies on effects of mindfulness therapy have shown *(Greenberg, M., "Become the CEO of Your Own Brain," Psychology Today, April 2, 2013)*.

We exercise POWER through our speech, and there are many ways to use it: denials, affirmations, prayer, praise, and thanksgiving. Here's a technique to help you apply the incredible effect of POWER. We call it the **3-P Formula of POWER,** and it defines in a very practical way we can use Power at the highest, most elevated level. The 3 P's stand for the words Positive, Passionate, and Proactive!

- *Positive*: Be diligent in ensuring that the words you speak are positive. This means focusing on what is going right, beholding the Divine in others, and looking for solutions rather than dwelling on problems.

- *Passionate*: Put energy into your words, and speak your vision with boldness and authority. You can only bring your thoughts into manifestation, and claim dominion over the world of appearance, by speaking with passion.

- *Proactive*: Evaluate the expectations and expansiveness of your words, to ensure you are speaking as a thought leader, regardless of your area of expertise. Focus on ways to move forward, and anticipate success as you claim your goals.

You have the power to create the appearance of monsters or miracles! When you use meditation and prayer to allow your Deeper Self (instead of personal ego) to guide, govern, and direct your thoughts and feelings, a charge of spiritual energy is infused in your words. Jesus understood the power of the spoken word: In Matthew 12:37, He said, "For by thy words thou shalt be justified, and by thy words thou shalt be condemned." Today He might say, "The words you use characterize your state of consciousness. And your state of consciousness can produce self-defeating thoughts, words, and actions—or life-affirming thoughts, words, and actions.

> The amygdala can read and identify the emotion in someone else's face within 33 milliseconds, and then just as quickly prime us to feel the same way
> *(Goleman, D., Social Intelligence, Bantam, New York, 2006, pg. 65).*

Here's another piece of advice to help you strengthen your POWER: **Refuse to be distracted**. A great example occurred during a visit from our grandson when he was five years old. During the course of his visit, we watched a TV show called *Wubbzy*, about a cute little critter who wanted to help his friends, but every time he had a task to do, he would get distracted by something—a butterfly, a bird, an ice cream truck... whatever it was he needed to focus on, he would always let something pull his attention away. When questioned about his inability to complete his tasks, little Wubbzy rationalized by saying, "I keep getting distracted!" Now—fast forward to the end of our grandson's visit, when his dad was ready to leave and was asking him to put on his shoes. It was taking a lot longer than expected, and our son finally said, "Come on Braeden—just put on your shoes!" And Braeden looked at him, so serious and sweet, and said, "But Daddy, I keep getting distracted!"

How often do we allow ourselves to become distracted by the world of appearance? We *know* our spiritual principles, but just when we are getting into the habit of meditating, BOOM, we get distracted by a busy schedule, a test we need to study for, a soccer practice we need to attend. We *know* the power of positive affirmations, but then that idiot driver takes the parking space we were getting ready to pull into; we *understand* the forgiveness concept, but then there's that coworker who stole our idea and got all the credit for it! It is so easy to get distracted from our spiritual practice—and when that happens, we just can't practice POWER from the highest and best level of consciousness. So refuse to be distracted! Create your own personal affirmation as your trigger to always bring you back to center! For example, "Wherever I am, God is ... and all is well." "I am healed, whole, and healthy. I am One in body, mind, and soul!" "My Consciousness is greater than any fear I may encounter!" "Peace, be still." "Be still and know." Find the one that works for you! Stay focused on your Oneness, and *refuse to be distracted!*

POWER From the Four Levels of Consciousness

Let's now review how POWER is used at various levels of consciousness:

1. **Unconscious POWER:** based on a cause in subconscious mind which consists of beliefs that are not in our moment to moment awareness. People at this level of unconscious POWER tend to be controlling in situations where unconscious beliefs are somehow activated or triggered. People who have subconscious low self-esteem tend to control situations in ways that confirm and reinforce this belief with "unconscious leakage." Alternatively, people may also be over-controlling to compensate for low self-esteem and overall low proficiency, without being aware of the impact of their actions.

2. **Conscious POWER from our senses:** based on something we see, hear, smell, touch, and/or taste. A young man watching other people snowboarding captures the fun and excitement of the sport. He gets excited, and decides he wants to learn how. So, through the use of conscious POWER, he is able to gain proficiency, and perhaps master the techniques needed to snowboard, while at the same time using POWER to dominate and control any fears and concerns he may have.

3. **Conscious POWER from our human personality:** based on thoughts, feelings, attitudes, and/or beliefs held in ordinary consciousness. A young woman decides she wants to follow in the footsteps of her parents, to become a doctor. So, she must master all that is required to become a doctor. She would also use her POWER to master and control any thoughts from her ordinary consciousness that she does not have what it takes to become a doctor.

4. **Conscious POWER from our True Identity, or Authentic Self:** based upon Divine Ideas, Laws, and Principles. We use POWER to master the concepts, Principles, and Divine Ideas involved in being the best person, the most proficient person, we can be. We also call on POWER to control any self-defeating thoughts to the contrary arising from the personality/ego.

> Studies link internal locus of control (what we would call POWER) with improved physical health, mental health, and quality of life in people with diverse conditions: HIV, migraines, diabetes, kidney disease, and epilepsy *(Maltby, J., Day, L., Macaskill, A., 2007. Personality, Individual Differences and Intelligence. Harlow, Pearson Prentice Hall).*

People sometimes express their concern to us about their inability to take control over their thoughts. We'd like to share a metaphor to make the point:

Imagine that you are sitting on the steps leading to your front porch. A car comes by and someone in the car says, "Get in!" You get in. You don't know where the car is going or who the people are, but you get in anyway.

Later that same day you are sitting on the steps again and an SUV drives by. Someone in the SUV says, "Get in." And so you get in. You're not sure where it's going, who the people are, or how long it will take, but you get in anyway.

Later that same day you are sitting on the steps to the front porch again and a truck comes by ... you get the idea! Here you are, allowing any vehicle that happens to drive by take control over you. You are just following blindly.

Suppose those vehicles represent your thoughts. Just because they 'drive by' in your consciousness, it doesn't mean you have to go with them.

This illustration symbolizes what happens when we *auction* our mind. It makes the point that mindless action can take us anywhere. We have many thoughts during the course of a day. Some thoughts 'drive by' like the vehicles in the story. Others linger or even repeat themselves. Our thoughts determine our inclinations, our inclinations lead to our choices, and our choices lead to our actions.

Thoughts like "I think I'll sleep 15 minutes later tomorrow" or "I'm going to floss after every meal today" or "I'm going to cheat on my diet today and eat a burger with fries" are all intentional thoughts. They may or may not lead to the actions they describe.

Sometimes we have emotional outbursts and fly off the handle: someone cuts in front of us on the Interstate or someone says something to us that sets us off. In each of these cases, our thoughts lead to our emotions. Emotions don't happen in a vacuum.

They are chosen. They are internal reactions to an outside stimulus. But the outside stimulus does not cause us to do anything. We can use our Power of POWER to take dominion over any outer situation, stimulus, or thought.

When we are fearful, we choose to be fearful. If we are envious, we choose to be envious. If we are joyful, we choose to be joyful. While it is our Power of WILL that actually makes the choice (more about WILL coming up), we use POWER to master our thoughts, emotions, and actions in order to transcend anything in the world of outer appearance.

Emerson said, "The ancestor to every action is thought." Henry Ford said, "Thinking is the hardest work there is, which is probably why so few engage in it."

We agree. And the thing about thinking is every thought we have either honors Truth or multiplies illusion. We talked about the Law of Mind Action earlier, in terms of how it related to LOVE. It comes into play with POWER as well. Thoughts held in mind produce thoughts after their kind. That is, they lead to thoughts which are similar to preceeding thoughts. Similar thoughts repeated often enough reinforce either Truth or perpetuate illusion—depending on the thoughts you are creating.

That is the Law of Mind Action and that's how *Mind Auction* works too! When we control our thinking through POWER, we control our thoughts. If we auction our thinking to the world of outer appearances we auction our lives to the world of wishcraft, quick fixes, and bailout promises.

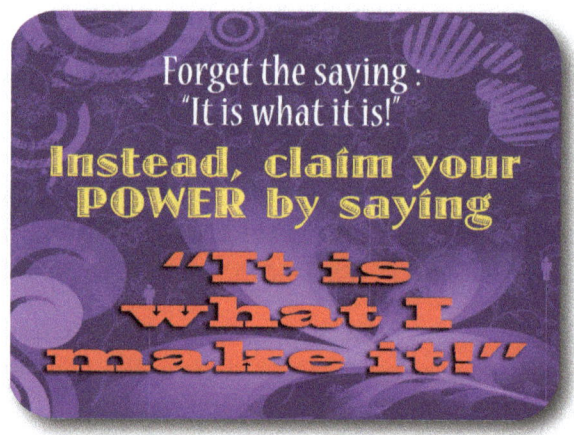

In a remarkable breakthrough study, researchers at Berlin's Bernstein Center for Computational Neuroscience claim they are the first to actually measure intentions we hold in our mind before the intentions are put into action.

When new information enters our brains, they say, it enters into our short-term memory field. The process is called synaptic transmission. The electro-chemical impulses ignite one neuron, which in turn ignites another neuron.

The new information is remembered only if the second neuron repeats the impulse back again to the first. This is most likely to happen when we decide that the new information is important. Affirmations are a perfect example of this repeat firing process.

If the neural 'echo' is sustained long enough it amps up the brain's neuroplasticity, which leads to lasting structural changes. This 'echo' hardwires the new information, forming memory grooves in our gray matter. These grooves are the physical results of our thinking. The question is, what kind of thoughts do we allow to flood through our consciousness?

It is a perennial spiritual teaching that if our human personality is not the product of a spiritual consciousness which springs from our divine connection, we tend to allow a cattle drive of materialistic thoughts to enter our consciousness and rob us of the happiness, inner peace, and prosperity we deserve. In other words when we deny our innate divinity, we auction off our thoughts to their lowest possible denominator — an outer appearance-focused, materialistic ego.

If we hardwire our thoughts only on what we see in the physical world, we create grooves of materiality in our consciousness which make it harder for us to see the abundance which is all around us.

When that happens we suffer from what is called the 'Pike Syndrome.' Researchers placed a Northern Pike in a fish tank and then put minnows in the tank. Pikes love minnows. It didn't take the Pike long to feast on the minnows.

Then the researchers placed a reinforced glass barrier between the pike and its food supply. The pike slammed into the barrier to get at its dinner, then circled and rammed the barrier again and again — until it gave up.

The researchers then pulled out the barrier and the pike found itself surrounded by the minnows. But it made no move to eat them. It was suffering from what is called learned helplessness.

So what does this have to do with POWER? When our POWER is under-developed, it can create a pattern of learned helplessness. This manifests as a giving-up reaction, a quitting response that follows from the belief that whatever you do doesn't matter. While the Northern Pike simply stopped beating its head against an imaginary wall, even to the point of starvation, people with an ineffective level of POWER may resort to what is called explanatory style — the manner in which you habitually explain to yourself why events happen (or why they don't happen). When it is used in a negative way, it is the great modulator of learned helplessness. According to Positive Psychology, an optimistic explanatory style stops helplessness, whereas a pessimistic explanatory style spreads helplessness. Your way of explaining events to yourself determines how helpless you can become, or how energized, when you encounter everyday setbacks as well as momentous defeats *(Seligman, M., Learned Optimism, Vintage Books, New York, 2006, pg. 16).*

We've all had those "What was I thinking?" moments ... when we look at the result of something we did .... and the results are NOT what we had expected or desired! We used POWER at an ineffective, underdeveloped or ego-centric level, and paid the price. Our explanatory style quite often reinforces the negative or ineffective results of our thoughts, words, and/or actions, and we move into learned helplessness.

Some people seem to live in that "What was I thinking" state of consciousness all the time! For example, consider these stories of "wanna-be" criminals who have to be saying, "What was I thinking?" (By the way, these are TRUE situations!)

> *A guy walked into a little corner store with a shotgun and demanded all the cash from the cash drawer. Then he saw a bottle of scotch that he wanted and told the cashier to put it in the bag as well. The cashier refused, saying "No, because I don't believe you are over 21." At this point the robber took his drivers license out of his wallet and gave it to the clerk, who checked it out, then put the scotch in the bag. As the robber then ran from the store, the cashier promptly called the police and gave the name and address he got off the license. The robber was arrested within the hour. WHAT WAS HE THINKING?*

> *A woman was reporting her car as stolen, and mentioned that there was a car phone in it. The police officer taking the report called the phone and told the guy who answered that he had read the ad in the newspaper and wanted to buy the car. They arranged to meet—and the thief was arrested. WHAT WAS HE THINKING?*

> *A man purchased a case of very rare, very expensive cigars, and had them included on his insurance policy. Within a month, having smoked his entire stockpile of cigars, he filed a claim against the insurance company, stating the cigars were lost "in a series of small fires." The insurance company refused to pay, citing the obvious reason that the man had consumed the cigars in the normal fashion. The man sued ... and won. In delivering the ruling, the judge agreed it was a frivolous claim, but because the man held a policy from the company in which it had warranted the cigars were insurable, including against fire, without defining what it considered to be "unacceptable fire" the company was obligated to pay the claim. Rather than endure a lengthy and costly appeal process the insurance company paid the man $15,000 for the rare cigars he lost in "the fires." But wait! There's more! After the man cashed the check, the insurance company had him arrested on 24 counts of arson. With his own insurance claim and testimony from the previous case being used against him, the man was convicted of intentionally burning his insured property and sentenced to 24 months in jail and a $24,000 fine. WHAT WAS HE THINKING?*

These stories seem unbelievable, but they are true. And all of us, at some times, walk around in a state of unconsciousness—operating from auto-pilot that is set on low-beam! We find ourselves hitting our head, loudly exclaiming, "What was I thinking?

But just imagine what would happen if we asked the same question (What was I thinking?) when we get GREAT results in our life? Consider how we could reinforce those wonderful experiences by becoming aware of what we were thinking, so we could replicate it! This is where our POWER comes into play, to help us take dominion over our thinking, and master our thoughts, words, and actions to ensure we are always operating from the highest level of consciousness.

So how do we move to that highest, most elevated level of POWER? Here are a couple of "adventures" you can try:

Create a Mental Shift: Make a shift from "What WAS I thinking?" (past tense) to that very present awareness: WHAT AM I THINKING?" This helps you become extremely aware of where your head is, where your thinking is, where your consciousness is, at every moment! You are paying attention—and setting an intention to keep your thoughts at the highest possible level.

Take the Fillmore Challenge: Both Charles and Myrtle Fillmore have been quoted as saying: "Never make an assertion, no matter how true it may look on the surface, that you do not want to see manifest in your life." Think about this phrase. It forces you to be really aware of what you are saying. And remember, POWER is located at the root of our tongue (larynx)—because it is through our power of speech, we command things into manifestation. So what are you saying? Even something as simple as "I am so tired" Or "I'm broke" give POWER to the wrong aspects of your experience. You don't want to see those things manifest, so don't say them! And by becoming aware of what you are saying, you are also becoming aware of what you are thinking! So we invite you to take the Fillmore Challenge, and "Never make an assertion, no matter how true it may look on the surface, that you do not want to see manifest in your life."

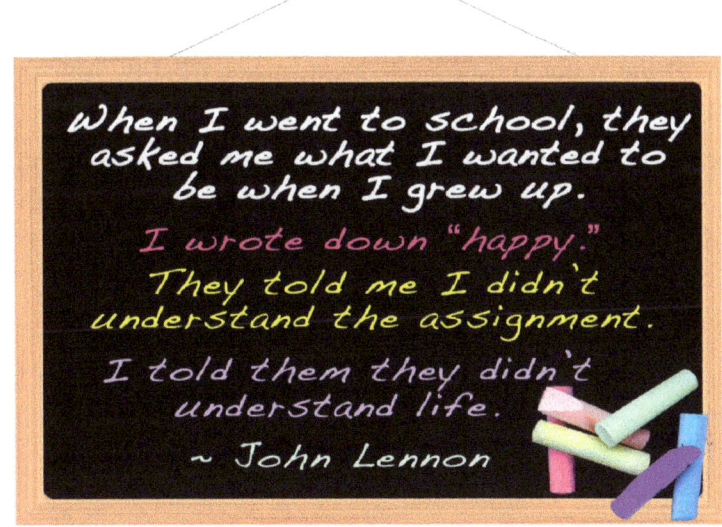

The secret is to replace those negative, self-defeating statements with positive, life-affirming statements. Create affirmations to claim, in positive, energetic ways, what it is you want to see in your life. People so often claim their affirmations don't "work." Actually, affirmations always work, in that our outer experience reflects the energy of our thinking. Every thought and word is a reflection of what we are giving energy to—so if you give 90% of your energy to error thinking and negative talk (whining, complaining, discussions about how bad things are...), and then throw in 10% positive affirmations, why would you be surprised when your experience outpictures in negative ways? We're just saying . . .

As Eric Butterworth so aptly says in *Spiritual Economics*, "Where you are in Consciousness has everything to do with what you see in experience. ... to pray for prosperity out of a sense of complaint or discouragement is to effectively compound the problem."

As you create your affirmations, be sure they are grounded in Spiritual Principles and focus on the essence of what you are seeking, rather than a specific material item. Again quoting from Eric Butterworth in *Spiritual Economics*, things "do not become true because you affirm them; you affirm them because they are true."

POWER:
Putting It Into Practice

POWER—Activity One:

Make a list of the skills you possess. Next, make a list of your favorite hobbies, activities, and interests.

As you look back over these two lists, think about what went into making these skills, hobbies, activities, and interests viable in your everyday life. How do your skills interact with your hobbies, activities, and interests? (For example, do you play the piano [skill] and accompany your church choir? [activity])

What steps did you take to gain a high level of proficiency over the particular skills, hobbies, activities, or interests you have? How can this help you in the future?

POWER—Activity Two:

As you think about the specific area you are working on throughout this course, identify toxic thoughts or beliefs you have that may be interfering with your success. How can you use POWER to deal with those testy thoughts and beliefs?

Now make a list of the skills you must master in order to be successful in the area of your choice. How can you use POWER to help you?

Example: Healthy Eating

Toxic Thoughts and Beliefs:

- I don't have the time to cook healthy food.
- I have never been successful at this before—why should this time be any different?

Life-Affirming Thoughts:
- I can use POWER to take control of the thoughts running amuck through my head.
- I can create powerful denial and affirmation statements to use whenever I become aware of these defeating statements in my consciousness: I use POWER to master my ability to cook healthy meals that are fast and easy to prepare.

Skills to master:

- How to prepare quick but healthy meals.
- Establishing regular times to eat—and sticking to those times, no matter what!

POWER Affirmation:

I claim POWER now. I use POWER to control my thoughts, words, and feelings to master Divine Ideas and be the best me I can be.

Quotes to Inspire POWER

A strong and focused personal power is essential to repairing physical tissue. Unearthing the positive is as effective a healing process as is clearing out the negative parts of our history. (Caroline Myss)

You will blaze your own trail, create your own gospel, be your own teacher, and follow your own master, which is the God-self of you at the heart of you which is created in the image-likeness of God who is love. (Eric Butterworth)

Power, we must understand, is not an end in itself, not a goal to be sought. Rather, it is simply a means that enables us to attain the end of bringing forth God ideas on earth. It is to be exercised not for the purpose of controlling others, but for the purpose of taking dominion over our own thoughts and feelings in order to come into a greater God awareness. (Winnifred Wilkinson Hausmann)

All power is in the midst of us, doing all things through us, right where we are in every experience. *(Sue Sikking)*

States of mind are not altered by changes in circumstances and surroundings, but circumstances and surroundings are altered by changes in our states of mind. (May Rowland)

All your happiness, all your health, all your power come from God. They flow in an unbroken stream from the Fountainhead into the very center of your being and radiate from center to circumference. (Emilie Cady)

Do you want to achieve mastery? You must determine that you can achieve it. Do not doubt it. Assert it. And keep on asserting it. (James Dillet Freeman)

The best years of your life are the ones in which you decide your problems are your own. You do not blame them on your mother, the ecology, or the president. You realize that you control your own destiny. (Albert Ellis)

To replace the random, endless negative chatter that filters into your mind each moment of the day, affirmations are conscious, preplanned, positive thoughts to direct your actions and behaviors in a productive way. Unless you direct your own thoughts, you leave much to chance. ... Affirmations are not self-deception; they are self-direction. (Jerry Lynch and Chungliang Al Huang)

*If one is master of one thing and understands one thing well,
one has at the same time insight into and understanding of many things.*
(Vincent Van Gogh)

Any fool can know. The point is to understand.

~ Albert Einstein

UNDERSTANDING

Overview

- Location: Front Forebrain
- Color: Gold
- UNDERSTANDING works with WISDOM and LOVE

UNDERSTANDING is the Power to comprehend and interpret knowledge; make cognitive connections.

From ordinary consciousness: The ability to comprehend; interpret knowledge; and make cognitive connections based on our senses, thoughts, feelings, and beliefs. We use UNDERSTANDING to comprehend and interpret the facts and figures, whether we're talking about building a bridge or an atomic bomb.

- *Underdeveloped UNDERSTANDING* results in a person who has difficulty comprehending and interpreting information easily, resulting in a diminished ability to perceive beyond the literal.
- *Egocentric UNDERSTANDING* results in a person who comes across as a know-it-all and perceives things that are not there ... literally or figuratively.

From elevated consciousness: The ability to comprehend; interpret knowledge; and make cognitive connections based on Ideas, Truths, Principles and Laws that are Divine in nature. We use UNDERSTANDING to interpret these Divine Principles to be the best person we can be.

When you say "I get it!" ... when you feel that "inner click" ... when you have one of those "I could have had a V-8!" moments—all of these are expressions of the Power of UNDERSTANDING.

People have different levels of understanding based on their experience, knowledge, learning, biases, intellectual capacity, and perceptual filters. In a report published by the Board of Scientific Affairs of the American Psychological Association in 1995 it was reported that "Individuals differ from one another in their ability to understand complex ideas, to adapt effectively to the environment, to learn from experience, to engage in various forms of reasoning, to overcome obstacles by taking thought" *(Neisser, U.; Boodoo, G.; Bouchard Jr, T.J.; Boykin, A.W.; Brody, N.; Ceci, S.J.; Halpern, D.F.; Loehlin, J.C.; Perloff, R.; Sternberg, R.J.; Others, (1998); "Intelligence: Knowns and Unknowns". Annual Progress in Child Psychiatry and Child Development 1997).*

The internet has become a really wonderful tool for learning about something new. The world is at our finger tips. Type in a few words, a click of the mouse, and we sometimes have more information than we ever needed or perhaps wanted to know. During this entire process, we are using our UNDERSTANDING. First, we have to comprehend the intricacies of using the computer. We must interpret what the words mean. We must know what we are looking up. Sometimes we know a few pieces of information, and then, as we add more and combine the pieces, they suddenly come together in a new way, just like a big jigsaw puzzle! This is UNDERSTANDING.

The Power of UNDERSTANDING is our ability to comprehend; interpret knowledge; and make cognitive connections. In today's slang, we might say that UNDERSTANDING means "I get it!" There are two types of UNDERSTANDING:

- Intellectual UNDERSTANDING, which is based on the cognitive awareness that characterizes the relative realm;

- Spiritual UNDERSTANDING, which is based on Oneness, Wholeness, and Connectedness that characterize the Absolute Realm.

Intellectual UNDERSTANDING is gained mostly through experience and the "school of hard knocks." It is subject to temptation and sometimes used for selfish ends. By combining reasoning with intellectual understanding, we are able to arrive at valid, practical conclusions.

Spiritual UNDERSTANDING is gained by investing time in the Silence. It results from the quickening of our Spiritual Nature, our Divine Nature. This type of knowledge sometimes includes, and always transcends intellectual understanding. This knowing comes swiftly and arises outside of the reasoning process. It comes as an internal knowing, or perhaps as a still small voice that may seem more like the reflection or echo of something we have heard and/or forgotten.

Emilie Cady, Unity minister and author of *Lessons in Truth* has this to say about spiritual UNDERSTANDING:

> You may say to yourself over and over again, that you are well and wise and happy. On the mental plane a certain "cure" is effective, and for a time you will feel healthy, wise and happy. This is a form of self-hypnotism. But until, down in the depths of your being, you are conscious of your oneness with the Eternal Presence, until you know within yourself that the spring of all wisdom and health and joy is within your own being, ready at any moment to leap forth at the call of your need, you will not have spiritual understanding."

She goes on to say that getting to this deeper understanding is necessary for our spiritual growth. And it cannot come from intellectual understanding. It must come from the wisdom of the heart.

As we've mentioned before, all the Powers work together, and it becomes difficult to separate each one to study independent of the others. UNDERSTANDING works very closely with two other Powers that will be discussed in the next two chapters: WISDOM and WILL. What distinguishes UNDERSTANDING from the others is its focus on what we know and our ability to put that information into the proper context. However, knowledge, no matter how well understood, is fairly useless unless it can be applied to our daily life and activities. That's when WISDOM comes in, which is more about knowing how to actually use the information in practical and productive ways. Then WILL becomes the Power with which we choose whether or not to actually use what we understand and know how to apply it.

So let's start the study of this triumvirate of Powers with UNDERSTANDING. When we have true UNDERSTANDING about something, we can grasp things more quickly and see results a whole lot faster! For example, think about ballroom dancing. We have enjoyed ballroom dancing for many years, and have competed as an amateur couple. We remember when we did our very first showcase routine—we had only been taking lessons for a few months (what *were* we thinking, signing up for a showcase?). Our coaches were teaching us a routine, and it took us forever to learn it, because, essentially, we were just memorizing the actual movements we were supposed to do.

Now, fast forward to a few years ago, with many showcases and competitions under our belts. By now, we understood more about the dances we were doing. We understood there were certain steps that, put together, created elements, which put together created a choreography. So instead of memorizing movements that looked ridiculously difficult, our instructors could play some music and say: "Okay, here you're going to do a twinkle into underarm turn, into a developé, roll out, then a syncopated grapevine..."—and we could see it in our mind's eye, making it fairly easy to create the routine. We could do it because we understood the movements, and it made everything easier.

With this kind of UNDERSTANDING, we could also recover more easily if something went wrong, like one of us forgets our steps. We can go into intuitive UNDERSTANDING and keep dancing until we get ourselves back on track.

Let's take another look at the Power of UNDERSTANDING from a more academic viewpoint. According to the Shorter Oxford Dictionary, 'to understand' means to comprehend, to apprehend the meaning or import of. From Merriam-Webster, we see: understanding is mental grasp, comprehension, especially the capacity to apprehend general relations of particulars. The definitions seem clear, and yet the language people use when they talk about how to help people understand something can be confusing.

Corroborating research by fifty-two researchers assures us that understanding, as a general mental capacity, involves the ability to reason, plan, solve problems, think abstractly, comprehend complex ideas, learn quickly and learn from experience. It is not merely book learning, a narrow academic skill, or test-taking smarts. Rather, it reflects a broader and deeper capability for comprehending our surroundings—"catching on," "making sense" of things, or "figuring out" what to do. In short, it's the ability to deal with cognitive complexity *(Gottfredson., L., (1997), Intelligence and social policy," Intelligence 24 (1): 1-12)*.

> Human intelligence is not only difficult to measure; it's also difficult to define. Most researchers, these days, will tell you that our intelligence is a combination of what we know (our knowledge), our skills and our ability to understand and reason -- and that our cognitive abilities continue to grow throughout our lives, rather than being set at birth. The basis of intelligence is likely a combination of several factors. For example, are you biologically destined to be only as smart as your parents? Biology, though important, is only part of the intelligence package. Other factors, including everything from what we eat to where we live, can also affect our intelligence and thus our understanding capabilities
> *(Trimarchi, M., Five Factors That Affect Human Intelligence, Curiosity, retrieved May 8, 2013)*.

Because of the nature of understanding and its relationship to comprehension, knowing, and perception, we believe there are a number of intelligences that contribute to our ability to understand anything intellectually and spiritually. The intelligences we're alluding to are the seven multiple intelligences that Howard Gardner refers to in his work:
- linguistic intelligence,
- logical-mathematics intelligence,
- spatial intelligence,
- musical intelligence,
- bodily-kinesthetic intelligence,
- interpersonal intelligence, and
- intrapersonal intelligence.

We all have these intelligences to some degree and singularly, or in combination, we use them to comprehend the world in which we find ourselves. The Power of UNDERSTANDING is truly a complex power and involves many aspects of our being.

Our notions of the Power of UNDERSTANDING are substantiated by seminal research by Robert Sternberg who suggests that "understanding is achieved by using combinations of analytical, creative, and practical intelligence" *(Sternberg, R.J. (2003) "A broad view of intelligence: The theory of successful intelligence," Consulting Psychology Journal: Practice & Research 55 (3): 139–154).*

We're sure it is becoming obvious UNDERSTANDING goes way beyond knowledge or facts. It is an inner knowing that provides information beyond the norm, helping us move through life experiences in an easier, more powerful way. Here's a great real life example. You may remember the earthquake that generated the great Indian Ocean Tsunami in December 2004. One of the many stories that came out of that event involves Tilly Smith, a 10-year-old English schoolgirl vacationing on the coast of Thailand with her parents and younger sister Holly. On the morning of December 26, the family was walking on the beach. But Tilly noticed something very different about the ocean ... how frothy it was, and not coming in and out, just coming in and in and in. She had recently studied about tsunamis in school, and she became very emotional, urging her family to return to the hotel. She kept saying, "It bubbles. The water bubbles!" She kept insisting there was going to be a tsunami, but her parents ignored her, until she finally convinced her father they should return to the hotel. As they neared their hotel, her father mentioned to a security guard that, strange as it sounded, his daughter was convinced there was going to be a tsunami. Thankfully, the guard listened, took it seriously, and began warning visitors. As people began streaming toward the hotel, Tilly and her family went to their 2nd story room, and watched from the balcony. At that moment, the massive tsunami surged toward shore. The giant tsunami killed a quarter-million people around the world that day, 10,000 of them in Thailand. There were several injuries at the Smith's hotel, but not a single fatality, which the British tabloids credited to Tilly, whom they dubbed the "Angel of the Beach."

How did Tilly KNOW? It came from something she saw and sensed at a different level than others around her. That is Divine UNDERSTANDING at work!

There is something really important to ... how else to say it, but—understand ... about UNDERSTANDING. You have to grow it to know it! Have you ever felt like Spiritual Principles appear to only work some of the time? It's because we do not fully understand the Principles. In fact, what we call "miracles" are simply demonstrations of Divine Laws which are currently beyond our knowledge and understanding of natural laws. If we don't "get it" we can't use it.

Here's a good metaphor to explain this. When our granddaughter was very young, she had a box with several different shapes cut into the top, along with blocks of all those different shapes. The goal was to fit the correct blocks into the matching shapes. We loved watching her play with this. She would take a block and struggle to force it into the wrong hole; but she was persistent (STRENGTH)! She would keep moving it around, trying different things, then move to another hole ... until all of a sudden, it would fall right into place and drop into the box. She would be so excited! But when she dumped the blocks back out, she went through the same process of trial and error. (Is any of this sounding familiar to the way we use Truth principles?)

We actually remember the moment when she got the a-ha! She was doing the usual routine, when a block dropped in. All of a sudden, she opened the lid and took that block out again—and stared at it, then stared at the hole, then put the block in the hole. Then she got another, stared at it, moved it around, stared at the lid, and put it in the right hole. She was then able to get all the blocks in the right holes easily. She "got it!" UNDERSTANDING! She could replicate it again and again. (Then she lost interest in that toy!!)

This is what happens when we "get it!" Knowledge gained through UNDERSTANDING is more stable when it is based on Divine Ideas, Principles, and Laws. Spiritual UNDERSTANDING is the ability to comprehend the Laws of Thought as well as the relation of Divine Ideas to each other. This type of knowledge is unchanging, because it is not based on the ever changing relative realm but on the immutable Laws of Spirit. Spiritual WISDOM is the ability to apply those Laws of Thought, recognizing the relation of one Divine Idea to another. It is also the ability to use and apply the knowledge that arises from that internal knowing that is outside and independent of intellectual reasoning.

UNDERSTANDING From the Four Levels of Consciousness

Now let's look at the use of UNDERSTANDING at the four levels of consciousness we have been exploring:

1. **Unconscious UNDERSTANDING:** based on a cause in subconscious mind which consists of beliefs that are not in our moment to moment awareness. This occurs when people subconsciously believe they are not worthy, and so, no matter what they do, they approach it with the unconscious knowing that they do not deserve anything positive.

   If we choose to focus on something that frightens us or makes us angry we can damage the neurons in our brain. Psychologists call this 'rumination' and it is clearly hazardous to our health *(J. Morgan and R. Banerjee, "Post-event processing and autobiographical memory in social anxiety: the influence of negative feedback and rumination," Journal of Anxiety Discord, 2008, Jan 9).* People often use the phrase "We get in our own way" or "We are our own worst enemy!"

2. **Conscious UNDERSTANDING from our senses:** based on something in physicality we are gleaning through our sight, sound, scent, touch, and/or

taste. For example, after experiencing the impact of going out into the cold without the proper clothing, a person knows what to wear the next time.

Believe it or not, this is not limited to humans! Anyone who has a dog will UNDERSTAND this UK study, which found that dogs are more likely to steal food when they think you're not looking, suggesting they understand our viewpoint. Dr. Juliane Kaminski of the University of Portsmouth's department of psychology found that when a human forbids a dog from taking food, the dog is four times more likely to disobey in a  dark room than a lit room, signifying dogs may take into account what humans can or cannot see.

The results have scientists questioning whether dogs have a cognizant understanding of other species' minds, an ability assumed limited only to humans. *(Kaminski. J.. et al.: Domestic dogs comprehend human communication with iconic signs. In: Developmental Science 12(6), 2009. pp. 831–837).*

3. **Conscious UNDERSTANDING from our human personality:** based on thoughts, feelings, attitudes, and/or beliefs held in ordinary consciousness. A woman believes she can become a real estate agent, and then goes about doing research in order to know what needs to be done to become a qualified, Board-approved agent.

4. **Conscious UNDERSTANDING from our True Identity, or Authentic Self:** based upon Divine Ideas, Laws, and Principles. This is when we begin to perceive and comprehend that there is more to us than a physical body and an ego, and we understand what it takes to be the best person, the most UNDERSTANDING person, we can be.

UNDERSTANDING: Putting It Into Practice

UNDERSTANDING—Activity One:

This one should be fun! Grab a piece of colored paper, and cut it into several big pieces, as if you were creating a jigsaw puzzle. Now, imagine that each piece represents some aspect of your job. When these pieces are put together, they will depict all the major components that make up the work you do. Take some time and write an aspect of your job on each piece of the puzzle you have created.

Now, imagine you are coaching someone who is interested in your job. How could you use this puzzle as a way to help that person understand what s/he would need to know or comprehend in order to have a grasp of what your work involves?

What did this activity tell you about the Power of UNDERSTANDING? What role does UNDERSTANDING play in successfully achieving your goals?

UNDERSTANDING—Activity Two:

As you think about the specific area you are working on throughout this course, brainstorm the specific things you need to know and understand to be successful. Include items from both the sense level and the more elevated spiritual level.

You might start by writing the sentence: In order to be successful in the area I am working on throughout this course, I need to know:

Now, complete that sentence ten different ways!

Example: Healthy Eating

In order to eat more healthily, I need to know what the recommended daily food requirements are; which foods meet these requirements; what amounts are appropriate each day; how to combine these foods into manageable, edible meals ...

From a spiritual level, I need to know how to develop my intuitive sense of knowing what to eat and when.

UNDERSTANDING Affirmation:

I claim UNDERSTANDING now. I spiritually know and comprehend how to use my Powers to be the best person I can be.

Quotes to Inspire UNDERSTANDING

There are two ways of getting understanding. One is by following the guidance of Spirit that dwells within, and the other is to go blindly ahead and learn by hard experience. Spiritual understanding is the ability of the mind to apprehend and realize the laws of thought and the relation of ideas one to another. (Charles Fillmore)

The reason why there is still poverty in this universe of lavish abundance is that many people still do not understand the basic law of life: they must radiate—give—in order to attract—receive. (Catherine Ponder)

Nothing in life is to be feared; it is only to be understood. Now is the time to understand more, so that we may fear less. (Marie Curie)

The great need in life for all of us is not so much to achieve the ability to set all things right, but to gain the perception to see them rightly. (Eric Butterworth)

Nothing can hinder (us) except our own lack of understanding. (Emilie Cady)

A special kind of understanding is called for if we are able to stand firm in our faith, and at the same time welcome the changes in contemporary thought and behavior that are good for (humankind). (James Decker)

With true understanding, we learn to keep a balance between the unseen and the seen and to meet appearances of lack on both the mental and material planes. (Georgiana Tree West)

A manifestation of spiritual healing is a miracle to one who does not understand its principles. But to many it is not an unusual event but a result of understanding and of compliance with law. (Richard Lynch)

There is a way to tell if we have entered the kingdom of heaven and found the pearl of great price: asking ceases. (Jim Rosemergy)

Nothing is so firmly believed as what we least know. (Michel Eyquem de Montaigne)

Keep looking below surface appearances. Don't shrink from doing so just because you might not like what you find" (Colin Powell)

Wisdom

The Power to practically apply what is known; intuitively discern and make heart connections

Color: Yellow

Location: Pit of Stomach

*I claim Wisdom now.
I use Wisdom to discern how to
apply what I understand, so
I am being the best I can be.*

*At times of challenge and uncertainty, nothing seems
more important than wisdom.
(Stephen Hall)*

To be truly happy, to bring peace to all, one must control one's mind. And to control one's mind to find enlightenment, one must be wise and virtuous.
~ Buddha

WISDOM

Overview

- Location: Pit of Stomach
- Color: Yellow
- Linked with LOVE, UNDERSTANDING, and WILL

WISDOM is the Power to practically apply what is known; intuitively discern and make heart connections.

From ordinary consciousness: The ability to practically apply what is known; intuitively discern and make heart connections based on our senses, thoughts, feelings, and beliefs. We use WISDOM to choose what we eat and wear. We also use WISDOM to be judgmental, discriminatory, and shrewd.

- *Underdeveloped WISDOM* results in a person who has difficulty making decisions, is indecisive, and perhaps cannot discern good from bad.

- *Egocentric WISDOM* results in a person who is highly judgmental, inappropriately discriminatory (as in being racist or sexist), and shrewd in dealing with people and situations. This person might also be highly critical of others, using WISDOM ineffectively as a tool to coerce others..

From elevated consciousness: The ability to practically apply what is known; intuitively discern and make heart connections based on Ideas, Truths, Principles and Laws that are Divine in nature. We use WISDOM to discern how to apply what we know at the highest, most effect level in order to be the best person we can be.

Until recently, wisdom has been relatively overlooked as a topic for serious scholarly and scientific investigation. And yet, it is difficult to imagine a subject more central to the highest aspirations of being human. The study of wisdom holds great promise for shedding light on and opening up new insights for human flourishing. Supported with funding from the John Templeton Foundation, six research projects led by University of Chicago faculty, in collaboration with scientists at other institutions, will investigate big questions in the field that have the greatest potential of influencing research, education, policy and professions: What is the relationship between expertise and wisdom? How does experience increase wisdom? What is the relationship between cognitive, social and emotional processes in mediating wisdom? *(Templeton Foundation and the Wisdom Research Network, University of Chicago, Chicago, Ill., March 4, 2013).* We can't wait to hear the results!

*H*ave you ever been with a group of friends, preparing to have lunch together, and someone poses the question, "Where do you want to go to eat?" It becomes very frustrating when everyone responds with, "Oh, I don't care. Whatever everyone else wants to do is fine with me." It can lead to a long decision-making period, and a short lunch time! Even with such simple situations as this, we can call on our WISDOM, which is the Power to apply what is known, evaluate, discern, or judge. The word "judgment" gets a bad rap these days, because it instantly calls up a vision of discrimination and unfair evaluation. We even use the words of Jesus to support our criticism of judgmentalness: "Do not judge, or you too will be judged" (Matthew 7:1, NIV). And yet, don't you think it's odd that Jesus would then turn around and call the Pharisees and Sadducees vipers and hypocrites? Sounds like judging to us!

The kind of judgment we are talking about when we discuss WISDOM is more of a discernment ... a deep inner knowing that goes beyond the facts. In fact (to play on words), sometimes facts can interfere with WISDOM.

We say, "Let's look at the facts." It sounds so simple. But wait ... what, exactly, is the truth? How do we know it when we hear it? It's not always as simple as it seems.

From reading this guide, you can tell that we are deeply immersed in the research related to neuroscience, Positive Psychology, and neurotheology. But even research can become confusing. For example, you would think research would confirm what is true. But we found clear, well-documented research that reported 5 cups of coffee a day may cut heart disease—and another equally well-documented study that indicated drinking five or more  cups of coffee a day increases the risk of having heart problems! One study claimed coffee is good for you because it helps prevent Parkinson's and diabetes, while another said coffee is bad for you because it contributes to osteoporosis. What's a coffee lover to do? Choose the research that supports what you want to do, of course!

And then there are the contrarians who want to dispute those life truths everyone knows and believes—what we know from our Power of WISDOM. For example, there is that truth about the positive effects of forgiveness. And yet, writer Bob Brody penned an article entitled "To Forgive Is Good...but sometimes I want to stay mad!" It says: "I believe in the healing power of the grudge ... I've discovered nothing feels quite as satisfying as a grudge well nursed. My grudge against a person balances out that injustice, somehow rights the universe" *(Brody, Bob, "To Forgive Is Good...but sometimes I want to stay mad!" Reader's Digest, April, 2010).*

Obviously this person is confusing forgiveness (what we do for ourselves) with condoning an action taken by someone (the impact of a consequence). We call this kind of thinking "Junk-o-logic!" For those who may not remember, Junk-o-logic is a

1950s advertising principle that says you can give someone any two unrelated ideas and act like they're related, and that person will make up a connection. Open a magazine, look at a billboard, or stop fast forwarding through TV commercials for a few minutes, and chances are you'll be seeing an image that has nothing to do with the product. Advertisers are hoping we are using WISDOM at the very lowest, most egocentric level as we watch their commercials!

And then, there are the truths that really are proven, but still seem so farfetched that we wonder—who cares? For example, did you know it is true that a duck's quack does not echo? Would you believe research has proven there are more plastic flamingos in the U.S. than real ones! And how about this? In 1939, Ernest Vincent Wright wrote a novel, *Gadsby* (not to be confused with the classic by F. Scott Fitzgerald, *The Great Gatsby)*, which contains over 50,000 words—none of which contain the letter E! A few more truths for you to ponder: The electric chair was invented by a dentist (totally believable!) ... If you yelled for 8 years, 7 months and 6 days, you would have produced enough sound energy to heat one cup of coffee ... which may or may not be good for you, depending on which research you believe!

Okay, by now you are probably asking, so what's the point? Here's the deal: Whether we are talking about research, personal opinions, politics, lifestyles, or religion, the result in the same: When we hear conflicting information, we must have the WISDOM to know the difference ... the WISDOM to discern the Truth!

That's what this Power is all about! Through this Power, we have the wisdom to know the difference between the short-lived satisfaction of revenge and the long-term peacefulness of forgiveness. With WISDOM, we know the difference between worrying about a situation, versus taking that situation into the Silence, claiming the Divine Ideas that bring solutions. With WISDOM, we can know the difference between playing the victim card, versus standing firm in our authenticity and integrity. With WISDOM, we can make the wise choices to live life grounded in the spiritual principles of our beliefs.

WISDOM is located in the pit of the stomach—and think about it: when you really *know* something, what do you say? "I feel it in my gut."

Research from Harvard Graduate School of Education has proven that sound judgment helps you:
- stay calm and centered;
- better manage uncomfortable feelings and difficult interactions;
- think more clearly and compassionately;
- discern where to direct your time and energy;
- sustain your enthusiasm; and
- achieve results.

These discernments will help you take stress in stride, make wise decisions, and savor the joy of leadership. Through guided mindfulness practices and exercises, meditation techniques, case studies, reflection, presentations, role playing, and large and small group discussion, you will become more discerning and able to renew your commitment to action, guided by the values that inspire you to make a difference.

Sound judgment helps you identify common patterns of overreaction, and then learn how to respond to difficulties with awareness, poise, and resilience. It helps you respond deliberately rather than react automatically, to be guided by your values rather than be derailed by your discomfort. It helps you explore skills for self-awareness and self-renewal so you can sustain your leadership and service to others with insight, wisdom, and warmth—and renew your incredible capacity for wise appraisal *(Faculty, Inner Strengths of Successful Leaders Program, Harvard Graduate School of Education, Fall 2013 Session)*.

Now, let's look at how WISDOM allows us to be judging and discerning machines. Our lives would be paralyzed into a numbing sameness if we did not constantly judge, evaluate, discern or appraise. In fact, we'd never get anything accomplished at all if we did not employ our Power of WISDOM. For example, have you ever been around someone who wants to get the best deal—so the individual keeps gathering data and evaluating information ad infinitum—and *never* makes a decision? Their WISDOM is on hold!

A Practical Look At Wisdom

Everything we do is wrapped up in our WISDOM Power. And our WISDOM is tightly connected to UNDERSTANDING and WILL, which are covered in other chapters. But for now, let's focus on WISDOM.

There is a difference between knowledge and WISDOM. Someone joked that knowledge was knowing a tomato was a fruit, and WISDOM was knowing enough to not use it in a fruit salad. So let's look at some practical examples of WISDOM in our everyday lives.

- Each of us makes some sort of evaluation about what time we get up in the morning. This decision is based on what we know about our morning habits, what the schedule looks like for the day ahead, and the responsibilities we have before we leave the house. The exact time we choose is a discernment which takes all the things we know into account.

- What clothes are we going to wear? We use WISDOM to select the clothing that will be most appropriate for the scheduled events, and we consider comfort, appearance, and utility. Sometimes people use their underdeveloped WISDOM to select 4 1/2" heels for a picnic in the park!

- When we need to complete a project at work, we use WISDOM to decide on a project plan, discern the key players for the team, and set a course of action for successful completion. When a team leader is operating from ego-centric

WISDOM, the team experiences a lot of criticism, micro-managing, and unnecessary rigidity.

- Parenting draws on the Power of WISDOM on a constant basis, as you make decisions about how to discipline, educate, nurture, and bond.

Think about how often we use this Power, often without even realizing it. All these decisions come from our Power of WISDOM, based on what we know, past experience, and expectations. If we allow ourselves to operate from default, we may find ourselves using our WISDOM in underdeveloped or egocentric ways that are ineffective and detrimental to our daily living.

What to do? The solution is to become truly conscious in this now moment about how we are using WISDOM. Awareness and self-knowledge go a long way to raising our consciousness. The key to the successful use of WISDOM is to get it under our wise control. We have been going about our lives blithely judging this, evaluating that, discerning one idea, and appraising something else. Sometimes our judgments are useful and good for our consciousness; other times, not so good. (Did you catch the judgment that happened just then? Was it good or bad? Hmmm?)

> Wise people know that one of the reasons for the failure of materialism to make us happier may be that even when people finally attain their monetary goals, for instance, the achievement doesn't translate into the increase in happiness *(Sheldon K., and T. Kasser, 1998, "Pursuing personal goals: Skills enable progress, but not all progress is beneficial," Personality and Social Psychology Bulletin 24: 1319-31).*

According to Tom Lombardo, Center of Future Consciousness, the cultivation of wisdom as a guiding light in our future psycho-social evolution will empower humanity to constructively, intelligently, and ethically address contemporary challenges as well as to realize the best within ourselves. Wisdom provides an enlightened, future- focused, and highly efficacious practical ideal for our evolution in the twenty-first century *(Lombardo, T., Wisdom in the Twenty-first Century: A Theory of Psycho-Social Evolution, Center for Future Consciousness, 2010).*

We cannot *not* use WISDOM; it is always at work. And that can be a good thing ... or not. Let's begin to explore WISDOM at a deeper level to demonstrate how we can use this Power more consciously and thus, more effectively.

Two notable research teams have examined WISDOM through a series of studies, and both conceptualize WISDOM in terms of specific kinds of knowledge and/or the application of knowledge. The late Paul Baltes and his colleagues at the Max Planck

Institute for Human Development (Berlin, Germany) have studied wisdom primarily in terms of life span psychology and gerontology. They define wisdom as "a highly valued and outstanding expertise in dealing with fundamental, that is, existential problems related to the meaning and conduct of life" *(Baltes, P. B., and J. Smith. 2008. The fascination of wisdom: Its nature, ontogeny, and function. Perspectives on psychological science 3:56-64).*

Baltes worked with another researcher, U.M. Staudinger, to identify six properties of wisdom: (1) a superior level of knowledge and judgment, including expertise in listening, evaluating, and advising; (2) the addressing of significant and difficult questions and strategies about the conduct and meaning of life; (3) knowledge about the limits of knowledge and uncertainties of the world; (4) knowledge with uncommon scope, depth, measure, and balance; (5) a synergy of mind and character; and (6) knowledge used for the well-being of oneself and of others *(Baltes, P. B., and U. M. Staudinger. 2000. Wisdom: A meta-heuristic (pragmatic) to orchestrate mind and virtue toward excellence. American Psychologist 55:122-36).*

As we consider this research, it is clear that, in a broad and general way, life boils down to a series of discernments. WISDOM is the innate ability by which we judge, evaluate, discern, use wisdom, appraise, and apply what is known. How we wisely evaluate, discern, appraise and apply what is known is what we base our decisions on. The actual choosing or deciding uses WILL ... more on that in the next chapter!

Underdeveloped WISDOM results in a person who has a crippled ability to evaluate anything. This person is wishy-washy, somewhat unpredictable, and perhaps lacks standards by which to discern or judge. This person could also be indecisive, like a leaf blowing in the wind.

For example, an employee in a job that provides no satisfaction, has low pay, and is led by an ineffective supervisor may continue to gripe and complain, but remain in the job because he/she cannot make a decision about what else to do or how to replace the health benefits the job provides.

W. Andrew Achenaum captured the essence of the impact of underdeveloped WISDOM on our lives with the following quote: "I am now realizing that—awakening, suffering, brokenness, renewal, remembering, reintegrating, and returning are in and of themselves pathways to growing wiser. How and why people may end up on one pathway and then another (or on none at all) remain a mystery" *(Achenaum, W. Andrew. "The Wisdom of Age An Historians Perspective." University of North Carolina Institute on Aging Distinguished Lecture Series, April 3, 1997).*

On the other hand, egocentric WISDOM comes across as judgmental, perhaps erroneously and overtly discriminatory, condemnatory, scheming, or manipulative.

We see this demonstrated by a person who uses inappropriate tactics to achieve a desired result. We knew one man who discovered an antique piece of furniture at a yard sale, priced by an unknowing seller at $25, when this man knew it was worth hundreds of dollars. Using his manipulative skills, he talked the sellers down to $5, then gleefully bragged about his great deal to others.

Let's make this really practical by taking a sensible look at how we use WISDOM in our everyday lives. Sometimes we use WISDOM in a positive way based on our ordinary thoughts, feelings, and what we are discerning, interpreting, and perceiving through our senses.

- A perfect example is flossing! We all know the infamous dental adage: only floss the teeth you want to keep! When you go to the dentist's office, we can guarantee you will get a reminder about the proper technique to use when flossing, along with a not-so-subtle reminder about how often to do it. You will probably even get a little case of dental floss along with your complimentary toothbrush and your bill! Now you have the UNDERSTANDING (covered in a previous chapter) about what to do, but up to this point, you are only borrowing the WISDOM of the dentist. As you make the decision to actually practice flossing on a regular basis (which is WILL—more on that in the next chapter), you notice how much fresher and cleaner your teeth feel. Then, on your next dental visit, you realize how much easier the cleaning is, and you receive kudos from the dental hygienist and your dentist. Now you have the WISDOM to continue making regular flossing part of your daily routine.

- A man may notice over time that foods containing certain ingredients cause heartburn (definitely a sense thing). He would then use WISDOM to apply what he knows and discern what foods to eat and what foods not to eat.

> Discerning mystics frequently speak of an overwhelming sense of being at one with the universe or with God, of glimpsing a holistic vision of reality, or of being in the presence of a powerful and loving influence. Most important, mystics claim they can grasp ultimate reality in a single experience, in contrast to the long and tortuous sequence of the logical-scientific method of inquiry *(Paul Davies, The Mind of God, New York: Simon and Schuster, 1992, pg. 227).*

We also can use WISDOM in negative, adverse ways based on beliefs derived from an erroneous interpretation or understanding of our thoughts, feelings, and what we are discerning and evaluating through our senses.

- A small business owner watches a hard-sell webinar advocating the benefits of a certain marketing program to build email lists. The presentation is packed with images of a rich life style, and testimonials praising the product. Based on the emotional impact of the webinar, the business owner jumps in and purchases the pricey product, without performing an adequate evaluation of it, assuming it will bring the same rich rewards as the webinar presenter promised.

While all of these examples certainly demonstrate some of the ways we use WISDOM in our lives, they do not give any indication of the best and highest way to use this important Power. However, Tom Atlee gives us a glimpse into what constitutes the highest way to use this extraordinary ability. He says:

> We are wise to see beyond isolated facts and linear logic into the whole fabric of life, using all the forms of knowing that are given to us, particularly intuition, heart, synthesis, spiritual experience, and the sciences that attempt to appreciate the whole and our relationship to it—such as ecology, living systems science, complexity and chaos theories, quantum mechanics and the consciousness sciences *(Atlee, Tom. "Some ways we can be wise." Co-Intelligence Institute. November 2003).*

In all our examples so far, WISDOM has been engaged based on what we are discerning and surmising from sense consciousness. This is important because awareness of how we are already using WISDOM in our everyday lives helps us know how to use WISDOM at ever higher levels of consciousness.

For example, we're going to take you to a quantum view of consciousness. In his book *The God Theory*, Bernard Haisch states, "It is not matter that creates an illusion of consciousness, but consciousness that creates the illusion of matter" *(Bernard Haisch, The God Theory, San Francisco:Weiser Books, 2006, pg. 137).*

The highest and best use of WISDOM is to evaluate and discern, moment by moment, how effectively we are being the best person we can be. We can also use WISDOM to see beyond the appearance of another person's personality/ego, attitudes, and actions, to discern the presence of their beautiful Divine Nature. Further, this Power is used to apply what we know about Divine Ideas, Laws, and Principles, making them ever more practical.

WISDOM From the Four Levels of Consciousness:

Now let's look at WISDOM as it is expressed from the four different levels of different levels of consciousness:

1. **Unconscious WISDOM:** based on a cause in subconscious mind which consists of beliefs that are not in our moment to moment awareness. An example is when we have a reaction to a person or a situation without being aware of a conscious, cognitive process.

2. **Conscious WISDOM from our senses:** based on something in physicality we are gleaning through our sight, sound, scent, touch, and/or taste. We eat luscious dark chocolate. We love the taste. So, nearly every time we see dark chocolate, we judge that it would be good to have some ... and do!

3. **Conscious WISDOM from our human personality:** based on thoughts, feelings, attitudes, and/or beliefs held in ordinary consciousness. A person

holds the belief that he/she will become a minister. He/she would then use WISDOM to make wise decisions on what courses to take to prepare for the ministry.

4. **Conscious WISDOM from our True Identity, or Authentic Self:** based upon Divine Ideas, Laws, and Principles. WISDOM would be used to evaluate how we are doing moment to moment, discerning the thoughts and actions that would demonstrate being the best we can be.

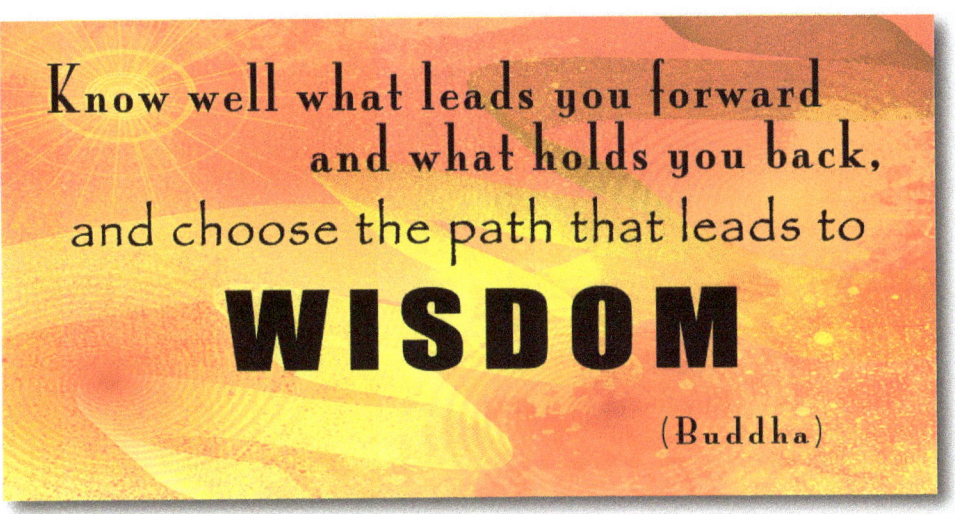

We had an interesting experience that brought home the whole meaning of WISDOM at a very practical level. On one of our Grandparent outings with our grandson, we walked down the cereal aisle with him on a spontaneous, unplanned stop. The aisle was a literal gauntlet of sugar. Each cereal box was lavishly colored and decorated to suit the fancies of kids who really don't need sugar highs.

We sharpened our 'NO' skills to cereals like: Addams Family Cereal by Ralston; Apple Zingaroos by Kellogg's; Baron von Redberry by General Mills; Batman Returns Cereal, a Ralston brand; Gorilla Munch by Nature's Path; Kung Fu Panda Crunchers, a Kellogg's brand; and Lucky Charms by General Mills.

We finally gave in to Pop Tarts by Kellogg's. It's our grandson's favorite. What are Grandparents to do?!

We had walked down a well-engineered gauntlet of temptation, quick fixes, and 'buy-me-nows' designed by advertisers and marketers who knew kids are easy marks when it comes to sugar.

We noticed all of the kid's cereals were shelved at kid's eye level or below—perfect for little sugar-crazed hands to grab them. The collusion between manufacturer, marketer, and merchant creates a billion dollar market for cereals.

Kids are targeted and parents/grandparents are just collateral damage! The industry's rhetoric is that they are just selling kids what they want. Their WISDOM is based on market research, focus groups, and bottom-line profit reports.

We thought about that, and then we thought about the temptations we adults face every day. We thought about the 'cereal aisles' we walk down. The aisles we're tempted to buy into. You know, the gauntlets we create for ourselves or allow others to create for us. Like:

- the 'aisle' called addiction and substance abuse;
- the 'aisle' called you'll never amount to anything;
- the 'aisle' called you can't do it because you're not good enough;
- the 'aisle' called you don't have the education it takes to succeed;
- the 'aisle' called it's too late to start over again;
- the 'aisle' called you'll never dig out from under your financial burden;
- the 'aisle' that says you'll never find that soulmate you're looking for because you're not worthy—who would want you anyway;

Have you ever been down one of those aisles? As you know, these aisles are well-crafted: aisles designed to steal your hope and joy; gauntlets designed to erode your happiness. You don't have to walk down those 'aisles.' You don't have to buy what the world is selling. You don't have to let someone's negativity rob you of joy, or hope, or happiness.

Any attempts to sell you incompleteness are error messages. They are rouses to keep you off balance. They are attempts to block your good. They are designed to steal your joy.

But just like the cereals which line the shelves on grocery store aisles, these subtle—and sometimes not so subtle—attempts to demean you, or use you, or limit you are only self-centered products of a worldly marketing consciousness that has lost its "wisdom teeth!"

Cereal boxes have nutrition facts posted on them—and so do the 'aisles of outer appearances' we just talked about. Check out the nutritional value of the next slight you get, or the next hurtful comment that comes your way, or the next slam that's leveled at your self-esteem.

You're going to find there's no—zilch—nada nutritional value associated with slights, demeaning language, fear messages, gossip, or hurtfulness directed at you.

"We live in darkness until we know that the Spirit of God within the depths of our being is moving," says Unity writer and minister Elizabeth Sand Turner, in her classic book *Let There Be Light*. "Our great need," she continues, "is for light, which represents illumination, intelligence, and wisdom. We can have no real comprehension until we tap into our inner wisdom."

Marianne Williamson, in *A Return to Love* predicts that, "Spiritual wisdom will be the key to wealth in the 21st Century. Thinking that we need the material world makes us slaves to the material world."

Both these wise ladies are right, of course. All of us have the inner WISDOM it takes to master the human experience. It's in our spiritual DNA. And there's something else in our DNA! There's a whole lot of "ELSE" in our DNA! Consider what Joel Primack, one of the world's leading cosmologists, and Nancy Ellen Abrams, a cultural physicist, have to say:

> Each of us is an atomic pastiche: the iron atoms in our blood carrying oxygen at this moment to our cells came largely from exploding white dwarf stars, while the oxygen itself came mainly from exploding supernovas that ended the lives of massive stars, and most of the carbon in the carbon dioxide we exhale on every breath came from planetary nebulas, the death clouds of middle-sized stars a little bigger than our sun. We are made of material created and ejected into the Galaxy by the violence of earlier stars. Human beings are made of the rarest material in the universe: stardust. Except for hydrogen, which makes up about a tenth of our weight, the rest of our body is stardust. Our bodies literally had the entire history of the universe, witnessed and enacted by our atoms *(Primack, Joel and Nancy Ellen Abrams, The View From the Center of the Universe, Riverhead Books, 2006, pgs. 94 and 99)*.

The Power of WISDOM goes so much deeper than what you know; it is the ability to listen to that inner voice that possesses the WISDOM of the ages, and speaks through your intuition. It calls into play your ability to listen—really listen—and know how to use what you know. Terry Dobbs shares an incredible story that captures the essence of WISDOM in action:

> The train clanked and rattled through the suburbs of Tokyo on a drowsy spring afternoon. At one station the doors opened, and suddenly the quiet was shattered by a man bellowing violent curses. The man staggered into our car. He wore laborer's clothing and was big, drunk, and dirty. Screaming, he swung at a woman holding a baby. The blow sent her spinning into the laps of an elderly couple. It was a miracle that the baby was unharmed.
>
> This so enraged the drunk that he grabbed the metal pole in the center of the car and tried to wrench it out. One of his hands was cut and bleeding.

I was young then, some 20 years ago, and in pretty good shape. I'd been putting in a solid eight hours of Aikido training nearly every day for the past three years. I thought I was tough. "People are in danger!" I said to myself as I got to my feet. "If I don't do something fast, somebody will probably get hurt."

Seeing me stand up, the drunk recognized a chance to focus his rage. "A foreigner!" he roared. "You need a lesson in Japanese manners!"

I gave him a slow look of disgust and dismissal. I planned to take this turkey apart, but he had to make the first move. He gathered himself for a rush at me.

A fraction of a second before he could move, someone shouted, "Hey!"

We both stared down at a little old Japanese man. He must have been well into his seventies, this tiny gentleman, sitting there immaculate in his kimono. He beamed delightedly at the laborer.

"C'mere," the old man said, beckoning. "C'mere and talk to me."

The big man followed as if on a string. He planted his feet belligerently in front of the old gentleman and roared, "Why should I talk to you?"

The old man continued to beam at the laborer. "What'cha been drinkin'?" he asked. "I've been drinkin' sake," the laborer bellowed back, "and it's none of your business!"

"Oh, that's wonderful," the old man said. "Absolutely wonderful! You see, I love sake, too. Every night, me and my wife—she's 76, you know—we warm up a little bottle of sake and take it out into the garden, and we sit on an old wooden bench. We watch the sun go down, and we look to see how our persimmon tree is doing. My great-grandfather planted that tree, and we worry about whether it will recover from those ice storms we had last winter." He looked up at the laborer, eyes twinkling.

As he struggled to follow the old man, his face began to soften. His fists slowly unclenched. "Yea," he said, "I love persimmons, too . . ."

"Yes" said the old man, smiling, "and I'm sure you have a wonderful wife."

"No," replied the laborer. "My wife died." The big man began to sob. "I don't got no wife, I don't got no home, I don't got no job. I'm so ashamed of myself." Tears rolled down his cheeks, a spasm of despair rippled through his body.

The train arrived at my stop. As the doors opened, I turned my head for one last look. The laborer was sprawled on the seat with his head on the old man's shoulder. The old man was softly stroking the laborer's filthy, matted hair. *("Another Way," from Chicken Soup for the Soul, p. 55-58)*

We share this story because it vividly illustrates the powerful impact of Divine WISDOM used in a very practical situation. We each possess WISDOM, like the old

Japanese man in the story, and each of us is able to see through uncertainty and chaos. We have the ability to remain calm in midst of a troubled world, and can move through difficult situations with ease and grace. This is true WISDOM for uncertain times: the WISDOM to risk reaching out; the WISDOM to risk listening, hearing, holding, and understanding. This is true WISDOM for chaotic times: the WISDOM to risk being heard, to risk being held, to risk being helped; to risk letting ourselves be vulnerable, to be fully present and poised in the midst of chaos. The WISDOM for knowing what to do and how to do it is in our DNA.

We can tell you with absolute certainty that you have a deep reservoir of WISDOM within you. And when you claim WISDOM at the highest, most elevated level, you'll achieve the inner peace, serenity, health, wealth, and happiness you seek.

WISDOM: Putting It Into Practice

WISDOM—Activity One:

Without over-thinking, jot down your immediate responses to each of the following statements:

Behaviors I find irritating, inappropriate, or offensive are:

Five attitudes or beliefs I really value are:

The best way to convince me of something is:

I base my decisions on:

When I'm not sure what to do, my "modus operandi" is:

Reflect on your responses, and see what they tell you about the ways you use discernment in your daily life. What is working for you? What would you like to change?

WISDOM—Activity Two:

As you think about the specific area you are working on throughout this guide, brainstorm a list of decisions you have made related to this area. Then ask yourself the following three questions, and reflect on the answers that arise:

- Is this really true?
- How is this decision serving me?
- What additional information do I need to be able to use my WISDOM at a more elevated level of consciousness?

Example: Healthy Eating

Decision: Carbohydrates are my enemy! Therefore, I should eliminate them from my diet.

Is this decision really true? Well, probably not. Carbohydrates provide energy power, but they also turn to sugar quickly, and in excess can pack on pounds. By totally eliminating carbs I could be robbing myself of necessary energy food.

How is this decision serving me? It helps me get sympathy from others ("Poor me! No carbs in my diet!") Hmmm... Is it sympathy I want? I am playing the role of victim, and sabotaging my own success!

What additional information do I need to be able to use my WISDOM at a more elevated level of consciousness? I need to gather good, sound medical information about the value of carbs, and how to add them to my diet in a healthy way. I can also create a checklist of criteria to use to evaluate food with carbs, so I can discern which ones are YES foods, and which ones I should avoid.

WISDOM Affirmation:

I claim the highest, most elevated WISDOM now. I use WISDOM to wisely discern how to apply what I understand, so I can be the best person I can be.

Quotes to Inspire WISDOM

I was privileged to see into the real nature of myself and all existence. When the veil of ignorance, which constitutes the ego, was lifted, it was revealed that my true, underlying identity is, and had always been, the one all-pervading Consciousness that is the Source and substratum of all that exists. (Swami Abhayananda)

Below everyday awareness is a shaman-like, childlike consciousness—weaver of dreams, keeper of instincts. Your subconscious holds keys to a treasure house of intuitive wisdom, clear insight, and untapped power. All you have to do is to look, listen, and trust, paying attention to dreams, feelings and instincts. (Dan Millman)

Judgment (WISDOM) is a faculty of the mind that can be exercised in two ways—from sense perception or spiritual understanding. If its action is based on sense perception, its conclusions are fallible and often condemnatory; if based on spiritual understanding, they are safe. (Charles Fillmore)

Guided by (Divine) wisdom we shall know when to express our spiritual ideas and when to keep them to ourselves. (Elizabeth Sand Turner)

The advancing human soul uses the keys of experience and discernment to solve unknown mysteries, moving them closer to the light. (Rebecca Clark)

Two people have been living in you all your life. One is the ego, garrulous, demanding, hysterical, calculating—the other is the hidden spiritual being, whose still voice of wisdom you have only rarely heard or attended to—you have uncovered in yourself your own wise guide. (Sogyal Rinpoche)

Divine Wisdom works in you if you do not cross bridges before you come to them. (Matthew Fox)

To act wisely when the time for action comes, to wait patiently when it is time for repose, put (us) in accord with the tides. Ignorance of this law results in periods of unreasoning enthusiasm on the one hand, and depression on the other. (Helena Petrova Blavatsky)

Spiritual illumination enables us to discern the spiritual reality where the human concept appears to be. Spiritual sense discerns the reality of that which is appearing as concept. The beginning of wisdom is when we draw our attention away from the outer world, from the world of effect or appearance, and begin to realize that power is not in it, but in us. (Joel Goldsmith)

Because you are spiritual beings with (the) freedom of choice, and with command of the power, faculties, and qualities of Being, you can determine just what will come into your life.
(Myrtle Fillmore)

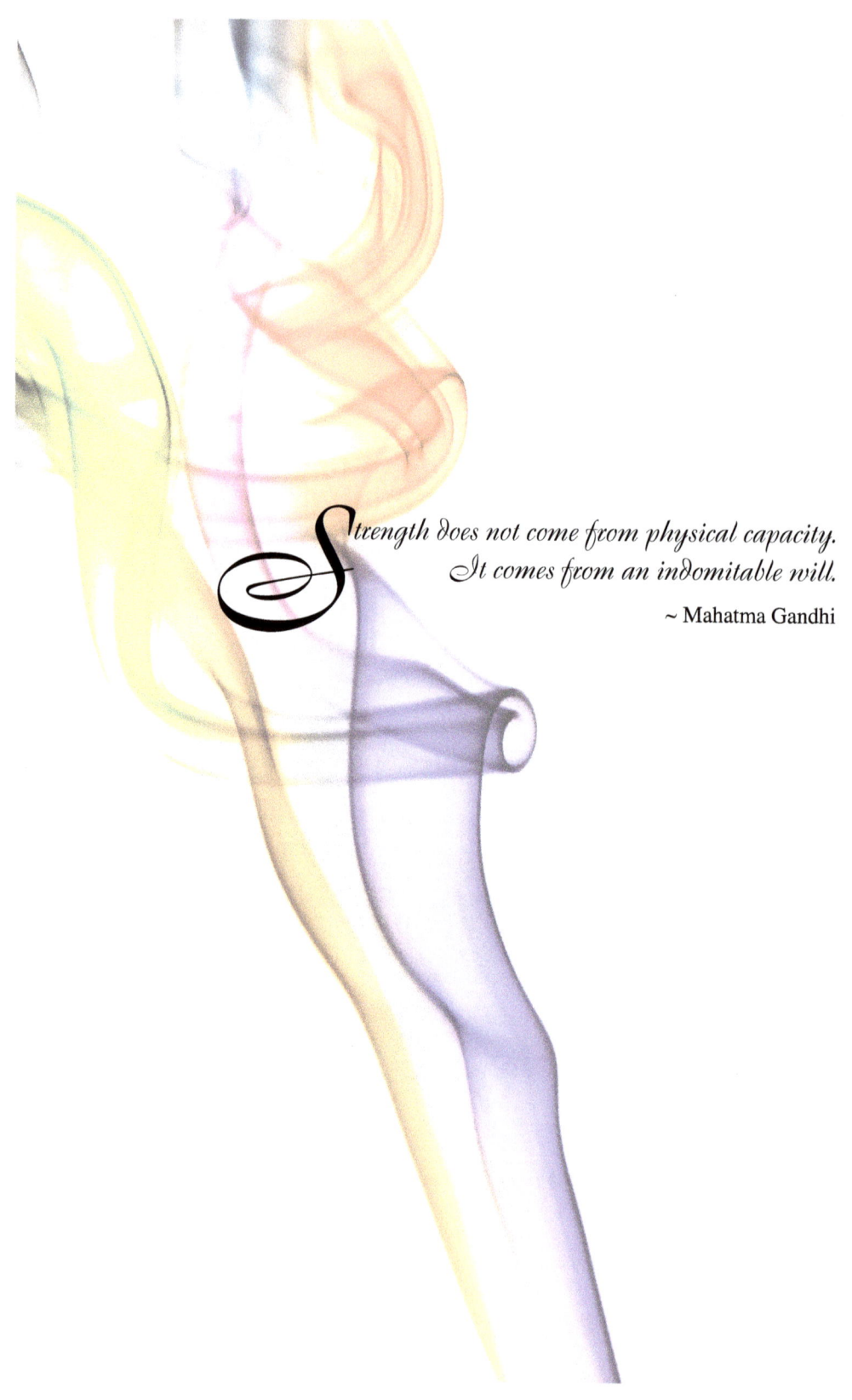

*Strength does not come from physical capacity.
It comes from an indomitable will.*

~ Mahatma Gandhi

WILL

Overview

- Location: Front Forebrain
- Color: Silver
- Works with UNDERSTANDING, WISDOM and LOVE.

WILL is the Power to choose; decide; direct; dictate; determine.

From ordinary consciousness: The ability to choose; decide; direct; dictate; and determine based on the senses, thoughts, feelings, and beliefs. We use WILL to make life-enhancing choices … or not. "Our power of choice," says Science of Mind philosopher, Frederick Bailes, "enables us to think like an angel or a devil, a king or a slave. Whatever we choose, mind will create and manifest."

- *Underdeveloped WILL* results in a person who is indecisive, wishy-washy and unable to make a decision.
- *Egocentric WILL* results in willful people who must have their own way all the time. They exhibit a "my way or the highway" attitude. They are obstinate, with a "don't confuse me with the facts" attitude. Once a decision is made they are reluctant to change it. They also tend to come across as bossy, telling everyone what to do.

From elevated consciousness: The ability to choose; decide; direct; dictate; and determine based on Ideas, Truths, Principles and Laws that are Divine in nature. We use WILL to choose and direct all thoughts and actions to be the best, most extraordinary person we can be.

WILL is all about our power of choice. The secret to living the life you want—to getting the most out of this earth experience—to attracting unbelievable happiness and prosperity—is to simply make the kind of choices that are life-affirming and growth-oriented, from our highest, most elevated consciousness. In his book, *Man's Eternal Quest*, Paramahansa Yogananda says: "(We) are engaged in an eternal quest for that 'something else' (we) hope will bring (us) happiness, complete and unending. For those who have made the choice to seek and find God within, the search is over: God is that Something Else."

We like to think of WILL as our great Director—the Power that says "Action!" As with all the Powers, we are constantly using our power of WILL. We can choose to live and act from our highest and best, or we can use it to choose to act from our ego. We can choose to meditate, or we can choose to vegetate—in either case, we are exercising our power of WILL. Think about the incredible number of choices you make every single day. From the moment you open your eyes in the morning (or whenever it is you choose to arise), you choose whether to get out of bed or hit the snooze button and snuggle under the covers for a few more minutes of rest; you choose what to wear; what to have for breakfast; what to read or listen to as you grab that breakfast you chose; and what your schedule will look like for the day. By the time you actually get your day started, you have already made hundreds of choices, mostly without any conscious thought at all! This is fine, because we could drive ourselves batty if we had to pay a lot of attention to every single choice we make.

However, the problem comes when we make important choices the same way we decide what to eat for breakfast: by default rather than intention. Imagine how powerful your life could be if you called on your most elevated level of consciousness to make the important choices in your life. That is what WILL is all about!

Making choices involves the Powers we have already explored and those that are yet to come; all of the Powers are in play in our choice-making. However, WILL is the one we use to actually *make* a choice. It is often called the executive power of mind. In addition to the ability to choose and decide, it is also the ability to command and direct. It actually moves all the other Powers into action. Think about it. We choose (WILL):

- What we believe, trust in, and spiritually intuit. (FAITH)
- When, where, and for what we persist in and stay the course. (STRENGTH)
- What we desire and need to harmonize, unify, and show affection for. (LOVE)
- What we visualize, conceptualize, and envision. (IMAGINATION)
- What we master or have control over. (POWER)
- What we know and comprehend. (UNDERSTANDING
- What we discern and when we apply what we know. (WISDOM)
- When and what we organize, sequence or adjust. (ORDER)
- What we let go of, disengage from, free ourselves from. (RELEASE)
- What we are passionate about. (ZEAL)
- What we vitalize or enliven. (LIFE)

We realize some of the Powers listed above haven't been covered yet ... this is a sneak peak into our future chapters! Hopefully, it will whet your appetite as we continue exploring each Power individually, and it will also help you see how all the

Powers work together, much like the cast of a play. You can easily see the appropriateness of the analogy of WILL as our Director.

This matter of choice is a very interesting one. Hopefully, most of us learn by experience over time how to make the wisest choices. However, have you ever discerned what would be best in a situation, then actually made another choice anyway? Many of us can remember when we were teenagers and did something even though we knew we shouldn't do it. (For example, perhaps you were grounded and decided to sneak out the window to meet with your friends. Of course, we never did that! We're just using it for illustrative purposes!)

The choice to go against our better WISDOM and UNDERSTANDING doesn't stop at the end of our teenage years. You, for example, probably know you shouldn't speed on a certain street because there is frequently a speed trap there .... yet you do it anyway. And we are appalled there needs to be a law prohibiting texting and driving! Who would have thought anyone would choose to do anything that would compromise their driving ability? And yet, lots of people drink, or text, or eat—and drive. Another example: we all know the countless benefits of healthy eating—yet choose to gobble down those burgers, fries, and shakes with a vengeance.

All these examples illustrate WILL in action. Even though we may know the right thing to do, we can still use our Power of WILL, the ability to choose, to make another choice! We think you'll agree this is a definition of insanity: knowing the best choice and then making an unwise one!

> As pointed out by researchers Amos Tversky and Daniel Kahneman in "The Framing of Decisions and the Psychology of Choice," no matter what the salient facts of a given set of choices, how the problem is presented and "framed" can influence the decision significantly. Thus, the "Power of Choice" may be rendered less powerful than is obvious by presentation, which is something that the marketing industry has known for some time and used to great advantage *(Tversky, A., and D. Kahnerman, The framing of decisions and the psychology of choice, Science, New Series, Vol. 211, No. 4481. Jan. 30, 1981; 453-458).*

At this point, we ask your indulgence while we take a bit of a side trip to clear up a common misunderstanding. In our experience teaching WILL, we have noticed a tendency on the part of some of our students to confuse the Power of WILL with what is referred to as God's Will. We hear people ask, "What is God's Will for my life?" This question comes from a belief that a "God out there" has a specific imposed script for them, a kind of Divine Plan or predetermination, where God has already made all the choices for their lives. From this perspective, their Power of WILL would be based on predetermined choices, choices that wouldn't be true choices at all.

We believe this whole idea stems from the religious practices in which people were raised. This kind of interpretation of God's Will implies a separation—a sense of an anthropomorphic God out there, micromanaging our lives. In actuality, the Will of God is non-specific for any of our lives and circumstances. The Divine Plan is for each of us to make the very best choices to express the maximum amount of Goodness, Godness, and elevated consciousness we can at our present level of awareness ... and we do this by using WILL at its highest level.

> Neither snap judgments nor sleeping on a problem are any better than conscious thinking for making complex decisions, according to new research. The finding debunks a controversial 2006 research result asserting that unconscious thought is superior for complex decisions, such as buying a house or car. If anything, the new study suggests that conscious thought leads to better choices *(Dijksterhuis, Ap, et al, Complex Decision? Don't Sleep on It, Science News, Science Daily Research, August 11, 2008).*

Thanks for indulging us! Now, let's get back to our discussion of WILL. As with all the Powers, we can use WILL from different levels of consciousness. Choices based on our sense consciousness, or ordinary consciousness, can range from very good and appropriate to the "what was I thinking" level of dismay! Since our senses tend to be rather selective in terms of accepting and sorting incoming information, what they seem to report should always be suspect. Because our shifting moods and focus tend to affect how we interpret incoming information, our human use of WILL should always be questioned.

When WILL is underdeveloped, it becomes difficult to make clear, decisive choices. People with underdeveloped WILL fall into the "I feel strongly both ways" style of handling decisions. They also have problems committing to a decision, thinking there may always be a better option around the corner. The following story illustrates this conundrum.

> A well-dressed young man saw a breath-takingly beautiful woman walk past Chicos in the mall. He was so smitten that he followed her as she made her way toward the center of the mall.
>
> The woman saw his reflection in the store windows as she passed them and finally turned and demanded: "Why are you following me?"

He declared innocently, "Because you are the most beautiful woman I have ever seen, and I have fallen madly in love with you at first sight."

The woman smiled and replied," I believe you need to look behind you at my younger sister who is ten times more beautiful than I."

The opportunistic suitor wheeled around quickly and saw what he considered to be an average looking girl walking toward him.

"She's no where near as beautiful as you," he lamented, "You lied to me!"

"No, you lied to me," she countered. "If you were so madly in love with me, why did you turn around?"

This young man illustrates the classic indecisive 'Definitely Maybe' attitude! He claimed he definitely thought the woman was the greatest thing since sliced bread—and then he thought maybe there's better sliced bread.

What's amazing is, people do this all the time. Indecisive Definitely Maybe people live their lives out of a chronic 'yes—no—wait—maybe' perspective. They short-change themselves because they undermine themselves. They are decisively indecisive.

We should also be aware of states of consciousness leading to the more negative side or down side of WILL. We certainly want to avoid becoming willful or stubborn. When we are willful, we force our decisions and choices upon another. When we are stubborn, we tend to ignore the facts and not change our minds (make another choice) for a variety of reasons, ranging from not wanting to be wrong (a.k.a. wanting to be right) to simply wanting our own way regardless of the consequences.

Some people have Ph.D's in making less than the best choice. They are well-credentialed in willfulness, stubbornness, and indecision. You probably know some of them. There are people who wear willfulness like a badge of honor. Others wear it like a straight jacket and struggle to get themselves out of a negative disposition.

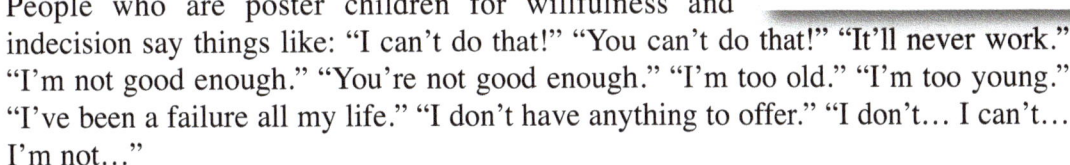

Willfulness and stubbornness come from a consciousness of lack, and fear, and anger, and hopelessness. People who are poster children for willfulness and indecision say things like: "I can't do that!" "You can't do that!" "It'll never work." "I'm not good enough." "You're not good enough." "I'm too old." "I'm too young." "I've been a failure all my life." "I don't have anything to offer." "I don't... I can't... I'm not..."

Here's the thing. All of us have grown up in those kinds of environments. We've been told we're not good enough, we're failures, we can't do or have certain things. And there's a part of us, that wounded child part of us, that asks—what if they're right?

We are affirming—no, declaring—no, categorically asserting—that anyone who willfully or stubbornly says you're not good enough is a negativity pygmy. They're short on joy, fun, happiness, and a zest for life. And they are short on Truth!

Negative, hurtful, willful, indecisive thinking is corrosive. It's the kind of thinking that soils our consciousness and spoils our spiritual walk. In their lowest forms willfulness, stubbornness, and indecisiveness are simply *whine-ology*. As you know, it takes strong WILL to stay positive in a world which has gone bonkers with negativity.

The use of WILL informed from a higher spiritual awareness allows us to claim the Truth of *What* (not who) we are: spiritual beings having a human experience. We have the capacity to so identify ourselves with Divine Mind (the eternal presence, God) that we can align ourselves in every thought and deed from the awareness of Divine Ideas, Laws, and Principles.

So how is it we get off course, and make ineffective, unwise choices? One area for vigilance is a tendency to subjugate ourselves to the will of another. Sure, there are some situations where this is appropriate, such as parents responsible for their young children and those with Power of Attorney for mentally incapacitated adults. And of course, there are many times when we use WILL to *choose* to go along with someone else's idea, or cooperate for the good of the whole, even if we aren't totally sold on their ideas. But this should always be a conscious choice; by and large, we don't want to allow others to determine our path and direction. And of course, the converse is also true: we do not want to inflict our will upon another.

If you would, take a moment to think back on a time in your life, when there was something you really wanted to accomplish, and you were successful. It might have been a skill you wanted to learn; or maybe training for some event, like running a marathon; or maybe an educational or a professional goal; or some negative habit you decided to eliminate. Think back on one of these things you *really* wanted—and then achieved. Now reflect on how it unfolded. One thing we notice is that once we make a decision to do something, it happens! We don't always know how, but it just happens. We don't mean it's easy, necessarily—we have to put in the effort. But regardless of the roadblocks that appear or the challenges we face, somehow we keep going and we achieve success. When that happens, we are exercising an elevated level of WILL.

What if we approached all of life from that same perspective? What if we really believed that we know what is ours to do—and we went forth to do it, without investing any energy in worrying about how we will do it ... just knowing the way will unfold? Imagine what we could accomplish! There would be no wavering ... no waffling. The secret to mastering the art of living is using WILL to set our intentions on the path of spiritual growth, and choose to take action!

We can think of two particular times in life when we need to quicken our Power of WILL and really focus on using it at the highest level: When we have something important we want to do, and when we have a difficult situation we want to move through.

The saying goes, "Where There's a Will, There's a Way." Here is a WAY Acronym that serves as a great memory peg to help you remember what to do when you are in one of those two situations in life, and need to call on and amp up your Power of WILL. Ready? Where There's a Will, There's a Way—W – A – Y!!

W = Work the Principles! For some reason, it seems like the times we most need to use our Principles and Spiritual Truths is when we least feel like doing it! When we are attempting a major goal, or when we are facing a difficult life situation—maybe at the same time—that's when we most need to go back to basics! We know there is One Power, all good. We know we are God expressing, and have all 12 Powers at our disposal. We know we are One, and there is no separation! We know all the resources we need already exist at the level of Spirit, and all the answers are there. So this is the time to work these Principles, from that place of claiming them as Truth!

A = Access Spirit. The answers are not "out there" but rather, they can only be found when we enter into the Silence. In other words, Be Prayed Up! We love that term! When we are "prayed up" we are ready, in an instant, to call on our inner Divine connection and Be Still and Know! When we are making those major choices in life, it is invaluable to Access Spirit.

Y = Yield to Divine Ideas, not to the world of appearance. Sometimes the challenges we face seem insurmountable; the world around us feels like it is falling apart; life looks bleak. But we know this is only the world of appearance, and through WILL we can take action to move forward.

WILL From the Four Levels of Consciousness

Now let's look at the use of WILL at the four levels of consciousness we have been exploring:

1. **Unconscious WILL:** based on predispositions in our subconscious mind which consist of beliefs that are not in our moment to moment awareness. Choices are made from unconscious/subconscious beliefs, by default rather than a conscious choice. For example, people who have a subconscious belief that they are unworthy and undeserving of awards and recognition will tend to make choices which unwittingly reinforce this belief. On the other hand, people who have a deeply embedded sense of self worth tend to make choices that serve to reinforce those beliefs.

2. **Conscious WILL from our senses:** based on an outside stimulus we experience through our sight, sound, scent, touch, and or taste. A man might decide to turn right instead of left because he notices there is unusually heavy

traffic to left, and he knows of another way to get home by turning right. Someone might choose to purchase a theater ticket based on a trailer viewed on the Internet. Of course, choices can be made that are not effective from this level of consciousness as well. For example, a person might choose to sabotage a diet plan after driving by a popular ice cream store and deciding to indulge!

3. **Conscious WILL from our human personality:** based on thoughts, feelings, attitudes and/or beliefs held in ordinary consciousness. A person believes he/she can be successful as an entrepreneur. After gathering the information and reviewing the requirements, he/she makes the choice to move ahead with that career option.

4. **Conscious WILL from our True Identity, or Authentic Self:** based on Divine Ideas, Laws, and Principles. We make choices and decisions that reinforce and confirm our belief in our True Nature, our Extraordinary Self..

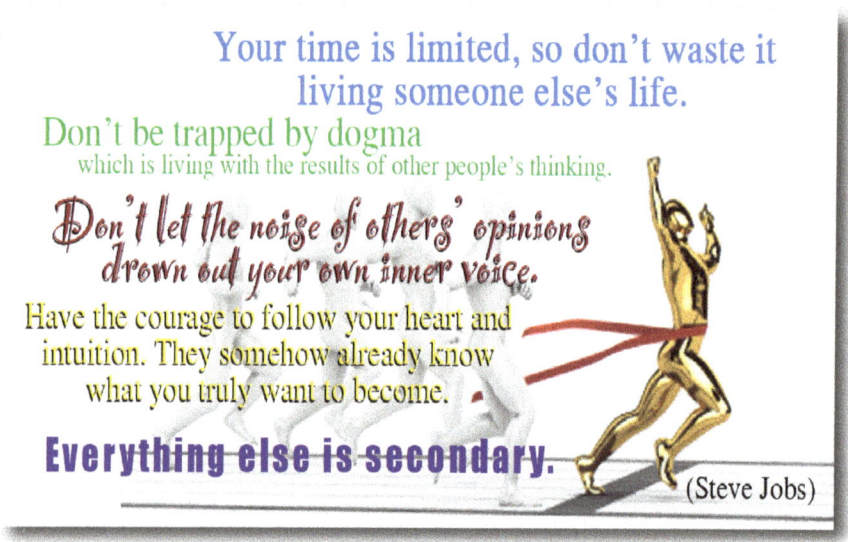

It's not rocket science to realize there's something better than constantly worrying about the economy. It's not rocket science to realize there's something better than going through life with a debilitating habit or addiction. It's not rocket science to know that there's something better than being bored and burdened by meaningless routines.

It's not rocket science to realize that there's more to life than debt; barely making ends meet; and the fear and doubt and disappointment which goes with a crazy economy. It's not rocket science to realize that we are the product of our thoughts, choices, and actions.

You may remember the film from the 80's, entitled ***Dead Poets' Society***, starring Robin Williams. The setting for the story is a prestigious boys' boarding school—a school in which the students are under heavy pressure to conform to the values and standards of success of their affluent parents.

Robin Williams plays a controversial, imaginative, new teacher at the school. He is determined to ignite the students' imaginations, and to encourage them to make life-affirming choices.

On the first day of class, he takes the boys from the classroom into the hallway where the school trophy case is located. In the case are pictures of championship teams and superstars dating back more than a century. He tells them to look very carefully at the faces in the pictures—to study them. Then he suddenly says, of the athletes in the pictures, "Food for worms, lads. They're all pushing up daisies—every one of them."

The boys are jarred. They make the connection between themselves and the boys in the pictures. It's not rocket science. The boys showcased in the trophy case have all made their transitions.

In a way, it was a harsh thing to do to these bright-eyed kids. But as you watched, you knew that it was a defining moment for these young men. They were being pushed by their parents, by the school, and by each other to become something that wasn't necessarily them. They were being pushed to conform to tradition, to make choices they didn't want to make.

It was the first step in getting them to think thoughtfully about their own lives and the contributions they can make. Were they going to spend their lives awake or asleep? Chasing rainbows or walking in their sleep? Living happily or haplessly? Were they going to be standing on the sidelines or standing in their truth? Were they going to live by the "I had no choice" code or the "I get to choose" code?

Those questions apply to us as well. Are we going to master the art of living or massacre the art of living? It doesn't take rocket science to know it's up to us. What will be, is what we will to be.

The secret to living the life you want—to getting the most out of this earth experience—to attracting unbelievable happiness and prosperity—is to simply to make the kind of choices that are life-affirming and growth-oriented.

Making the "Right" Choice

We are confronted with a multitude of choices every day. The options that face us can sometimes seem overwhelming just by their sheer numbers. Research confirms that providing one with the ability to choose increases an individual's sense of personal control and feelings of intrinsic motivation. This personal control and intrinsic motivation, in turn, have been associated with numerous physical and psychological benefits. Conversely, the absence of choice and control has a variety of detrimental effects on intrinsic motivation, life satisfaction, and one's wellbeing *(Deci E, Speigel N, et al. "The effects of performance standards on teaching styles: The behavior of controlling teachers." Journal of Educational Psychology 1982 74: 852-859; Schulz R, Hanusa B. "Long-term effects of control and predictability-enhancing interventions: Findings and ethical issues." Journal of Personality and Social Psychology 1978 36: 1194-1201).*

But other research conducted by choice research expert Dr. Sheena Iyengar stresses that too many options may actually paralyze people or push them into decisions that are against their own best interest *(Iyengar, S., The Art of Choosing, NY: Twelve, Hachette Book Group USA, 2010).*

So how can we ensure we are making the best possible choices? Some decisions are more mundane (Do I drink Coke, Pepsi, or Dr. Pepper?) Others can impact our life (Which job do I take? Do I blow the whistle on unethical behavior?)

What does making the right choice mean? Simply, and perhaps naively put, it means thoughtfully using the right information at the right time under the right circumstances with the right intentions to the best of your ability, given the dual demands of conscience and expediency. Of course, what makes something right (or wrong) is a theoretical issue. Whether something is right (or wrong) depends on the wise use of moral compasses like good intentions, sound judgment, abiding faith, and a positive attitude ... and using WILL at the highest level of consciousness. The concept of right choice implies moral obligation and concern for the welfare of others as well as yourself.

We have created **The Choice Map™** to help you exercise WILL from a high level of consciousness and intention. It is not meant to be the absolute, authoritative source, nor is it a fail-safe template to guarantee the right choice will be made 100 percent of the time. However, it will broaden your decision-making perspectives so you can make more informed and sophisticated choices. Although each question can be used independently of the others, the entire set of questions operates like a moral calculator to significantly improve your chances of making the right decision.

For best results, prayerfully consider each question before you determine your course of action. You have a much better chance of making the right choice if you have answered the entire set of questions.

Suggestion: Choice doesn't need to be focused on what has to be avoided, but rather on what can be done.

Reminder: One bad choice doesn't necessarily make you a bad person—nor does one act of generosity necessarily make you perfect.

The Choice Map™

1. What harm could come from this decision, and if there should be harm, how can I minimize the harm?
2. Which choice best represents what I stand for, and is consistent with the kind of person I want to be?
3. What would the wisest, most ethical person I know do in this situation?
4. What effect will my choice have on my family, my friends, my co-workers, my community, and the environment?
5. What effect will my choice have on my reputation and credibility?
6. Is my choice driven by facts or assumptions, feelings or peer pressure, conviction or consequences?
7. Is this choice the right thing to do, or am I bowing to expediency?

WILL: Putting It Into Practice

WILL—Activity One:

For one day, make decisions quickly and act on them. For example, when you are getting dressed, walk into your closet and choose the first thing you see. What movie to see? Pick one right off the top of your head; when you are in a restaurant, glance at the menu and choose something immediately. You get the idea!

At the end of the day, reflect on your experience:

- What role did WILL play?
- What impact did some of the other Powers we've discussed have (especially WISDOM and UNDERSTANDING)?
- How accurate were your snap decisions?
- How did it feel to make decisions so quickly?
- What does this tell you about your Power of WILL and how effectively you use it?

WILL—Activity Two:

As you think about the specific area you are working on throughout this course, make a list of some of the important choices you have made up to this week, and evaluate how effective they have been.

- What choices would you like to change? Can you? If so, how?
- What choices do you need to make at this point, to move you forward in being successful with your goal? Use the Choice Map™ to help you work through the more difficult choices you are facing.

Example: Healthy Eating

Key Choices up to this point:
I chose to set boundaries about how I can get the support I need on my journey toward healthy eating. (Effectiveness: Excellent! I got all of the support I could have hoped for—and have come up with some healthy variations of some of my old favorite recipes!)

Choice I'd like to change ... and how:
I chose to go with my friend to Dairy Queen, and I caved! I ordered a large chocolate chip cookie dough Blizzard ... and ate the whole thing! (I can't change it since I've already eaten the whole thing ... but I can learn that this is a potential temptation for me. I want to prepare a way to handle future invitations such as this more effectively.)

WILL Affirmation:

I claim WILL now. I use WILL to make wise choices so I can be the best I can be.

Quotes to Inspire WILL

Through your power to choose what kind of thoughts you will think, you can think in ways that will gradually convert the prison of habit into a powerhouse of freedom and newness in mind and body. (Russell Kemp)

People, places, conditions, and events cannot keep your God-given prosperity and success from you, once you decide to deliberately employ prosperous thinking as your ally for success. (Catherine Ponder)

The WILL moves to action all of the other faculties of mind. I AM is expressed through I WILL; it is the business of I AM to know when the I WILL activities are ideally true. (Charles Fillmore)

Be miserable. Or motivate yourself. Whatever has to be done, it's always your choice. (Wayne Dyer)

You must make the great decision to affirm your unity with the Infinite. (Eric Butterworth)

Living the beautiful way of life calls for discriminating choices. So, choose wonders that build you up, not those that tear you down. Choose only those things that fulfill your own very special needs. Become a master in the art of being and building yourself. (Charles Lelly)

Choose the way of wholeness. Choose the way of all good in life. Decide to initiate right actions. Make decisions and stick with them. Choose your God essence over your ego self. (Donald Curtis)

The most important phase of good— the very foundation and essence of all the good that can possibly come into my life—is not some manifestation that is poured out upon me. It does not come to me through any external channel; it lies within me, and whether or not I use this good and exercise control over it is a matter absolutely within my own jurisdiction, a matter of my own volition and action. (Dana Gatlin)

There is an innate knowing that one's spiritual, emotional, and even physical well-being depend upon heeding the call and making the commitment to endure whatever is necessary in order to attain the treasure and the transformation. (Mary-Alice Jafolla)

There is a great depth of splendor within us, but it must be unfolded through self-realization and self-discipline. There is no synthetic shortcut to the Kingdom. (Eric Butterworth)

The divine idea of order is the idea of adjustment, and as this is established in [our] thought, [our] mind and affairs will be at one with the universal harmony.
~ Charles Fillmore
Revealing Word, p. 143

ORDER

Overview

- Location: Navel
- Color: Olive Green
- Works with LOVE to create harmony

ORDER is the Power to organize; align; sequence; adjust; arrange

From ordinary consciousness: The ability to organize; align; sequence; adjust; and arrange based on our senses, thoughts, feelings and beliefs. We use ORDER to organize the garage or create a logical sequence to accomplish something ~ or, we can use it to be obsessive compulsive in our behavior.

- *Underdeveloped ORDER* results in someone who cannot organize, balance, or make adjustments easily. You might call people with underdeveloped ORDER disorganized, disorderly, or even (to the extreme) slovenly. They find it very difficult to adjust to change, and often become hoarders.

- *Egocentric ORDER* results in someone who is overly fastidious about their immediate environment, must make sure everything is just so, and may be obsessive compulsive, as well as hyper-detailed about nearly everything. For example, this person obsesses over things like ensuring every picture is perfectly level and in precisely the right position; bathroom towels and wash cloths are spaced perfectly and hung evenly; and books on shelves are alphabetized by author's last names.

From elevated consciousness: The ability to organize; align; sequence; adjust; and arrange based on Ideas, Truths, Principles, and Laws that are Divine in nature. We use ORDER to organize and prioritize our thoughts, feelings, and actions to be the best, most organized person we can be.

Think about the messiest place in your home. We know, this is not the most enjoyable thing you could be thinking about! But bear with us for just a moment. It might be the garage, the office, a bedroom, a closet, or maybe just that catch-all drawer in the kitchen. How many times have you had thoughts about getting that particular area in order? You were using your ORDER linked with IMAGINATION to envision it. And when you actually start the clean-up process, ORDER kicks in even more, since you use it to match what you imagined as you go about the clean-up. As you invest your time and energy creating a special place for each item, you can literally feel a sense of organization and balance flow through your very being! It feels so good ... so why don't we keep things in order all the time?

People experience this same phenomenon in the workplace. According to author Alice Hudson, three common but solvable time-wasting environmental factors in the office are:

- email notifications,
- playing telephone tag and
- keeping a messy work area.

Her tips to manage these issues calls on the use of ORDER at the highest level. For example:

- Turn off your email notification to avoid being distracted by it. Instead, identify specific times during the day to check your emails, keeping you in control of the email instead of it controlling you.
- Avoid leaving countless uninformative "please call me back" messages when you have to leave a message for someone. Instead, explain exactly what you need. It gives the person more to go on and frees up more time for you to manage other projects.
- Messy desks mean time wasted looking for things. Even when you are busy, get into the habit of having an allocated place for everything and avoid letting junk pile up around you *(Hudson, A., How to Handle Multiple Projects and Deadlines, eHow.com, May 9, 2013).*

ORDER, like so many of the other Powers, is often misunderstood. People sometimes interpret ORDER to be synonymous with the phrase Divine Order, meaning Divine Predetermination or Divine Proclamation. As stated in the book, *Get Over It,* co-authored by Paul Hasselbeck and Bil Holton:

> Divine Order is often used in the traditional sense, [meaning] there is a God separate from us ordering everything that happens in the universe, including our daily lives. The idea is that there is a set order for our lives and that all of our activities are governed by it. This is not an enlightened view.

This misunderstanding of Divine Order leaves one feeling resigned rather than empowered. Understood in a different and more empowering way, Divine Order is the orderly sequence by which everything comes into existence: Mind-Idea-Expression. Everyone ... and we do mean everyone ... uses this sequence; we cannot *not* use it! First there is an idea or thought in mind; we experience it; and then we go about bringing the thought or idea into physical existence—or not. In the case of cleaning out that messy area we envisioned to kick off this chapter, you probably thought about cleaning it a lot prior to actually bringing the act into physical existence! In fact, you may still be thinking about it!

ORDER is the ability to organize, and it shows up in our lives in the way we organize our living space, work, files, and lives. We might use it to sequence a series of activities to reach a goal, to schedule the classes we need to take to complete a degree, to arrange the ingredients we put into a recipe, or to schedule our time in order to get things done.

We use it to make plans as well as to adjust those plans according to what we encounter along the way. For example, if you are driving to a friend's house and find your usual way obstructed by emergency road work, you will, in that moment, use ORDER to adjust to this new situation and re-sequence the way you get to your destination.

> Research confirms that people who meet deadlines consistently have the ability to prioritize tasks, delegate, coordinate resources, and adjust schedule demands *(Suttle, R., Organization skills in the workplace, Small Business Chron, retrieved May 9, 2013)*.

When ORDER is underdeveloped, you will not be able to create much balance in your life, nor will you find it easy to adjust to changes. Further, there will be the inhibited ability to sequence events and activities. As a result, you will feel disorganized, and find yourself backtracking or re-doing things in order to finish a project. Your home and work environments may well be messy and disorganized, even though you probably claim that you know where to find everything you need!

Two of the best methods we've found to rectify this are the **Ten-Minute Jump Start** and the **ABCDE Method**. Here are quick recaps of each method for you to try.

The Ten-Minute Jump Start is very simple. Select a project you have been wanting to accomplish, but for one reason or another have never completed. Then set a timer, watch, alarm, or clock for ten minutes. Work like crazy on the project until the timer rings. When the alarm sounds, you have permission to stop working on the project. At least 90% of the time you

won't want to stop because you will have become involved in the project. You see, the problem with procrastinators does not lie in actually *doing* the project ... the issue is in getting started! *(Holton, Cher, and Bil Holton, The Manager's Short Course, Wiley and Son, New York, 1992).*

A word to the wise: You must be honest with yourself when you use this technique. If you really want to stop when the alarm goes off, do it! Allow yourself to feel a bit more satisfied ... guilt-free ... and productive. Otherwise you won't reap the full benefits of this strategy. Walk away ... and return later for another 10-minute jump start. Eventually you will get it done! Use this Ten-Minute Jump Start Technique to successfully employ ORDER to move beyond procrastination into organizing—and accomplishing—the things you need to do.

Another good method for setting priorities, once you have determined your major goals or objectives, is the **ABCDE Method** by Brian Tracy. Place one of the letters below in the margin beside each of the tasks on your list to rank them before you begin:

- "A" stands for "very important;" something you must do. There can be serious negative consequences if you don't do it.
- "B" stands for "important;" something you should do. This is not as important as your 'A' tasks. There are only minor negative consequences if it is not completed.
- "C" stands for things that are "nice to do;" but which are not as important as 'A' or 'B,' tasks. There are no negative consequences for not completing it.
- "D" stands for "delegate." You can assign this task to someone else who can do the job instead of you.
- "E" stands for "eliminate, whenever possible." You should eliminate every single activity you possibly can, to free up your time.

When you use the ABCDE method, you can very easily sort out what is important and unimportant. This then will focus your time and attention on those items on your list that are most essential for you to do *(Tracy, B., Brian Tracy International, retrieved November 10, 2008).*

When ORDER is overdeveloped, you tend to be very fastidious and obsessive about everything having a place and being in it ... to perfection. There will be a compulsiveness about things being done in a certain way and order. Think about a person who sits down to dinner in a restaurant, and re-organizes the place setting while defining their space. They adjust the location of the water glass, and even where the salt and pepper shakers are at the center of the table. If you happen to be dining with this person and move the salt and pepper shakers, they will invariably move them back to where they had originally positioned them.

In terms of neurological research, the prefrontal cortex is the most recently evolved part of the brain. It controls the functions of attention span, impulse control, organization, learning from experience, self-monitoring, priorities triage, and follow-through *(Morgenstern, Julie (2004). Time Management from the Inside Out: The Foolproof System for*

Taking Control of Your Schedule—and Your Life (2nd ed.). New York: Henry Holt/Owl Books). Obviously this area is working overboard in people who exhibit an underdeveloped Power of ORDER.

ORDER From the Four Levels of Consciousness

It is useful to review how ORDER is used at various levels of consciousness:

1. **Unconscious ORDER:** based on a cause in our subconscious mind which consists of beliefs that are not in our moment to moment awareness. In this case, you would organize, sequence, and adjust your life to conform to a belief you are not even aware of. For example a person who has a subconscious belief in unworthiness might win the lottery, and then organize, sequence, and adjust their actions so the money is lost in a short period of time. Then they would say, "I don't know why this happened to me!"
2. **Conscious ORDER from our senses:** based on something in physicality we are gleaning through our sight, sound, scent, touch, or taste. This is demonstrated by a person who must have the picture just so, the place setting exactly right, or the garage in perfect order. Perfect examples would be the character of Monk on TV, or the mystery fiction detective Hercule Poirot, created by Agatha Christie.
3. **Conscious ORDER from our human personality:** based on thoughts, feelings, attitudes and/or beliefs held in ordinary consciousness. If an individual wishes to become a doctor, the person will organize, sequence, and adjust life in order to obtain the goal. He/she will take all the pre-med courses

in the right order, and then take the pre-med exam (Med-Cat) the next time it is available. Classes and residency will follow, all designed to lead to achieving the goal of becoming a physician.

4. **Conscious ORDER from our True Identity, or Authentic Self:** based on the Divine Ideas, Laws, and Principles. Here, we use ORDER to organize, balance, sequence, and make adjustments so we can be the Authentic Self we already are. We might notice that we are showing up in very egotistic and unproductive ways, and then choose to consciously readjust our thoughts and actions to be the best we can be. We might also adjust our schedule to create a specific time for meditation and spiritual study.

> Multitasking is a weakness, not a strength. In 2010, a study by neuroscientists Etienne Koechlin and Sylvain Charron of the French biomedical research agency INSERM in Paris showed that when people focus on two tasks simultaneously, each side of the brain tackles a different task. This suggests a two-task limit on what the human brain can handle *(Koechlin, E, and Charron, S., Science, Vol. 328, No. 5976, 16 April 2010).*

There's a reason why ORDER is so important! If we don't approach things in ORDER, we notice it becomes:
- Harder to learn, because we don't have a strong foundation to build on;
- Tougher to experience results in our growth; and
- Easier to get frustrated and give up!

Think about this: what if, in Kindergarten, the teacher said, "Don't worry—we'll come back and pick up what the numbers are later. But this Calculus is really cool, and I want you to experience it!" How many math wizards do you think we'd have? Or what if, on your first piano lesson, the teacher placed a sheet of Mozart in front of you and said, "Okay, I know most teachers start by teaching you the notes and scales, but I love this piece and it is so much more interesting that those pesky Hanon Piano drills!" How many children would continue with their lessons?

Any new skill you learn—golf, tennis, dance, knitting, a new language—demands going from simple to complex. You start with the basics, create a strong foundation, and are then able to build on it! It's important to approach things from a place of ORDER! Our Spiritual growth is exactly the same! If you try to jump right in on a 20-minute meditation, you'll probably give up really quickly! First you need to develop the skill of how to focus, and how to handle that monkey mind that occurs. Then you can build on this foundation by using a variety of meditation techniques, learning to master them as you practice.

ORDER

As you seek to call on ORDER at the highest, most elevated spiritual level in your life, here are two powerful tips:

- Make yourself your top priority! Work on bringing YOU into alignment with Truth, so your world will be right.
- Don't compare yourself with anyone but yourself! One of our favorite quotes comes from the great ballet master Mikhail Baryshnikov, who said, *"I don't try to dance better than anyone else, only better than myself."* If life seems to be out of sync, look within first. If you are having relationship issues, look within first. If you're having prosperity or health issues, look within first. If you feel separated from Spirit, look within first. If the Principles don't seem to be working, look WHERE? Within first.

As you look within, ask yourself these questions:

> - Is everything in order?
> - Am I practicing the basics?
> - Is there some forgiveness work to be done?
> - Is there some time in the Silence to be scheduled?
> - Does my self-talk need to be edited?
> - Am I at peace within?

Setting life priorities is an important business. Each stage of life brings new challenges that have the potential to add to our happiness or dampen our growth. What we choose (which goes back to WILL) ultimately becomes part of our destiny. When it boils down to choices, priorities bring order to our lives and help us clear the confusion by putting things in the right perspective. This is where ORDER comes into play. When we know what is important for us in our lives, our efforts and energy become streamlined in a definite direction to help us achieve what we consider important. Using ORDER to set priorities in life and organize how we want to do things are skills which help us remain focused, centered, and productive.

Where there is an appearance of disorder—where it seems like the Principles are not working—this is when we can call on ORDER, and use a process we call Spiritual Alphabetical Order! Let us explain! Most sequential processing is identified by using alphabetical order. Steps are identified as A, B, C... In life, there are all kinds of "alphabetical orders," when you think of it in terms of creating the proper sequence of things. For example, "Cooking Alphabetical Order" would be the sequence of how you combine  ingredients to create the final dish you are making. You don't mix the cream cheese icing of a carrot cake in with the cake batter!

A nail technician has a very specific order designed to create the perfect looking nails. That would be "Manicure Alphabetical Order." You don't do filing after you apply polish! And carpenters follow a very specific order when building a house. They do not wait to lay the foundation after the attic is completed! They are using "Carpentry Alphabetical Order." You get the idea! Every sequential process has its own Alphabetical Order. So let's talk about "Spiritual Alphabetical Order."

When we think about our spiritual growth, affirmations always come up as so important. A great technique we like to use is called Glamour Grammar. Anytime you are sensing yourself in a diddlysquat order kind of experience, just think of the alphabet. Then, for each letter of the alphabet, brainstorm positive, powerful, spiritual words. For example, for A you might use Awesome; B could be Bodacious; C might be Creative. Then create affirmations, using the words you selected and placing "I am..." in front of them. For example, I am Awesome; I am Bodacious; I am Creative... And become aware of the energy flow you feel as you affirm the Truth of who you really are, and notice the change you experience in your ability to bring a sense of ORDER to whatever you are doing. (By the way, this is particularly effective when you are stuck in traffic! Simply look at the license plates on the cars around you, and come up with positive words for the letters on those plates! Honest—it is transforming!)

These affirmations are great—if they are done in the right Spiritual sequence! But have you ever used affirmations, and felt like they were meaningless? It might be because they weren't grounded in the Intuitive Guidance that comes from your time in the Silence, from your awareness of your oneness! That's why it's important to know the secret to "Spiritual Alphabetical Order" which, put quite simply, might look like this:

A. Be Prayed Up! (Time in the Silence, at Headquarters)
B. Follow Your Intuitive Guidance (which comes from being prayed up!)
C. Affirm the Truth of Who You Really Are (which you know that you know because you are prayed up.)

When we approach life in this sequence, the Divine Ideas we recognize will always be grounded in the strength of our awareness of our Oneness, and we will have the guidance of Spirit to direct our out-picturing of those ideas. That way, we end up with Divine ORDER instead of diddlysquat order—and we can affirm with confidence: *I am mastering the art of living with ORDER as I walk the spiritual path on practical feet.*

ORDER: Putting It Into Practice

ORDER—Activity One:

Go back to that area of messiness you thought of at the beginning of this chapter. If you did not choose a specific area yet, this is the moment. Choose an area in your living environment that is out of order, cluttered, untidy, and somewhat chaotic.

Schedule a block of time, and put it in order. Create a space that is balanced, orderly, neat, and efficient for what you need.

Once you are done, grab your journal and jot down answers to the following questions:
- What inner feelings did you experience as you ordered this area of your life?
- What other Powers did you see interacting with ORDER, to help you achieve this goal, and how did they complement each other?

ORDER—Activity Two

As you think about the specific area you are working on throughout this course, identify the areas involving organizing, aligning, sequencing, adjusting and arranging that are necessary to achieve your goal successfully. Create a schedule (that would be using ORDER) to address the areas that need some work.

Example: Healthy Eating

I need to create an eating plan for the week, so I can plan my grocery shopping, my cooking, and the foods I will be eating. I also need to coordinate my work schedule in with my eating plan, to plan for those meetings that are conducted in restaurants.

ORDER Affirmation:

I claim ORDER now. I use ORDER to align and organize my surroundings, my thoughts, and my feelings so I can be the best, most orderly person I can be.

Quotes to Inspire ORDER

(Our) body is made up of centers of consciousness—of light—and if arranged so they radiate the light within (us), (we) will shine like a diamond. (Charles Fillmore)

Order establishes the right sequence for events. Some divine ideas must become manifest before other divine ideas can become manifest. Everything has its right place, and when by some means it is in wrong relationship to the things about it, order makes an adjustment to reestablish the right relationship. (Hypatia Hasbrouck)

I've learned that we can do anything, but we can't do everything ... at least not at the same time. So think of your priorities not in terms of what activities you do, but when you do them. Timing is everything. (Dan Millman)

Order is a rightness, a right outworking of things, and this is what we are to affirm and hold to. Our affirmation of order reveals to us what our part is in bringing about the proper adjustment and right conditions in some situation. Ordering positive actions acts as a catalyst to start things in the right direction. (Martha Smock)

We feel the weight of worldly matters, but we also hear the call to come up higher. Let us respond not by living apart and isolating ourselves from the human family and the world, but by seeing earthly matters from a higher point of view. In this way, we will not forsake the world; we will assign it its proper place. After all, even mystics have bills to pay. (Jim Rosemergy)

Order cannot possibly be brought about through conformity to a pattern, under any circumstances. (Jiddu Krishnamurti)

Not out of right practice comes right thinking, but out of right thinking comes right practice. (Annie Besant)

My message is of hope, courage, and confidence. Let us mobilize all our resources in a systematic and organized way and tackle the issues that confront us with determination and discipline. (Muhammad Ali Jinnah)

The condition of our outer world is always the perfect outpicturing of our inner world. If we do not like the outer us, we can change it by going within and putting our thoughts and feelings in order. (Margaret Pounders)

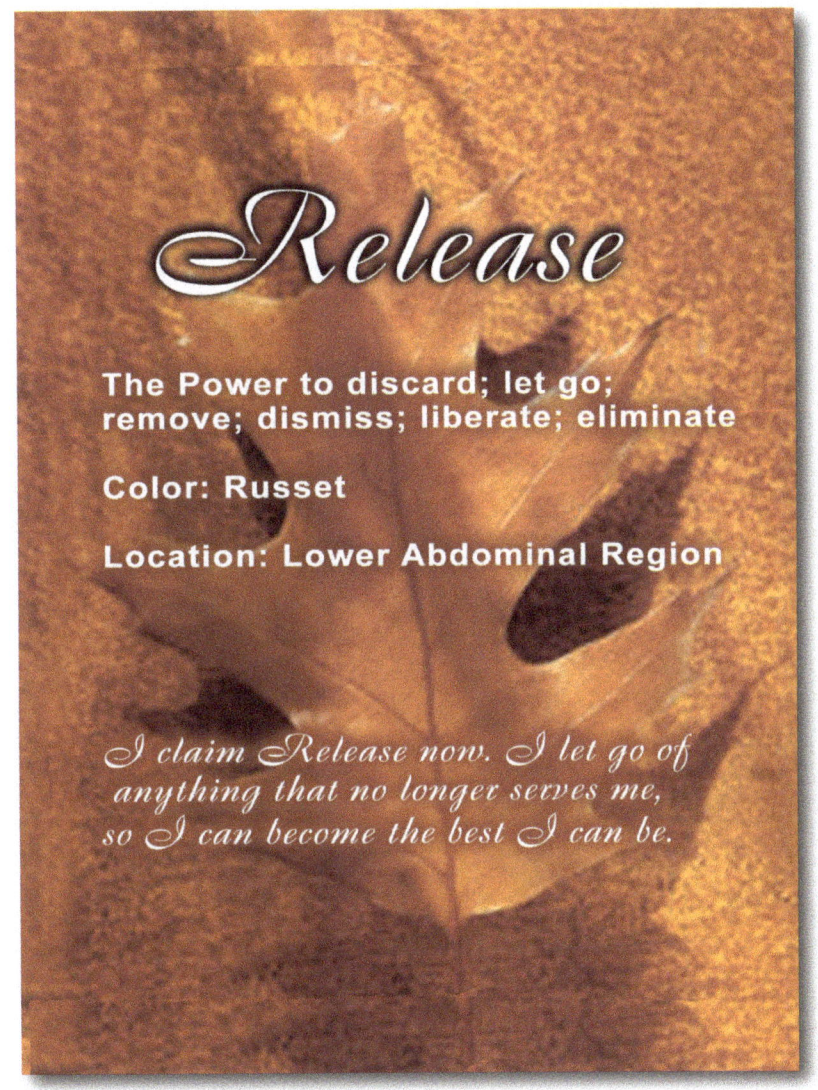

Sometimes letting things go is an act of far greater power than defending or hanging on. (Eckhart Tolle)

Letting go gives us freedom, and freedom is the only condition for happiness. If, in our heart, we still cling to anything—anger, anxiety, or possessions—we cannot be free.
~ Thich Nhat Hanh

RELEASE

Overview

- Location: Lower Abdominal Region
- Color: Russet

RELEASE is the Power to discard; let go; remove; liberate; dismiss; eliminate.

From ordinary consciousness: The ability to discard; let go; remove; liberate; dismiss; and eliminate based on our senses, thoughts, feelings, and beliefs. This Power releases and lets go of things that are not working or are no longer useful in our lives. We use RELEASE to eliminate a destructive habit like smoking or biting our nails—or, ironically, we may use RELEASE to let go of things that *are* working, like an exercise program or meditation practice.

- *Underdeveloped RELEASE* results in the classic pack rat: people who have difficulty getting rid of anything. They live in a perpetual mess of disorder and chaos. People with underdeveloped RELEASE often have a difficult time ending a relationship, job, or other situation ... even when it is obviously abusive or destructive.
- *Egocentric RELEASE* results in person who is rash about letting things go , resulting in premature endings of relationships and jobs. This person could be wasteful, purging all the time, and often tends to throw the proverbial baby out with the bathwater.

From elevated consciousness: The ability to discard; let go; remove; liberate; dismiss; and eliminate based on Ideas, Truths, Principles, and Laws that are Divine in nature. We use RELEASE to let go of anything that interferes with these Ideas or erroneously uses Divine Laws and Principles. We use RELEASE to let go of old beliefs, embedded theology, and aspects of our ordinary consciousness that hinder being the best person we can be.

*S*tuff! It is one of the most popular words in today's culture—and by definition, has no definitive definition! It can be used in a variety of ways to describe a multitude of concepts or items. We did a File Name search on our own desktop computer for the

word "stuff" and got 112 results—112 files on our own computer that we'd named which included the word stuff! We obviously love that word! But hey! We aren't alone! Shakespeare even used in *The Tempest*, when Prospero says, "We are such stuff as dreams are made on" as he indicates his feelings about this life being illusion. (As a little bit of dramatic arts trivia— take note that Prospero says "made on," not "made of," despite Humphrey Bogart's famous last line in *The Maltese Falcon*, when he misquoted, saying "The stuff that dreams are made of." Bogart suggested the line to director John Huston, but neither seems to have brushed up their knowledge of Shakespeare. Film buffs may think "made of" is the authentic phrase, but that's just illusion!)

So why are we ranting on and on about stuff? It relates specifically to the Power covered in this chapter: RELEASE. Release is our ability to eliminate, let go, remove, or deny. We use it to let go of things that are no longer serving us, and on a spiritual level, we use this Power to let go of error thinking or incorrect applications of Divine Laws and Principles.

How many of you can look around your home and admit you might just be a little overwhelmed with "stuff?" It is amazing that even in what has the appearance of a difficult economy, the storage companies are doing great, raking in money so people have a place to store their stuff! Of course, there are legitimate uses for storage units, but our ability to rationalize using them really pushes this particular Power to its limits.

We recently read a story about a woman named Sarah. Convinced that she would be able to sell, donate or otherwise dispose of her extra stuff during the "First 30 Days Free Rent" period that her storage company offered, Sarah moved her "stuff" into four of the cheapest storage units available. Fast forward 5 years! She never moved out ... until she finally did the math ... 5 years x $200 a month per unit x 4 units = $48000. And that total doesn't even account for the money spent on gasoline to get her to and from her storage or all the late fees she's paid on other bills because she chose to pay her storage bill on time so her incredible stuff wouldn't be seized for non-payment.

Now there's nothing wrong with having stuff, as long as stuff doesn't have you! But there is something incredibly freeing about getting rid of stuff that is no longer serving you. It is important to recognize that our material stuff is actually an outer manifestation of what is going on inside. If we have a lot of stuff that is no longer serving us, perhaps we also have some thoughts, ideas, or emotions that aren't serving us either! We invite you to consider the concept of "Less is More..." and identify areas where we could all have less stuff. In Matthew 6:19-21, Jesus as the Christ tells us: "Lay not up for yourselves treasures on earth, where moth and rust corrupt, and where thieves break in and steal; but lay up for yourselves treasures in heaven, where neither moth nor rust corrupt, and where thieves do not break through nor steal; for where your treasure is, there will your heart also be."

Let's look at this advice from a metaphysical interpretation: "We should not judge our self worth by our net worth, because egocentric thoughts steal our sense of worthiness and contentment. Instead, we must build our prosperity consciousness, realizing that God is the Source of our supply and that Truth and error cannot occupy the same place at the same time" *(The Gospel of Matthew, New Metaphysical Version)*.

Please hear us say: There is nothing wrong with having things! That's not what RELEASE is about, nor should there be any guilt about what people possess. (We have our share of stuff, too!) The question is, "Does your stuff get in the way of the abundant life you deserve? Are you working just to keep your stuff? Are you spending hard-earned dollars to protect stuff you don't even use? Does your stuff create such a mess that you are not even able to wade through it to efficiently accomplish the goals you set? When our stuff takes over, it's time to call on our Divine Power of RELEASE and say, "Wait a minute! Less is more!"

We see examples all around us of people who try to just cover up the old stuff that no longer works: flood-damaged cars that have been refurbished to look like new; a fresh coat of paint over a termite-infested house; a great make-over for a person so they look terrific—but still have the same old negative attitude! Just covering something up with the new doesn't cut it! We have to be willing to let go of what is no longer serving us, to make way for the new!

> We are all searching for answers, but the reality is there's no quick fix. But there are time-honored interventions that can help mend the wounds, mend the fences, close painful chapters, and move on to a life of peace, health and serenity. The first of those interventions is to let go of the reluctance to let go *(Creagan, E., To mend you must let go of anger and resentment, Mayo Clinic Health News, Mayo Clinic, February 20, 2013)*.

In order to say yes to inner peace and spiritual enrichment, we must also be able to say no to things that no longer serve us. Please read that sentence again, and allow it to internalize! (Go ahead, we'll wait!) Using RELEASE allows us to say no to the things that no longer serve us, including thoughts, beliefs, people, and stuff! We use

RELEASE to say no, whether it is to something material in the outer physical realm, or to something in consciousness. It is every bit as important—in fact, we maintain it is even more important—to renounce, eliminate, and say no to inappropriate or ineffective thoughts and beliefs in our minds and consciousness, as it is to eliminate useless material stuff from our lives. Of course, WISDOM must be engaged, to evaluate whether it is appropriate to say yes or no.

Check out this interesting example that illustrates how critical it is to employ RELEASE at the highest, most elevated level of consciousness. A few years ago the city council of Monza, Italy barred pet owners from keeping goldfish in curved goldfish bowls. (You'd think the council could find something better to do with their time! Our question when we read about this was: Do you suppose one of the council members sold large, non-curved fish tanks and aquariums?) In any case, the council justified the decision by claiming that it is cruel to keep a fish in a bowl with curved sides because the fish would have a distorted view of reality. An object we humans would see that was moving in a straight line would be seen by goldfish as moving along a curved path.

It is true, goldfish have a goldfish view of reality. (And dogs have a dog's view; and cats a cat's view). For all we know, fish may even formulate scientific laws and religious doctrines from their 'fishbowl' frame of reference. They could make predictions based on those laws and organize their Facebooks, swimming, dating, and child-rearing around a curved perspective.

If their curved fish tank was large enough, a human could swim with them. But the human would very readily see that their view of reality was different. It would seem distorted. Myopic. Full of flaws.

If the fish were moved to a larger, more rectangular tank, their view might be less distorted. If they were moved to fresh water or sea water they would have an entirely different view of reality. There would be distortions, but not of the kind they experienced in the small curved fish bowl.

Each 'fishbowl' environment has its own hazards, its own rules, its own belief systems, its own assumptions, its own limits.

We humans are also in a fishbowl. It's called skin school. Our fishbowl is planet Earth. And our view is distorted by the lens we call the human personality.

The size of our world depends on the band width of our perspective. And the band width of our perspective depends on how expanded our awareness is. And how expanded our awareness is depends on how expanded our consciousness is.

We can choose to remain in a fishbowl of anger, in a fishbowl of unforgiveness, in the fishbowl of hatred. We can stay in an ocean of self-doubt, and fear, and worry. But the view from these fishbowls is distorted. Living in these environments is what quantum physicists refer to as interference. Hatred, self-doubt, worry, and fear interfere with joy, inner peace, health, and well-being. Their interference patterns affect our happiness, and cause disturbances in our spiritual growth.

Fishbowls are for those who choose to live limited lives. They are for those who settle for self-imposed enclosures, fences, and walls. The result is spiritual cataracts.

Small fishbowls, like limited perspectives, are for people who want to live in the past. They're for people who are afraid to give up old perspectives and worn out beliefs ... who are fixated on old assumptions ... who wear misinformation like badges of honor.

In his book *The Concentric Perspective*, Eric Butterworth reminds us that if we want to progress spiritually, we must get rid of old frames of reference. He says, "If you insist on holding onto things like an anthropomorphic God or the need to nurture past hurts and disagreements, you will look outside yourself for answers instead of within."

He continues, in the strongest possible terms, "Truth is at the center of you. It is the mystical point where God becomes you. *(Yes, he actually said "where God becomes you!)* You are the activity of God expressing and pressing out into visibility as you."

Butterworth wasn't trying to trick you. And neither are we. Be willing to release the old you, the small fishbowl you. Break the bonds of the past that interfere with your being the best YOU you can be. The Power of RELEASE is therapeutic. It's cleansing. It unclutters your consciousness and your life.

RELEASE is the Power behind the practice of denials. It is the ability we use to disempower self-negating thoughts, feelings, and beliefs. If we truly want to grow in the awareness of our Spiritual Nature, we must be able to deny, disempower, and let go of any thoughts, feelings, and beliefs that hinder or hold us back, or keep us tied to our personalities/ego. We cannot effectively claim our True Nature if at the same time we believe we are simply personalities inhabiting physical bodies.

"(Humankind) must know the reality of the divine Existence, and then know—not only vaguely believe and hope—that his/her own Innermost Self is one with God, and that the aim of life is to realize that Unity" *(Annie Bessant, Esoteric Christianity, pg. 22)*. The same sentiments are offered by Sufi mystic Ibn Arabi: "When the mystery of the oneness of the soul and the Divine is revealed to you, you will understand that you are not other than God ... For when you know yourself, your sense of a limited identity vanishes, and you know that you and God are one and the same" *(Ibn Arabi, Divine Governance of the Human Kingdom Including What the Seeker Needs and The One Alone. Louisville: Fons Vitae, 1997)*.

All of us carry conscious or subconscious beliefs that we chose at some time in our lives as a way to take care of ourselves. At some point, these beliefs are no longer useful. Many people were raised in a belief system consisting of an external God that is a supernatural Being having absolute control and power over them. For some, this belief system serves them well their entire lives, while for others, this belief system loses its appeal. This leads them to search for, and hopefully find a new belief system that works better. However, since the old belief system was held in consciousness for so long, it may still have a hold at barely conscious, if not subconscious levels. By using their Power of RELEASE, these people are able to disempower and eliminate every aspect of the old belief system in order to fully embrace the new.

> Even if we've unlearned a negative experience, it still leaves an indelible trace in our brain. That residue lies waiting, ready to reactivate if we encounter a similar fear-provoking experience *(G.J. Quirk, C. Repa, and J. E. LeDoux, "Fear conditioning enhances short-latency auditory responses of lateral amygdala neurons: Parallel recordings in the freely behaving rat," Neuron, 1995; 15: 1029-1039).*

There are many examples of the Power of RELEASE at work in the physical world. Our physical bodies are a great example. When we breathe in, we acquire oxygen and we must let go of carbon dioxide in order to survive. We take in food and give off waste. If we did not release these metabolic waste products, we would surely die. When we exercise, we release excess heat through perspiration and heavy breathing. If we did not do this, we could become overheated and die. We bring groceries into our homes and we release garbage, keeping our homes neat and tidy. Where there is inflow or increase, there also must be outflow and release. The Dead Sea is void of life because there is inflow but no outflow.

Underdeveloped RELEASE is demonstrated by people who are pack rats or hoarders. They collect and hold onto everything ... even useless and broken stuff. In fact, you could get a nosebleed climbing over their stacks of newspapers and magazines! Sometimes these folks become emotionally attached to their stuff, and become upset or distressed at the very suggestion of releasing it. This phenomenon is so common there are TV shows designed to force hoarders to let go of the mass of material possessions threatening to suffocate them.

Underdeveloped RELEASE is also evident in people who simply cannot end things like jobs or relationships, even when they are harmful. These people might be able to sort the wheat from the chaff, the good from the bad—but they find it extremely difficult to eliminate any of it. They just keep hanging on, justifying it by assuming that at least they know what to expect.

What's really incredible is the way we tend to hang on to things which we have already replaced! For example, someone might have a perfectly good refrigerator, but decide to replace it with a more efficient contemporary model. This person has the new refrigerator installed, and then, guess what? That good, old refrigerator sits in the garage or basement, because it might come in handy some day, doing no good to anyone and taking up storage space, simply because this person could not part with it. If the refrigerator example is too big a stretch for you, what about this one? How many articles of clothing hang in your closet unused for years, even though you have newer, more up-to-date, better fitting clothes to replace them? (Are we getting too personal?)

Here's one more powerful example! It isn't always something negative or useless we need to let go of ... sometimes we get so caught up in what we have—because it's so good—that we blind ourselves to something even better! We keep ourselves in a Spiritual Box, and get stuck there. Here's a personal example from our experience: We built our dream house ... planned to live there forever. Then we made some changes in our careers, and decided to make the move to another area. The decision to sell our "dream home" was extremely difficult ... but now we live in a fabulous home that meets our needs perfectly ... and we love it! The lesson we chose to learn from this experience was Let go of your good for your GREATER good!

Let's look at this from a spiritual point of view. We may clearly believe in God being Divine Mind—not an external supernatural male Being. We may believe in Oneness—One Power and One Presence. And, yet, in some of our actions, like prayer, we are still holding on to the "old God" by addressing God as "He" or "She" and as a Being who is separate and apart, expecting guidance and direction from "out there." Even the phrase "Father/Mother God" alludes to some sort of anthropomorphic Being out there" to whom we call for guidance and help.

As we learn to recognize a mismatch between our beliefs and our actions, we can use RELEASE to let go of our past beliefs and embedded theology, and create the space to embrace a new, more spiritually enriching practice which supports our current beliefs and Truth pronciples.

Egocentric RELEASE results in getting rid of things prematurely. For example, have you ever eliminated some perfectly good possessions, then later needed to re-purchase them? The egocentric Power of RELEASE can also manifest as denying valuable ideas and beliefs before really understanding their usefulness. For example, someone could be taking a class and learning some new metaphysical principles, and dismiss them out of hand. Another case involved a man who needed new flooring in his lower level living area and kitchen. A trusted friend suggested simply putting a high grade finish on the concrete. The man quickly said no, without really investigating or considering the idea.

RELEASE From the Four Levels of Consciousness

Let's examine how RELEASE is used at various levels of consciousness:

1. **Unconscious RELEASE:** based on a cause in our subconscious mind which consists of beliefs that are not in our moment to moment awareness. If a person has an unconscious or subconscious belief based on something from the past, s/he might unconsciously eliminate things that challenge that belief. A great example would be a woman who clips coupons and saves every penny, won't release any extra funds for things she really needs, and does not even leave a tip at a restaurant—even though she has plenty of money flowing in her life. She eliminates any signs of prosperity in her life, because of a subconscious fear of lack, arising from her parents who went through the depression.

   Research tells us we all have a reason for doing what we do. Even the things we hate to do—even the things we try to let go of—remain in our lives because something in us believes we want it. Yes, we always do what we want to do. If you have not yet let go of your attachment, it is because part of you believes, for some reason, that you are better off with it. In other words, by holding on to your bad habits, you are trying to accomplish something, to get desires met, to get feelings of safety and control satisfied, or to remain comfortable *(Mazarin, J., Nine Practical and Spiritual Tips for Letting go of Unhealthy Attachments, PsychCentral, April 30, 2013).*

2. **Conscious RELEASE from our senses:** based on something in physicality we are gleaning through our sight, sound, scent, touch, and or taste. We have all probably smelled something spoiling in our refrigerators and proceeded to eliminate its source. Another example is a woman who saw herself doing a presentation on videotape. Based on the way she looked, she decided to institute a diet and exercise program to eliminate her excess weight, and achieve a more desirable body image.

By the way, did you know your fat has a brain? Seriously. And it's trying to kill you. Body fat is just an inert layer of blubber, right? If only. New research shows that it's more like a toxic parasite that doesn't want to let go. In any sedentary, inactive person—including people who aren't actually obese—fat invades the muscles, slipping in between muscle fibers like the marbling in Wagyu beef. Worse, fat infiltrates individual muscle cells in the form of lipid droplets that make the cells sluggish. According to Gerald Shulman, M.D., a prominent diabetes researcher at Yale, these pools of fat, which occur in both the liver and the muscles, block a key step in the conversion of glucose. There seems to be a "diseasome" of inactivity, a collection of nasty health consequences stemming from lack of exercise—independent of an individual's body weight *(Gifford, B., Your Fat Has a Brain. Seriously. And It's Trying to Kill You, Outside Magazine, March 5, 2013)*. (Aren't you delighted we shared that?)

3. **Conscious RELEASE from our human personality:** based on thoughts, feelings, attitudes and/or beliefs held in ordinary consciousness. A person might believe that walking under a ladder causes bad luck and so eliminates walking under ladders. A woman married a man she thought was her perfect partner. Over time he became physically and mentally abusive. She believed he would physically harm or even kill her, and used her Power of RELEASE to leave him.

    An article published in *Psychology Today* reinforces the fact that the most amazing things can happen to you as the direct result of facing the crippling terror of letting go of something. Whether a relationship, a job, or a story about what you're not good at, the best things in your life can come when you've chosen to hold your breath and dive under the terror, even if you've tried hundreds of times before and failed *(Kirk, M., The Power of Letting Go, Psychology Today, March 24, 2013)*.

4. **Conscious RELEASE from our True Identity, or Authentic Self:** based on Divine Ideas, Laws, and Principles. Once aware of how to be the best we can be, we would then eliminate activities, thoughts, feelings, and beliefs that inhibit reaching that goal. We become aware of situations in which we get angry or fearful and realize that these reactions hinder our being the best we can be. So, we first discern the beliefs that fuel the anger or fear, and then use RELEASE to disempower and remove them from our consciousness.

Finally, we'd like to share two stories, apocryphal or not, that help capture the essence of the Power of RELEASE. The first involves a mynah bird.

A mynah bird developed a very distressing cough. So, his concerned owner took him to an exotic bird vet, who listened to the mynah's cough.

Then she checked the bird's throat, and examined the bird's eyes and feather coating. The vet raised her eyebrows and with a sigh said to the owner, "Let me hear you cough."

It was the same cough.

So, the doctor said with a smile, "You get over your cough, and the mynah will get over your cough, too!"

It works the same way with us. If we want to manifest the things we want in life, we've got to get over our 'coughs.' That is, we've got to get rid of 'coughs' like negative thinking, and anger, and unforgiveness. We've got to move beyond self-doubt and bad habits. We've got to let go of lack of confidence, old self-defeating patterns of behavior, and false beliefs. You know, coughs like that.

We could also refer to these 'coughs' as 'critters.' And that takes us to the second story:

> Three campers were setting up their campsite when a bear suddenly appeared. Two of the campers saw the bear and climbed a nearby tree. The third camper, who was not as observant, wasn't fast enough to escape.
>
> He threw himself on the ground and pretended to be dead. He had heard that bears will not touch dead bodies, so he laid as still as he could and held his breath. He tried his best to control his trembling, too.
>
> His life passed before him as the bear sniffed at his clothing and then moved up to his face. The camper lay as still as he could.
>
> To his astonishment, the bear whispered something in his ear. After a few moments, when he opened his eyes, the bear was gone. When the coast was clear, the other two campers climbed down out of the tree and rushed over to their comatose comrade.
>
> "Are you okay?" the taller one asked.
>
> The prone camper nodded. He was still too frightened to move.
>
> "It's okay," the third camper replied, "the bear's gone."
>
> The two helped the frightened camper to his feet.
>
> "By the way," the taller one said, "I could have sworn I saw the bear whisper something in your ear. I know that sounds crazy, but am I right?"
>
> The camper who had the close encounter with the bear nodded.
>
> "You're kidding," his comrades exclaimed in unison. "A talking bear. No way! Like we're going to believe that," they laughed.
>
> Their comrade replied, "He told me never to travel with 'friends' who desert you at the first sign of trouble."

The story is obviously apocryphal, but it represents an important point we want to make about the Power of RELEASE. It's about releasing critters that get in the way of your happiness and success. The more critter control you have—the happier, safer, more balanced, and prosperous your life will be.

The critters we're talking about are just as ferocious as the bear. They are false assumptions, engrained beliefs based on those false assumptions, self-defeating habits, feelings of unworthiness, fears, doubts in your ability to prosper, negative thinking, and a host of other wild and untamed thought and feeling critters.

These are all critters that keep you flat out or up a tree instead of living confidently and happily at the speed of your common sense and sound judgment. A bear of a doubt or a grizzly of a false assumption can keep you immobilized or up a tree for years.

So, use your Power to RELEASE anything that compromises your greater good seriously.

RELEASE:
Putting It Into Practice

RELEASE—Activity One:

Part 1:

Here is a little experiment to try. In your journal, write the following word:

NO

Say the word out loud. Say it again, louder. Shout it out, with power and gusto! There! You have proved you know how to say no!

Now, write the following word:

KNOW

Say that word. Say it again, louder. Shout it out, with power and gusto!

Did you notice that the two words sound the same? Here's the deal: if you find yourself having trouble saying "No" to things you need to eliminate, just say "Know!" Other people will hear the sound of "NO" ... and so will your subconscious mind.

Now let's take it a step further, because there is a very important principle at work here. The key is: *if you KNOW why you want or need to say NO to something, it is a whole lot easier to say it.* In other words, if you have an image of the extraordinary you clearly in your consciousness, have clarified your goals, and understand your values, you know what will help facilitate those desires, and what is getting in the way. This makes it much easier to say "NO" and release those things which are no longer serving you.

Part 2:

Brainstorm a list of specific things you are willing to let go of, consciously using the Power of RELEASE, in the following areas:
- Physical (material things, a.k.a. STUFF):
- Mental (attitudes and emotions you are hanging on to):
- Spiritual (outdated beliefs about God; embedded theology).

RELEASE—Activity Two:

As you think about the specific area you are working on throughout this course, identify anything that is no longer serving you in achieving your goal. Write these things down, and conduct a some kind of ceremony, such as giving the actual items away; burning them (or a list of them) in a bowl or fireplace; conducting a symbolic burial; or performing some other ritual to help you release and let these things go!

Example: Healthy Eating

I release and let go of my belief that only chips, crackers, and other high-calorie/high-carb munchies can be tasty snacks.

I will create a list of my favorite unhealthy munchies, and perform a bowl burning, releasing any power I have given these items that prevent me from eating in a way that supports my health goals. I will also conduct a ritualistic clean-out of my cupboards, and either throw out opened packages of these items, or donate uponened ones to a food bank.

I release my "big size" clothing that I'm keeping "just in case" I gain back weight.

I will pack these clothes up, perform a blessing over them, thanking them for their service to me. Then I will donate them to a thrift shop, affirming that someone else will find them and get a lot of wonderful use from them.

RELEASE Affirmation:

I claim RELEASE now. I deny and eliminate anything that I have empowered to hinder my being the best person I can be.

 # Quotes to Inspire RELEASE

Lay not up for yourselves treasures upon earth, where moth and rust doth corrupt, and where thieves break through and steal; but lay up for yourselves treasures in heaven, where neither moth nor rust doth corrupt, and where thieves do not break through. For where your treasure is, there your heart will be also. (Jesus)

Thoughts are things; they occupy space in the mental field. A healthy state of mind is attained and continued when the thinker willingly lets go (of) the old thoughts and takes on the new. (Charles Fillmore)

(Unfortunately), it (is) apparent how much modern research yet clings to, and cannot release, the external side of phenomena, and is not at present able to build a bridge to that which permeates the universe spiritually. (Hans-Werner Schroeder)

Our life is frittered away by detail ... Simplify, simplify. (Henry David Thoreau)

You don't need to die in order to enter the kingdom of heaven. In fact, you have to be truly alive in order to do so. And that requires releasing anything that blocks your availability for entering the kingdom. (Thich Nhat Hanh)

If you want greater good, form a vacuum to receive it. In other words get rid of what you don't want to make room for what you want. (Catherine Ponder)

When I let go of what I am, I become what I might be. When I let go of what I have, I receive what I need. (Tao Te Ching)

You can only lose what you cling to. (Buddha)

You cannot let go of anything if you cannot notice that you are holding it. Admit your 'weaknesses' and watch them morph into your greatest strengths. (Neale Donald Walsch)

To change skins, evolve into new cycles. Learn to discard. If one changes internally, one should not continue to live with the same objects. They reflect one's mind and the psyche of yesterday. Throw away what has no dynamic, living use. (Anaïs Nin)

Respect yourself enough to walk away from anything that no longer serves you, grows you, or makes you happy. (Robert Tew)

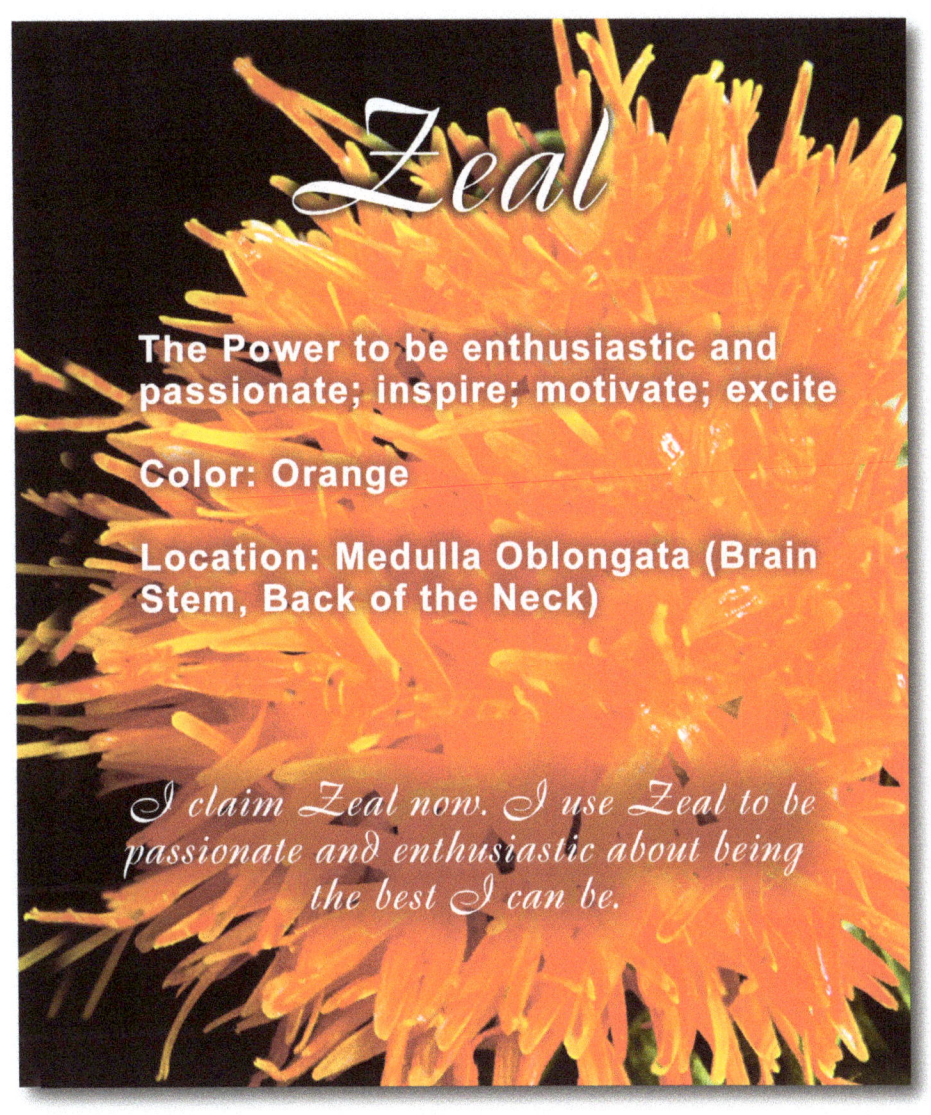

Daring enthusiasm and abiding cheerfulness can accomplish everything on earth without fail.
(Sri Chinmoy)

I fairly sizzle with zeal and enthusiasm and I spring forth with a mighty faith to do the things that need to be done by me!

~ Charles Fillmore
Written at age 94

ZEAL

Overview

- Location: Medulla Oblongata, Brain Stem, back of the neck
- Color: Orange

ZEAL is the Power to be enthusiastic and passionate; inspire; motivate;excite.

From ordinary consciousness: The ability to be enthusiastic and passionate; inspire; motivate; and excite based on our senses, thoughts, feelings, and beliefs.

- *Underdeveloped ZEAL* results in a person who is listless and has little zest for life. This person is personally unmotivated, experiences difficulty in getting started on any type of project (even something fun), and is unable to inspire excitement or passion in others. Should this individual actually bring him/herself to the point of starting something, he/she rarely is able to see things through to completion.

- *Egocentric ZEAL* results in a person who is zealous, impulsive, ruthless, compulsive, and overly ambitious. This individual often comes across as being pushy, and ends up appearing to be insincere and phony.

From elevated consciousness: The ability to be enthusiastic and passionate; inspire; motivate; and excite based on Ideas, Truths, Principles, and Laws that are Divine in Nature. We use ZEAL to put energy into our spiritual and personal enrichment practices, to enthusiastically be the best, the most passionate, energized, glowing, spirited, vibrant, zestful person we can be.

There's an impatience that goes with the sizzle of ZEAL: an energy that is compelling and expansive... an energy that gains momentum as it connects and interacts with out-of-the-box thinking, deeper spiritual understanding, and the harmonics of a deeply felt love for all of humankind.

It is an impulsive Power that is zealous, vibrant, and spirited. The Power of ZEAL is one that excites people—and communities, and nations—because it resonates with

something deep inside of them. We are wired for ZEAL. It's in our spiritual DNA. And to explain why it's in our DNA we're going to take you back 13.7 billion years ago to an event quantum physicists call the Big Bang.

We're going to start by referring you to the night sky. When you look at a starry sky the light coming from those stars is hundreds of millions of years old. Billions of years old. You are looking back in time billions of years.

By its very nature the universe is expanding. It is filled with supernovas, singularities, quasars, galaxies, parallel universes, cosmic inflation, black holes, binary star systems, and rare quantum beings like us.

In what quantum physicists now believe was just 'a' beginning, a tiny bubble of space-time popped spontaneously into existence out of the cosmic womb. It was believed to be a billion-trillion-trillionth of a centimeter across.

This tiny space bubble was seized by an intense antigravitational force which caused it to explode. In scarcely more than a billion-trillionth of a second, our universe swelled to about the size of a small grapefruit. You know, about the size of the grapefruits you find in grocery stores.

Up until now it was believed that our universe was the only universe and that it was created by the Big Bang. Most physicists today agree that there were a number of little Big Bangs—one of which was ours.

Cosmologists have recently proposed that our universe is part of a multiverse which has always existed. A multiverse, they speculate, is a unified field which contains many universes. "Baby universes," says quantum physicist Paul Davies, "can arise spontaneously as a result of quantum fluctuations, and therefore one may envision a 'mother universe' giving rise to progeny" *(Paul Davies, The Mind of God, New York: Simon and Schuster, 1992, pg. 221)*.

They believe that instead of one Big Bang, a series of little big bangs occurred 10 to 15 billion years ago in our region of the multiverse. One of these little big bangs was our universe. And it was a special universe because it created at least one planet that is conducive to human life—our planet.

In Genesis 1:31 we read that on the sixth day of creation 'God saw all that had been created and behold it was very good.' That's actually one of two mistranslations in the Genesis account.

In the original Aramaic, the verse does not read 'behold it was very good,' but 'behold it was a unified order.' Sounds quantum, doesn't it? And the other mistranslation is the second word in Genesis 1:1. It says, "In the beginning..." The 'the' is the mistranslation. In the original Aramaic it says, "In *a* beginning..." which squares with the 'unified order' theme, and also with the multiverse theory in quantum physics.

This 'unified order' refers to the multiverse and our place in it. "In a beginning" refers to the birth of our universe along with the births of many other universes. Are you still with us? The multiverse was giving birth to many universes, one of which was ours.

Why have we taken you back billions of years to explain the Spiritual POWER of ZEAL? Because that's where spiritedness, expansiveness, and explosiveness began. The multiverse holds the key to the Spiritual Power of ZEAL.

> When we hear the word "universe," we think that means everything: every star, every galaxy, everything that exists. But in physics, we've come upon the possibility that what we've long thought to be everything may actually only be a small part of something that is much, much bigger. The word "multiverse" refers to that bigger expanse, the new totality of reality, and our universe would be just a piece of that larger whole
> *(Physicist Brian Greene, The Hidden Reality: Parallel Universes and the Deep Laws of the Cosmos, 2011).*

Did you know that less than 1% of the universe is made of visible matter? It appears to have always been that way. The planets, suns, galaxies, trees, the chairs on which you are sitting, the meals you'll consume today—are part of the 1% visible matter.

What's more, our bodies literally hold the entire history of the universe in our cells, atoms, and molecules. The helium and hydrogen atoms in us are the Adam and Eve atoms, the parent atoms of all other atoms which came out of our little Big Bang. The iron atoms in our blood carrying oxygen to our cells came from exploding white dwarf stars. The oxygen we breathe came from exploding supernovas. Most of the carbon in the carbon dioxide we exhale came from planetary nebulas.

We are truly made of star stuff. We are made of the super-charged energies of the little big bang event that created our known universe. These planetary energies fuel our physical being. We come wired for movement. And that's why we've taken you back 13.7 billion years in time. We are micro-universes of exploding potential.

Just like the universe, less than 1% of our entire being is physical. We are 99% spiritual. That may seem hard to believe, but it's true. There is much, much more to us than mere flesh and blood, pimples, and backaches. Most of us is invisible!

There is more to us than the lives we are currently living. We are much more than we appear. When you look at another person, you're only seeing the visible 1% of his or her make-up. And they're only seeing the visible 1% of you.

The only thing different between us and the great spiritual teachers is that they have harnessed the primordial energies of our little Big Bang by right of consciousness. They were able to use their 99% spiritual energies to master the 1% of their human energies. And Jesus, Buddha, Krishna, and others, have shown us how we can do it.

We are bundles of potential, expansion, and growth. Our whole being is wired for expansion and growth. We are born as sparks of Spirit with an inborn urge to return as quickly as we can to our true nature. This inborn fire is the passion and ZEAL Charles Fillmore talks about ... the ZEAL that is one of our twelve Powers.

> Because all organisms are made out of atoms and molecules, you and I and every living thing are radiating energy (vibes). That means molecules, which are made up of atoms, are vortices of energy as well; so cells, which are made up of molecules, are also vortices of energy; and finally, human beings, each of whom is made up of trillions of cells, are ... vortices of energy. We are literally energetic beings
> *(Bruce Lipton, Stem-Cell Biologist, author of The Biology of Belief).*

Unfortunately, when times get tough, people find themselves fizzling instead of sizzling. Have you been there? Many people feel overwhelmed, despondent, lost. They want to give up.

They find themselves becoming critical of their own talents, skills, and abilities. They may even allow the gravity of their situation to crush their hopes and dreams. People tend to get down on themselves. They think they can't do something or be something or have something.

But here's the thing. By nature, we are spiritual beings with sizzle in our genes. Our genetic make-up is wired for action, and movement, and sizzle—not fizzle.

So, how can we make this quantum sizzle work for us today? Those who are students of New Thought, the Course in Miracles, Eastern thought, and Native American spirituality already know. The open door to our sizzle is our consciousness.

The sizzle is here. It's just waiting for us to turn up the HEAT. And the HEAT we're talking about is an acronym for turning up the sizzle, and calling forth your Power of ZEAL to the highest, most elevated level.

Here's the formula for turning up the HEAT, using the word HEAT as an acronym:

H = **Honor your own uniqueness.**
E = **Eliminate old beliefs, habits and assumptions that block your good.**
A = **Adopt a bias for action.**
T = **Temper your ZEAL with WISDOM.**

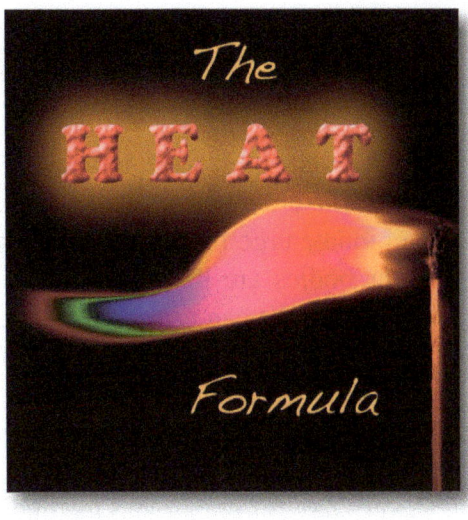

Let's go into a little detail, so this all makes sense.

H = Honor your own uniqueness.

How many times have life coaches and motivational speakers told you this? There's no one else quite like you. And that's a good thing, you probably tell yourself! You are unique. In quantum terms, you are a singularity. One of a kind.

You can turn up the sizzle by being your Authentic Self—not a copy of someone else. Honor the inner pull to be you. Listen to your uniqueness. Take a lesson from an oak seed. A typical oak seed has a cosmic blueprint that guides its growth. As it fulfills its destiny, it gets many opportunities to be true to its oakness. If it should happen to fall into a crevice or on rocky soil, it will find a few ounces of fertile soil. And against all odds, it will actualize itself by the sheer uniqueness of its genetic blueprint.

It will tenaciously take hold, expressing its oakness. That may mean splitting the rock that would have imprisoned it, or wrapping its roots around a crevice that would have limited its growth. The seed asks no questions. Points no accusing fingers. Offers no excuses. It simply goes about the business of becoming the best oak tree it can be.

So it is with you! To use ZEAL at the highest, most elevated level, honor your uniqueness.

E = Eliminate old beliefs, habits and assumptions that block your good.

It's not so much unanswered questions that stunt our growth. It is unquestioned answers. Organizations make the same mistake. For example, National Cash Register enjoyed 80% market share in the 1950's and 60's. In 1971 NCR was still clinging to the soon to be obsolete electromechanical technology that made them famous.

They had the resources to totally dominate the 70's market—if they had gotten serious about a new technology—computers. A combination of the recession of the 1970's, IBM's introduction of its 360 model, and customer demand, caused NCR to lose almost all of its market share.

Clinging to old technology and antiquated beliefs buried them. And the same thing happens to us. We must release any and all beliefs, assumptions, and habits that dampen our sizzle. (This calls on our Power of RELEASE.)

That may mean changing the way we see things and do things. It may mean changing friends and changing jobs. It most certainly means stopping bad habits and replacing them with ones that will bring us health, wealth, and happiness.

To use ZEAL at the highest, most elevated level, eliminate old beliefs, habits and assumptions that block your good. If you need help with this one, just go back and re-read the chapter about the Power of RELEASE!

A = Adopt a bias for action.

The atoms which make up our bodies are wired for action. That means we have an innate urge for the do-able. That primordial Big Bang energy primes us for sizzle. Our bodies are humming with activity, waiting for us to tap into our natural-born energies. We can turn up our inner rheostats by choosing growth over stagnation.

Surround yourself with people who energize you instead of drain you. Quantum physicists would say to stop hanging around "interference patterns."

Realize that prayer and meditation are engines of sizzle. They are the most accelerated forms of mind action. So make the commitment to schedule specific time every day for prayer and meditation, and make it non-negotiable.

The important thing to remember is that if you want to be, do, and have more than you've got—if you want to use ZEAL at the highest, most elevated level—you've got to adopt a bias for action.

T = Temper your ZEAL with WISDOM.

Zeal serves as an excellent example of how our Powers work together. Taking action without giving thought to the consequences of those actions is a dumb program. ZEAL without WISDOM leads to impulsive behavior. What usually happens is that you do something you wish you hadn't done ... although there are always exceptions. The following story is about one of those exceptions:

A young salesman is called into his manager's office. She tells him, "Richard, you are an excellent salesman, and you have a lot of natural talent. But you need to be more enthusiastic. Your sales are average but you're better than that. You could be the best salesperson we've ever had if you'd just be more enthusiastic. Are you open for a suggestion?"

"Yes, of course," Richard responded. "I appreciate your help."

"Okay. This is what I want you to do. When you get up tomorrow morning I want you to jump out of bed, stand in front of the mirror, and say to yourself: 'I'm great, I'm great. I'm great.' Then I want you to get dressed enthusiastically, run down the steps, eat a high energy breakfast, and come to work all charged up with energy. Can you do that?"

"I'll certainly try," he responded enthusiastically.

The next morning Richard was two hours late for work!

His manager was devastated. "Richard, what happened? Why are you two hours late?"

"I did exactly as you told me," he defended himself. "I jumped out of my bed; I stood in front of the mirror; said—'I'm great, I'm great, I'm great;' I got dressed; I rushed down the stairs, I kissed my wife enthusiastically … and *that's* why I'm two hours late for work!"

Sometimes impulsiveness can lead to wonderful results. But it's generally best to temper our ZEAL with WISDOM.

ZEAL is like the first stage of a two-stage rocket, when the burst of energy lifts the rocket off the launch pad. After getting the rocket going, the fuel is spent and the second stage must take over. ZEAL is like this! Our zeal or enthusiasm for something can burn out quickly, leaving things undone.

For the rocket, the second stage keeps things going until the rocket reaches its goal, using its escape velocity, and orbits around the earth. With ZEAL, we combine a few other Powers to ensure this second phase kicks in. We use LIFE (which we discuss in more detail in the next chapter) that enlivens and energizes whatever we are doing. In addition, when ZEAL starts to wane, we must engage STRENGTH to stay the course and keep on going. We could say that STRENGTH is the determination to see something through to the goal after we used ZEAL to get us started. We may also engage POWER and WILL to control any thoughts or feelings about quitting.

Think about what we like to "lovingly" call "the spiritual flavor of the month." It's when some new spiritual book or concept is released, surrounded by lots of hype and marketing. You read about it and get very excited. In fact, you may even get zealous about it, telling all your friends and writing testimonials on Amazon. Then, when the next idea, book, or class comes along, the teachings of the previous guide are all but forgotten as you now zealously embrace the new one. In this case, you certainly had plenty of enthusiasm for the new guide and its teachings, but fell short of continuing to energize these teachings because you are now giving your intention and attention to the next offering.

Someone with underdeveloped ZEAL has little zest for life, can be listless, and has difficulty getting started with anything. This person probably has a slew of unfinished projects around the house, or a long to-do list of things which have not even been started. Not only does this person lack self-motivation; inspiring others is difficult or seemingly impossible.

Egocentric ZEAL shows up as *excessive* passion for something. In fact, these people can be seen as a bit obsessive-compulsive. However, even this can be used in productive ways. The Ringling Brothers Circus museum, located in Sarasota, Florida, is home to the world's largest miniature circus, captured down to the minutest detail. The Howard Bros Circus Model is a 3/4-inch scale model depicting Ringling Brothers and Barnum & Bailey Circus when it was at its largest (circa 1919-1938). Occupying 3,800 square feet, it contains eight main tents, 152 wagons, 1,300 circus performers and workers, more than 800 animals, and a 57-car train. Howard Tibbals, the creator of this masterpiece, invested an incredible number of hours over a 50-year period to create this model. He must have had a mighty passion to complete such a marvelous project. One could perceive this as either a magnificent passion or an obsession. Whatever the view, it still resulted in a wonderful gift for all to see.

ZEAL From the Four Levels of Consciousness

Let's explore how ZEAL is used at various levels of consciousness:

1. **Unconscious ZEAL:** based on a cause in our subconscious mind which consists of beliefs that are not in our moment to moment awareness. A person with unconscious ZEAL would be enthusiastic about doing something, and clueless about the reason. For example, a person may get excited and totally enthusiastic about a piece of music, and be totally unaware that the response is triggered by a belief or memory from the past. For example, we have noticed that whenever we enter a hotel ballroom, we feel an immediate surge of excitement and passion. We've been known to stop what we are doing and dance a few measures to imaginary music. This automatic response is totally unconscious, and stems from the years we spent as amateur competitive ballroom dancers.

    Another example is a person who argues passionately for a certain political stand, without even knowing why. This may be the result of their upbringing, and listening to parents fight for certain causes. Anger is another emotion that often comes from our subconscious mind. Research has shown that what makes anger particularly dangerous is that it blinds you even to the fact that you're angry; thus it gives you a false sense of certainty, confidence, and optimism *(Lerner, J.S., Tiedens, L.Z., Portrait of the angry decision-maker: How appraisal tendencies shape anger's influence on cognition," Journal of Behavioral Decision Making, 2006: 19: 115-37)*.

2. **Conscious ZEAL from our senses:** based on something in physicality we are gleaning through our sight, sound, scent, touch and/or taste. For example, realtors suggest burning scented candles or baking cookies prior to a person viewing a home for sale because these aromas can ignite enthusiasm to buy the home.

   Another example from our own experience: As we delve more and more into these Twelve Powers, we find ourselves enthused whenever we see a product that is very colorful. As we connect what we are seeing with our passion for the Twelve Powers, we often end up purchasing the item.

3. **Conscious ZEAL from our human personality:** based on thoughts, feelings, attitudes and/or beliefs held in ordinary consciousness. A young man knows and believes that exercise is good for his body, and believes eating all the right foods is the very best for his health. As a result, he is zealous about getting his exercise and eating right, even in the face of a multitude of temptations and distractions.

4. **Conscious ZEAL from our True Identity, or Authentic Self:** based on Divine Ideas, Laws, and Principles. Once you get a glimpse and experience of your Spiritual Nature, you experience a passion and zeal about learning more to become the best you can be. You passionately start to research, understand at a deeper level, and put time into your spiritual practice, so you can have more of these experiences.

> People who are optimistic about their abilities and expectations of success and can release old failures have more T cells and natural killer cells, which support immune responses that destroy substances that are poisonous to cells *(S. C. Segerstrom, S.E. Taylor, M.E. Kemeny, and J. L. Fahey, "Optimism is associated with mood, coping, and immune change in response to stress," Journal of Personality and Social Psychology, 1998, 74 (6): 1646-1655)*.

ZEAL: Putting It Into Practice

ZEAL—Activity One:

This is a "High Five" Activity!
Part 1: Grab your journal and respond quickly to the following questions:

- What are five things I really enjoy doing?
- What are my five strongest skills and/or gifts?
- Who are five people I find inspiring and motivational?
- What are five of my favorite books, movies, TV shows, websites, and/or sporting events?
- What are five of my favorite quotes?

Part 2: Reflect on your responses above, using the following thought provokers to help you:

- What do the answers to the questions above tell me about myself, in terms of what inspires and motivate me?
- What are common themes or patterns, in terms of how I experience ZEAL in my life?
- How does ZEAL manifest as I express it?
- How can I begin to consciously call on ZEAL when I may not be feeling it?
- How are the other Powers interacting with ZEAL, as I am involved in my favorite activities identified above?

ZEAL—Activity Two

As you think about the specific area you are working on throughout this course, identify ways you can claim and activate ZEAL to help you be successful. Here's an interesting side note: When he was 94, Charles Fillmore wrote this statement: *"I fairly sizzle with zeal and enthusiasm, and spring forth with a mighty faith to do the things that ought to done by me!"* This is a powerful affirmation! What affirmations could you write to spur you to action? Come up with a few, and then say them often, using lots of enthusiasm and excitement. We are serious here! You might even over-act it! Say the affirmations as if you were a college football coach at half time, spurring the team on to victory! Get excited, and use your ZEAL to bring energy to your statements. Notice the difference it makes in your ability to be successful!

Example: Healthy Eating

One way to spur myself to action by using ZEAL is by having a friend who supports my goal go with me to restaurants. Together, we can play a game zealously and passionately, finding the healthiest combination of foods on the menu. We can create an award for ourselves whenever we successfully consume a healthy meal in a restaurant!

Affirmations I can use:

- I am radiantly healthy, and feel great because I eat food that is good for my body.
- I love and accept my body completely! I am good to my body and my body is good to me!
- Nothing tastes as great as healthy feels!

ZEAL Affirmation:

I claim ZEAL now. I use ZEAL to be passionate and enthusiastic about being the best person , the most Authentic Me, I can be.

Quotes to Inspire ZEAL

Do not let your zeal run away with your judgment. When zeal and judgment work together, great things can be accomplished! (Charles Fillmore)

Every cell in your body should be radiant with light, love, and peace. When it is, you enjoy perfect health. The very joy of living animates you. You radiate the spirit of wholeness to others. (Clara Palmer)

We are driven to do what we do and be what we are by great drives that originate in the very core of us. In the heart of every living cell, there is a fire. In the heart of everyone alive, there is a fire. (James Dillet Freeman)

Enthusiasm is not an emotional state. It is a spiritual commitment, a loving surrender to our creative process. Enthusiasm—from the Greek, filled with God—is an ongoing energy supply tapped into the flow of life itself. (Julia Cameron)

Zeal is a volcano, the peak of which the grass of indecisiveness does not grow. So, rest in reason, move in passion. (Khalil Gibran)

There is no passion to be found playing small—in settling for a life that is less than the one you are capable of living. (Nelson Mandela)

Is not life a hundred times too short for us to bore ourselves? (Friedrich Nietzsche)

Your work is to discover your work, and then with all your heart to give yourself to it. (Buddha)

Follow your bliss. Find where it is and don't be afraid to follow it. (Joseph Campbell)

Today, the middle is moving forward, the mainstream is starting to awaken spiritually, and race consciousness is shifting. We are riding a cresting wave of good that is strong enough and powerful enough to transform our world. (Wendy Craig-Purcell)

How do you go from where you are to where you wanna be? I think you have to have an enthusiasm for life. You have to have a dream, a goal. And you have to be willing to work for it. (Jim Valvano)

There is a vitality, a life force, an energy, a quickening, that is translated through you into action, and because there is only one of you in all time, this expression is unique. (Martha Graham)

Life is divine, spiritual, and its source is God, Spirit. The river of life is within [us] in [our] spiritual consciousness. [We come] into consciousness of the river of life through the quickening of Spirit. [We] can be truly quickened with new life and vitalized in mind and body only by consciously contacting Spirit. This contact is made through prayer, meditation, and good works.

~ Charles Fillmore
Revealing Word

LIFE

Overview

- Location: The Generative Organs, External Reproductive Organs
- Color: Red

LIFE is the Power to maintain vitality; sustain energy; make whole; enliven; quicken.

From ordinary consciousness: The ability to maintain vitality; sustain energy; make whole; enliven; and quicken based on our senses, thoughts, feelings, and beliefs. We use LIFE to energize worthwhile projects and activities, and to manifest healing in our bodies. Conversely, LIFE can be used to energize troublesome projects like fueling an emotionally damaging relationship or manifesting an illness!

- *Underdeveloped LIFE* results in people who have little energy to accomplish anything. They are often apathetic, listless, and uninterested in anything. They may run into problems with illnesses and diseases.

- *Egocentric LIFE* results in people who demonstrate a frenetic kind of energy, coming across as hectic, feverish, and even be a bit chaotic. They have an unhealthy concern about their physical well-being, and may do things such as taking overdoses of vitamins, exercising to the extreme, and even experiencing burn-out.

From elevated consciousness: The ability to maintain vitality; sustain energy; make whole; enliven; and quicken based on Ideas, Truths, Principles, and Laws that are Divine in nature. We use LIFE to energize and enliven our good intentions, goals, and desires to take and sustain action to be the best person, the most enlivened, vitalized person we can be.

LIFE at this level can even contribute to our wellbeing and overall attitude toward living. Research confirms that depression and other mental illnesses can be treated by rewiring the neural pathways in the brain instead of flooding the brain with problematic drugs *(Sharon Begley, Train Your Mind, Change Your Brain, New York: Ballantine Books, 2007, pg.24)*.

In the broadest and most important sense, LIFE is that great indefinable "something" that enlivens and energizes every living thing. We know that all living things, from viruses to human beings, clearly demonstrate life; however, scientists still cannot truly define what "life" actually is, other than perhaps a form of energy.

The good news is that we have a mind and a brain that can transform energy. Each of us is unique and has a unique brain. Our brains can combine elements of plasticity and hardwiring based on how we objectify our human experience, enabling our brains to adapt to the world around us. The brain's hundreds of trillions of neural switches drive interconnected networks that evince our senses, feelings, thoughts, and identities. By setting goals, learning about our own motivations and behaviors, and changing our behaviors in light of our motivations to help reach our goals, we can harness the insights of neuroscience to master the art of living.

We can describe in detail how a myriad of life forms replicate themselves, and yet we still cannot say with certainty what is happening. For humans, we say that the baby begins to "have life" with the union of the egg and sperm. And, yet, the egg and the sperm independently demonstrate this thing we call LIFE.

Perhaps one becomes most focused on LIFE at the time approaching the death. A growing amount of research on the dying process. As people move closer towards death, there may be a sudden and unexpected surge of energy as they get nearer. They may want to get out of bed and talk to loved ones, or ask for food after days of no appetite. This surge of energy is usually used as a dying person's final physical expression before moving on. The surge of energy is usually short, and the previous signs become more pronounced as death approaches. Breathing becomes more irregular and often slower. As the last breath is taken, you can sense the life energy leave the loved one's physical body *(The Hospice Foundation of America, The Dying Process: A Guide for Caregivers, 1990).*

If you have ever been in the presence of a person as they are making their transition, you become aware at the moment of death that something invisible leaves the body. The physical body is still there, and it looks like the same person, but somehow you just know the person is no longer present. The "life" or energy is gone. But since energy cannot be destroyed, this "life"—this energy—must somehow continue, because that is the transformational nature of energy.

There is also a similar, yet different way we speak of LIFE. Have you ever used the phrase "breathe life into a project?" It means we give it an energy, a force, that generates excitement and results. We can also breathe life into the thoughts, feelings, ideas, and beliefs we hold. Clearly it is easy to see that all of the Powers need to be brought into play in their most supportive and positive aspects, so we can enliven and energize our lives and our actions for the highest good for ourselves and others. In fact, you could say that LIFE actually is used to energize all the other Powers! That makes it difficult to discuss on its own ... but we're going to give it a shot!

Let's look at LIFE first from the aspect of how we use it to energize projects, activities, and interests. It is easy to confuse ZEAL and LIFE in this aspect, but if you will recall our chapter on ZEAL, we made a strong distinction between these two Powers. We use ZEAL to initiate and have passion about thoughts, ideas, beliefs, and projects. ZEAL was that first stage of the rocket that gets it off the launching pad. LIFE is the second and even third stage of the rocket that gets it into orbit. Most of us are enthusiastic about starting something new (which is our ZEAL); once we get started, LIFE enlivens and vitalizes that job or project.

> This is my work, my blessing, not my doom; of all who live, I am the one by whom this work can best be done in the right way. (Henry Van Dyke)

Another very essential aspect of LIFE is how it enlivens our mind and body, to achieve complete health, wholeness, and vitality. When you feel a cold coming on, you can claim and speak LIFE to every cell and atom of your being, to manifest an energy that restores wholeness and health.

You can also practice acts of kindness. You might ask, what does this have to do with LIFE? Performing generous acts makes the giver, the receiver, the connector, and the observer happier, and increased happiness has a host of benefits. Specifically, happiness promotes numerous successful life outcomes, including superior physical and mental health, enhanced creativity and productivity, higher income, more prosocial behavior, and stronger interpersonal relationships *(Lyubomirsky, Sonja, The How of Happiness, Penguin Books, New York, 2008)*.

LIFE is underdeveloped in people who have little or no energy to engage in daily activities ... perhaps they are classic "couch potatoes!" It could be they have the zeal and passion to get something going, but have little or no LIFE to energize and maintain it. Have you ever been guilty of creating incredible goal lists and collages picturing your success, but then getting bogged down in the details and never actually taking action? People with underdeveloped LIFE Power find their projects are done in a lack-luster way, and may not ever be completed. These people may experience a higher level of illness in their lives, and run into problems with low stamina. They find it difficult to move through the least little barrier or challenge, and often see themselves as victims.

The impact of underdeveloped LIFE can be seen in the workplace. According to the American Institute of Stress, workplace-related stress costs the U.S. over $300 billion annually due to increased absenteeism, employee turnover, lower productivity, medical and legal insurance expenses, and Worker's Compensation payments *(Paul J. Rosch, ed., "The Quandary of Job Stress Compensation," Health and Stress, American Institute of Stress, March, 2001; 3)*. Clearly, when LIFE is not employed at the most elevated levels, all areas of our being are affected.

From a health and wholeness standpoint, an example of underdeveloped LIFE Power might be a man who constantly catches colds and flu bugs because of low resistance. His thought pattern is probably something like this: "I always catch colds! I get every flu bug that comes along."

> A neurological approach suggests that the (Deeper Self) is not the product of a cognitive, deductive process, but was instead "discovered" in a mystical or spiritual encounter made known to human consciousness through the transcendent machinery of the mind *(Andrew Newberg and Eugene D'Aquili, Why God Won't Go Away, New York: Ballantine Books, 2001, pg. 133)*.

Egocentric LIFE shows up as restlessness, nervousness, and hyperactivity. People in this category might energetically flit from one project to another, or be frenetic about completing something. Strong emotional reactions, impulsive behavior, and a short span of attention are typical for a hyperactive person. Some people may show these characteristics naturally, as personality differs from person to person. Nonetheless, when hyperactivity starts to become a problem for the person or others, it may be classified as a medical disorder *(Hallowell, E., and J. Ratey, Driven To Distraction: Recognizing and Coping with Attention Deficit Disorder from Childhood Through Adulthood, Pantheon Books, New York, 1994)*.

Egocentric LIFE can also manifest as "panic attacks," or as individuals who simply cannot sit still. Panic attacks are not fun experiences. As a matter of fact, according to the research, experiencing a panic attack has been said to be one of the most intensely frightening, upsetting, and uncomfortable experiences of a person's life and may take days to initially recover from *(Bourne, E., (2005). The Anxiety and Phobia Workbook, 4th Edition: New Harbinger Press)*.

LIFE in the ineffective egocentric form could also demonstrate as someone who is excessively busy, busy, busy ... but never really gets anything accomplished. When this becomes an extreme or chronic behavior, the person can reach the point of burn out.

From a health and wholeness standpoint, a person expressing egocentric LIFE might obsess over doing all the things related to health, to the extreme. This person would work out at the gym three times a day, eat only raw vegetables, always have a bottle of water available, and take mega doses of vitamins daily. The phenomenon of addiction to exercise is real and it is one of the risks of obsessive recreational physical activity. It is more common in men, especially those undertaking intense aerobic workouts *(Annett, J., B. Cripps and H. Steinberg (Eds.), Exercise addiction. Motivation and participation in sport and exercise (pp. 1-5). Leicester: The British Psychological Society)*.

> In the 1980s, the best tool for looking at neurocircuitry was to take a piece of removed tissue and look at single neurons. We now can see multiple neurons, and we can actually see how the cells talk to one another. Functional magnetic resonance imaging, f.M.R.I., lets you see what's happening on the whole brain level. In the last three years, we've gotten connectomics, where people are taking a bit of tissue and mapping every connection in it. And the science of optogenetics is where you express some fluorescent protein in some tissue that allows us to see individual cells and watch the change. And, so, the neuroscience of everyday life is here *(Wang, S., The Neuroscience of Everyday Life, The Great Courses, New York, 2010)*.

LIFE From the Four Levels of Consciousness

It is useful to review how LIFE is used at various levels of consciousness:

1. **Unconscious LIFE:** based on a cause in subconscious mind which consists of beliefs that are not in our moment to moment awareness. A case in point: a person who gives a lot of energy to self-deprecating remarks might have an unconscious need for outside validation. (An interesting sidebar from scientific research expounds on this by claiming the biggest reason people aren't more self-compassionate seems to be they are "afraid they'll become self-indulgent," says Dr. Kristin Neff, an associate professor of human development at the University of Texas at Austin. "They believe self-criticism is what keeps them in line. Most people have gotten it wrong because our culture says being hard on yourself is the way to be" *(Parker-Pope, T, Go Easy on Yourself, A New Wave of Research Urges, The Well, February 28, 2011)*.

2. **Conscious LIFE from our senses:** based on something in physicality we are gleaning through our sight, sound, scent, touch, and/or taste. A woman enjoys a massage because of the way it feels, the scent of the massage oil, and the soft background music. As a result. she invests energy in making massage a part of her regular routine.

   Another example of the impact of the senses: Research has shown that music has a profound effect on your body and psyche. In fact, there's a growing field of healthcare known as music therapy, which uses music to heal. For example, the change in brainwave activity levels that music can bring can also enable the brain to shift speeds more easily on its own as needed, which means that music can bring lasting benefits to your state of mind, even after you've stopped listening *(Misic, P., D. Arandjelovic, S. Stanojkovic, S. Vladejic, and J. Mladenovic. "Music Therapy." European Psychiatry 1.25 (Jan. 2010): 839. Academic Search Premier. Web. 9 November 2011).*

3. **Conscious LIFE from our human personality:** based on thoughts, feelings, attitudes, and/or beliefs held in ordinary consciousness. If you believe in the power of affirmations to contribute to your on-going health, you will create powerful affirmations and use them regularly to energize your body and deny giving power to illness.

   Research confirms that the mere repetition of a sound, affirmation, or short phrase over a period of time significantly reduces symptoms of stress, anxiety, depression, and anger, while improving the practitioner's perception of the quality of life and spiritual well-being *(R. Spencer, T. Verstynen, M. Brett, and R. Ivry, "Cerebellar activation during discrete and not continuous timed movements: An fMRI study," Neuroimage, 2007, June, 36 (2): 378-87).*

4. **Conscious LIFE from our True Identity, or Authentic Self:** based upon Divine Ideas, Laws, and Principles. At this level, we give energy to the pursuit of being the best person we can be. We invest time and energy learning about spiritual principles and laws, create continuity through our commitment to practice, and model the lives of people who have demonstrated a high level of consciousness. We practice wholistic health and choose our food wisely to ensure the flow of LIFE throughout our being. Most importantly, we enliven our thoughts and actions to apply what we have learned, to manifest results in our own lives.

Most people are herded by their secular activities instead of being heralded by their spiritual ones. They have allowed Good Morning America, The Today Show, and drive time radio to occupy the time slot once reserved for morning affirmative prayers and centering affirmations. Late night TV hosts like Jay Leno, David Letterman, and Jimmy Kimmel help news junkies and entertainment groupies say their "amens" to busy, tiresome, and generally unfulfilling days. Giving prayer and meditation back their "time slots" so we can "practice the Presence" will connect us with Spirit and bookend each day with an awareness that we are one with the Abiding Presence. You become truly grounded in Spirit by spending time in the Silence. You'll find that by spending time in the Silence, you begin getting messages, insights, ideas, strength, wisdom, and resources you need. By giving time to Spirit, you gain a life of spiritual growth, inner peace, and pure joy.

We believe that when you invest the time and energy it takes to realize an elevated consciousness, you will agree with physicist Amit Goswami: "The higher we develop, the more ego-less we become, until at the highest level there is no discernable identity with the ego at all. Thus a profound humility characterizes the levels of being beyond ego" *(Amit Goswami, The Self-Aware Universe, New York: Penguin Putnam Books, 1995, pg. 208). It is that "being beyond the ego" that we'll find when we align ourselves with our True Identity, our Extraordinary Self.*

As we wrap up this chapter about the Power of LIFE, and recognize how intricately all twelve of the Powers work together to bring out the best YOU you can be, we want to share a special secret you can use on a regular basis to guarantee you are living life and living it abundantly. The secret is actually quite simple ... but not so easy to implement! It involves taking one question, and keeping it uppermost in your mind at all times. Are you ready for the BIG questions that can keep you on track, focused on living from your Spiritual Center of Being? To ensure you are putting your Twelve Powers to use at the highest, most elevated level, simply use the following Big Questions technique. Begin by stopping often through the day to ask:

> Am I showing up in this moment as my Highest Self?
> A corollary: If not, what do I need to change, right this moment, to shift to my Highest Self?

Every evening, as you review your day, invite these questions into your awareness:

> Did I show up as my Highest Self in every situation?
> If not, how could I handle things differently NEXT TIME?
> And is there anything I need to do
> to make amends for anything I did today?

Make extra time in every day to go into the Silence, meditate, and allow yourself to "be present" with Spirit ... be still and know. When you do this, you will be able to show up as the best YOU you can be ... and your incredible future will unfold before you, as you master the art of living, walking the spiritual path on practical feet.

LIFE:
Putting It Into Practice

LIFE—Activity One:

Part 1:

In your journal, respond to the following question by writing down as many answers as you can think of:

What am I giving energy to—and how is it serving me?

Part 2:
- Reflect on your answers, and assess what they are telling you about how you are showing up for life, and what you are experiencing.
- What would you like to change?
- In order to make that change, what do you need to give energy to, calling on your Power of LIFE?

LIFE—Activity Two:

As you think about the specific area you are working on throughout this course, identify specific activities that have been difficult for you to work through and complete. Reflect on the following two questions:
- How has LIFE been involved, and how can you call on it to help you move toward success?
- How is LIFE impacting your other 11 Powers as you work on your specific area?

Example: Healthy Eating

What has been difficult: The toughest area has been committing the time to fixing healthy meals at home. I get excited about it as I look through recipe guides (lots of ZEAL), and I even go to the store and buy the food. But then the food sits in the refrigerator and goes bad, because I can't seem to generate any interest in actually creating the meals.

How to use LIFE and the other Powers to move toward success: I want to use FAITH to clearly claim the belief of the benefits of eating healthy; I call on STRENGTH to stay the course through actually preparing the meals. And finally, I invoke my Power of LIFE to enliven my ability to energetically prepare these healthy meals and maintain excitement, interest, and continuity.

I will use affirmations to excite myself, and envision how these foods will help me create the healthy, attractive body I desire.

LIFE Affirmation:

I claim LIFE now. I use LIFE to energize and enliven my pursuit of being the best person I can be.

 Quotes to Inspire LIFE

Your body is the ground and metaphor of your life, the expression of your existence. It is your Bible, your encyclopedia, your life story. Everything that happens to you is stored and reflected in your body. (Gabrielle Roth)

The ability to resign, to let go of obsolete responses, of exhausted relationships and of tasks beyond one's potential is an essential part of the wisdom of living. (Fritz Perls)

Because we are part of the web of life, we can draw on the strength—and the pain—of every creature. This interconnection constitutes our deep ecology. It is the source of our pain for the world as well as our love and appetite for life. (Joanna Macy)

The words "I am" are potent words; be careful what you hitch them to. The thing you're claiming has a way of reaching back and claiming you. (A.L. Kitselman)

Here is the test to find whether your mission on earth is finished. If you're alive, it isn't. (Richard Bach)

We ought to dance with rapture that we should be alive, and in the flesh, and part of the living, incarnate cosmos. (D. H. Lawrence)

Avoiding danger is no safer in the long run than outright exposure. Life is a daring adventure, or nothing. (Helen Keller)

Fortunately psychoanalysis is not the only way to resolve inner conflicts. Life itself still remains a very effective therapist. (Karen Horney)

Life is like a ten-speed bike. Most of us have gears we never use. (Charles Schultz)

Invent your world. Surround yourself with people, color, sounds, and work that nourish you. (Sark)

Slow down and enjoy life. It's not only the scenery you miss by going too fast—you also miss the sense of where you are going and why. (Eddie Cantor)

Every time you don't follow your inner guidance, you feel a loss of energy, loss of power, a sense of spiritual deadness. (Shakti Gawain)

Save Time by Learning From Our Case Example

$\mathcal{O}$n the next few pages, we explore one fictitious example to illustrate how the Powers may be brought into play at the four levels of consciousness we explored in each of the preceding chapters. Each table focuses on a single level of consciousness, and identifies each of the Twelve Powers with the resulting action—how the Power "shows up" or is applied.

The Case Example ~ Synopsis

We will be using a fictitious person, Mary, who has been overweight for much of her life. Not only is Mary overweight, she grew up in a family where her parents and siblings are also overweight. They are definitely not height and weight proportionate. As witnessed by old family photographs, Mary's grandparents on both sides were also overweight.

We will begin by looking at Mary's subconscious or unconscious beliefs at the point where she finally decides—one more time—to lose weight. Yes, Mary has also been a yo-yo dieter/exerciser. We will look at how Mary uses each of the Powers to either maintain her current weight or gain more weight fueled by these subconscious beliefs. Yes, that's right! Since we cannot *not* use these Powers, Mary, too, must have been using them to maintain her weight or gain more weight. These Powers work … it is up to Mary to decide *how* she wants to apply them. Moreover, these subconscious beliefs are the underlying reason her past attempts to diet and exercise have failed.

Subconscious Belief of the Cause

Mary is unaware of the causes of her being overweight because of one or more subconscious beliefs. Mary is totally unaware of two subconscious beliefs that fuel her weight issues:
- Belief that she inherited slow metabolism because of old family photographs showing all of her grandparents being overweight.
- Belief she is and always will be heavy because she sees that everyone in her immediate family is overweight.

Power	Action (How the Power is used)
FAITH Believe	Mary's lifestyle choices are driven from these subconscious beliefs resulting in not eating right, eating too much of the wrong thing, and not exercising.
STRENGTH Persevere	Mary unconsciously uses STRENGTH to support and hang onto her beliefs. This includes holding onto all the bad habits that maintain her weight or even add more weight.
LOVE Desire; attract	Mary unconsciously desires her subconscious beliefs. She uses LOVE to want and desire everything and anything that supports these beliefs. She desires the wrong foods and desires to be sedentary, and attracts herself to those desires.
IMAGINATION Visualize; conceptualize	Mary visualizes herself being overweight. In fact, she looks in her mirror and sees herself even heavier than she actually is.
POWER Master; have dominion	Mary unconsciously masters the art of eating poorly and not exercising. Also, she unconsciously dominates and controls any thoughts and feelings that are contrary to her subconscious beliefs.
UNDERSTANDING Know; comprehend	Mary unconsciously knows just what to do and what to avoid in order to support her subconscious beliefs.
WISDOM Discern; apply what is known	Mary unconsciously discerns what to do in order to continue supporting these subconscious beliefs. It may seem strange and counter intuitive, but she would "wisely" choose foods that keep her heavy as well as shun exercise—even avoiding the steps in favor of the elevator.
WILL Choose	Mary unconsciously chooses foods based on what she knows (Understanding) and evaluates (Wisdom) to support her subconscious belief. Obviously, she chooses not to exercise.
ORDER Organize; prioritize	Without even realizing it, Mary organizes her life insuring that there is no time to exercise nor time to eat right.
RELEASE Remove; let go	Through a litany of excuses, Mary eliminates, denies and dismisses any thoughts about eating right and getting exercise. She even allows healthy foods to spoil so she can toss them.
ZEAL Inspire; motivate	It may seem odd, but, Mary is "passionate" about maintaining her beliefs and lifestyle. She is passionate about foods that are not good for her.
LIFE Enliven; vitalize	Mary is vitalizing these beliefs with every choice she makes to eat poorly and not exercise, thus bringing about self-criticism, illness and depression along with the weight gain.

Case Example

Conscious Belief of an Outer Cause

Mary believes the main cause is from the outer, physical realm. She decides it is time, once again, to lose weight. Totally unaware of the subconscious beliefs and the power she is giving them, Mary looks to her outer actions and the outer realm for the cause of her being overweight. With all the conscious information she has, Mary consciously thinks and feels the cause of her being overweight is because she does not eat right or get enough exercise. Mary now believes (FAITH) she will lose weight if she only eats right and exercises.

Power	Action (How the Power is used)
FAITH Believe	Based on her belief that she is heavy simply because she does not eat right nor exercise, Mary begins a diet and exercise program, (or, she may choose surgical procedures: liposuction, lap-ban surgery, or laparoscopic obesity surgery to change her outer appearance).
STRENGTH Persevere	Mary uses STRENGTH to stay the course with her decision to diet and exercise, (or, get surgery).
LOVE Desire; attract	Mary uses LOVE to desire to lose weight. She also uses it to attract herself and desire to eat right and exercise, (or to want and desire to get surgery).
IMAGINATION Visualize; conceptualize	Mary use IMAGINATION to see herself exercising and dieting as well as imagining what she will look like when she has lost the weight, (or visualize herself doing what she needs to do to have the surgery).
POWER Master; have dominion	Mary uses Dominion to master exercising and dieting, (or to master what she needs to know and do in order to get surgery).
UNDERSTANDING Know; comprehend	Mary uses Understanding to know about various exercise programs (or surgery, doctors, and surgery centers).
WISDOM Discern, apply	Mary uses Wisdom to discern how to exercise and diet, (or to figure out the best doctors and surgery centers).
WILL Choose	Mary uses Will to choose her belief in an outer cause as well as to choose a diet and exercise program, (or to ultimately choose her doctor and surgery center).
ORDER Organize; prioritize	She uses Order to sequence and organize her life so that she can diet and exercise, (or organizes her life and affairs so she can get surgery).
RELEASE Remove; let go	She uses RELEASE to remove and deny any doubt she can do this as well as to eliminate inappropriate foods and habits, (or to eliminate any fears and concerns about the surgery).
ZEAL Inspire; motivate	She uses ZEAL to start and be enthusiastic about her diet and exercise program, (or to begin the process for surgery and be enthusiastic about it).
LIFE Enliven; vitalize	She uses Life to enliven and energize her diet and exercise programs, (or to vitalize and energize the entire process of getting surgery).

Conscious Belief of a Cause in Consciousness

Mary notices, once again, that her diet and exercise plan begins to work and then she backslides and goes back to her old ways—it begins slowly and subtly and then accelerates until she is no longer dieting and exercising. This yo-yoing is inevitable since Mary is totally unaware of the subconscious beliefs that are "working against her." Or, more accurately, she is unconsciously using her Powers to sabotage her efforts to lose weight. Her long standing subconscious beliefs are fueling her behaviors that work against her beliefs in dieting and exercise. For example, since STRENGTH is most effective when linked to something we firmly believe, her use of STRENGTH to stay the course with the new beliefs will not be as effective because the subconscious beliefs are still supporting the use of this Power to stay the course with her former ways of eating and exercise.

Wisely, Mary begins to wonder and reflect on why all her efforts to diet and exercise do not work. She definitely knows that she is the one who decides to start eating poorly again, as well as to miss more and more days of exercise. Upon reflection and perhaps with some help from her therapist, Mary finally surfaces the subconscious beliefs. She becomes aware that she has been using her actions to hold and reinforce the beliefs that she inherited slow metabolism and that she will always be overweight because her entire family is overweight.

Mary now knows that she has work to do with the beliefs she is holding in consciousness in order to permanently lose weight. She also knows that she must disempower and eliminate the formerly subconscious beliefs while claiming a new belief.

Power	Action—How the Power is used. *Disempowering* Old, Unwanted Beliefs	Action—How the Power is used. *Claiming* New Beliefs
FAITH Believe	Now, Mary begins to disempower the unwanted beliefs: • Belief she inherited slow metabolism, because from the photograph she is able to see that all her grandparents were overweight. • Belief she is and will be heavy because she sees that everyone in her immediate family is overweight. (See the Power of RELEASE).	Mary begins to claim the beliefs she wants: • I have a normal and health-promoting metabolism. • I am whole and healthy, demonstrated by being height and weight proportionate Her deep realization of these beliefs is coupled with the use of affirmations such as, "I am whole and perfect, my body is height and weight proportionate.
STRENGTH Persevere	Mary sticks with her inner work to transform her unwanted beliefs into wanted beliefs. She sticks with consistently using her denials. Every time she is aware of acting or even thinking in ways that support the unwanted beliefs she applies her denial.	Mary sticks with and perseveres with her inner work to claim the new beliefs by using her affirmations. She would also be sticking with her diet and exercise programs.
LOVE Desire; attract	Mary desires and wants to change her beliefs, thoughts and feelings.	She effortlessly desires and wants to support these new beliefs as well as to eat right and exercise.

Case Example

IMAGINATION Visualize; conceptualize	Mary conceptualizes how to release the beliefs she does not want, visualizing them flying out of her mind. She sees herself using her denials effectively.	Mary conceptualizes how to claim the new beliefs. She sees herself claiming the new beliefs.
POWER Master; have dominion	Mary controls any thoughts and feelings that support her old beliefs.	Mary masters her new beliefs, thoughts and feeling.
UNDERSTANDING Know; comprehend	Mary knows the beliefs she wants to let go. She knows how to construct a denial.	She knows the beliefs she wants to acquire and own. She knows how to construct an affirmation.
WISDOM Discern, apply what is known	Mary has already discerned and judged which beliefs to remove. She knows how to use a denial.	Mary already wisely discerned which new beliefs she wants to claim, and wisely chooses her food and exercise. She knows how to use an affirmation.
WILL Choose	Mary chooses/decides which beliefs to release. She decides to use denials.	She decides which new beliefs to clam. She decides to use affirmations.
ORDER Organize; prioritize	Mary organizes her process to effectively disempower and eliminate old beliefs. She is aware of the Law of Divine Order: Mind-Idea-Expression.	Mary organizes her process to be effective at claiming and owning the new beliefs. She adjusts to changing situations in regards to her diet and exercise.
RELEASE Remove, let go	Mary uses denials to disempower the unwanted beliefs. Example: I give no power to the belief I inherited low metabolism. I give no power to my family being heavy.	Mary uses her power of RELEASE to remove and eliminate any thoughts of doubt about being able to complete her program as well as to maintain her weight loss. She also eliminates any foods or temptations to have foods that are not on her diet.
ZEAL Inspire; motivate	Mary is passionate about disempowering and eliminating the old beliefs.	She is passionate and starts to claim the new beliefs as well as to start a new diet and exercise program.
LIFE Enliven, vitalize	Mary enlivens and invigorates disempowering the beliefs she no longer wants.	Mary enlivens and invigorates claiming and owning the beliefs she wants.

Conscious Belief in a Higher Cause

While working to disempower her old subconscious beliefs, claim new beliefs, and continue her diet and exercise programs, Mary becomes aware that there is only One Power and One Presence, the Truth of What she is. Mary begins to believe in the Truth of her innate Divinity, even if this belief is merely the size of a mustard seed. She begins to loosen and disempower her belief in her personality or ego. As this new state of awareness gets more and more solidified, it affects the personality as well as the physical body.

Power	Action (How the Power is used)
FAITH Believe	Mary begins to own the belief in her innate divine nature.
STRENGTH Persevere	Mary stays the course and supports her belief in her divine nature, no matter what her senses seem to be informing her.
LOVE Desire; attract	Mary desires and demonstrate her highest and best. This includes desiring to be, do, and say the things that demonstrate she is divine in nature.
IMAGINATION Visualize; conceptualize	Mary visualizes and conceptualizes what it is like to be the best person she can be, using vision boards as a reinforcement.
POWER Master; have dominion	Mary masters the belief, thoughts, and feelings in regard to living as One with Spirit. She also controls any thoughts and feelings to the contrary.
UNDERSTANDING Know; comprehend	Mary knows both intellectually and spiritually what it is to be the best person she can be.
WISDOM Discern, apply what is known	Mary discerns when she is operating from her highest level of consciousness and when she is not. She applies what she knows about the Twelve Powers to her every-day life.
WILL Choose	Mary chooses to be the best person she can be in the big picture as well in the moment-to-moment choices that support this belief and every decision.
ORDER Organize, prioritize	Mary organizes and adjust her life so that she can be the best person she can be.
RELEASE Remove, let go	Mary eliminates and denies any emerging thoughts, feelings and beliefs that work against her being the best person she can be.
ZEAL Inspire; motivate	Mary is passionate about being the best person she can be. She uses affirmations to maintain her enthusiasm and excitement.
LIFE Enliven; vitalize	Mary enlivens and vitalizes every aspect of her life so she can be the best person she can be.

Appendix 1:
Historical Background on the Twelve Powers

Written by Rev. Eric Page, M.H.A.M.S.*

Emma Curtis Hopkins, Annie Rix Militz, and other New Thought writers used the symbols of the numbers seven and twelve for spiritual attributes. Hopkins taught Militz as well as Charles and Myrtle Fillmore. Both Hopkins and Militz wrote for Unity. Hopkins operated a seminary in Chicago and lectured throughout the country. Militz worked at Unity before founding the California-based Homes of Truth.

Information about Charles Fillmore's private experiences with the Twelve Faculties is limited. Certainly the ideas of body centers were being discussed prior to Charles writing about the concepts. The Fillmores were part of a group of individuals who read and discussed concepts from eastern thought. Fillmore acknowledges Hinduism for the idea of seven centers or chakras in his writings.

Charles Fillmore does not mention colors related to the Twelve Powers in his 1930 guide, *The Twelve Powers of Man*, though Unity writers were writing about colors. In her 1896 Unity article, "Twelve Lights," Mary E. Griswold explores Twelve Spiritual Attributes represented by the colors of twelve jewels. A 1903 program given to graduates of an early Unity course includes affirmations and colors for seven objective centers. Colors were also included in a description of controlling centers in 1917. Colors are also outlined in a 1934 series in Unity magazine. One group of colors has been attributed to Joel Baehr in 1971. He noted that businesses were beginning to use colors for filing at the time. Baehr used a color key program at Unity Christ Church in St. Louis, Missouri and the color key program was adopted by the Association of Unity Churches International. [The Association carries Twelve Power Candle sets for use in Unity Churches.]

---

* *Rev. Eric Page is the archivist at the Unity Library and Archives, Unity Village, MO. He has a Master of Historical Administration and Museum Studies from the University of Kansas, and Master of Divinity with ordination from Unity Institute, Unity Village, MO.*

Appendix 2:
Additional Commentaries

Commentary on the Colors Associated with the Powers

The colors that are associated with the Twelve Powers were not part of the original system as put forth by Charles Fillmore. They were created by Rev. Joel Behr many years ago. A person does not have to relate to the color system in order to understand and apply the Powers; however, many individuals find the colors associated with the Powers provides an added inspiration and depth.

There is an incredible amount of research to support the impact of color in nearly every aspect of our lives. There are several reasons why colors are able to influence how we feel. According to Leslie Harrington, executive director of The Color Association of the United States, which forecasts color trends, "We react on multiple levels of association with colors—there are social or culture levels as well as personal relationships with particular colors. You also have an innate reaction to color. For example, when you look at red, it does increase your heart rate. It is a stimulating color. This goes back to caveman days of fire and danger and alarm" *(Bender, R., "How Color Affects Our Mood,: Huffington Post, May 28, 2013).*

As a result of the psychological effects of color on human being, the use of color has become an important marketing tool. In fact, according to recent research cited by Mimi Cooper, and quoted in The TABS Journal article, "How Color Affects Marketing," by Channa Leichtling, "color is ranked among the top three considerations in the purchase decision" *(Leichtling, C., "How Color Affects Marketing," The TABS Journal, http://legacy.touro.edu/tabs/journal02/tabs5c.pdf).*

As you work with the Twelve Powers, you can strengthen your focus and awareness by integrating color into your study. For example, when you want to strengthen a specific power, you can make the associated color a major focus. Choose to wear something of that color; eat foods that are that color; place items in your home or office featuring the predominant color you are focusing on. You may even want to use a pen with that particular color of ink to write with! While this may sound somewhat superficial and feel a little strange at first, allow yourself to give it a try before making a judgment. Pay attention to the impact your focus on color has on your ability to use that particular Power at its highest, most elevated level.

Commentary on the Body Locations Associated with the Powers

In addition to color, each of the Powers is located in a specific area of the body. Many people find these associations to be quite a stretch. However, a particular logic is found when taken in the context of the Unity teachings.

Appendices

1. Everything begins in Divine Mind as Divine Ideas.
2. The physical body is manifested using Divine Ideas according to the level of consciousness manifesting it.
3. Therefore it makes sense that there is a center associated with each Power located in the body.

Charles Fillmore believed that each of these centers enlivens and controls the associated functions in and around that location. Some of the associations make intuitive sense. For example, POWER (Dominion, Mastery) is located in the throat, base of the tongue, and larynx. When we are using our ability to manifest or control our surroundings, thoughts, feelings, or beliefs, we use strong affirmations to call forth what we are claiming. Thus, placing POWER in the location of the larynx/voice box is consistent with its purpose. Similarly, LOVE is located in the heart; STRENGTH is housed in the lower back. Interestingly, in some cases recent science is backing up Fillmore in regards to the locations he discerned. Fillmore located the Power of Will, along with Understanding, in the front forebrain. Recently, scientific studies on the brain have located the will to be in this part of the brain. "Cognitive control and value-based decision-making tasks appear to depend on different brain regions within the prefrontal cortex," says Jan Glascher, lead author of the study and a visiting associate at the California Institute of Technology in Pasadena, referring to the seat of higher-level reasoning in the brain *(Szalavitz, Maia, "Making Choices: How Your Brain Decides," TIME Healthland, September 4, 2012).*

Having a color and a body location can be a useful way to focus on a Power during Meditation; or even while consciously employing one during everyday waking life.

> When you are inspired by some great purpose, some extraordinary project, all your thoughts break their bonds: your mind transcends limitations, your consciousness expands in every direction, and you find yourself in a new, great, and wonderful world. Dormant forces, faculties and talents become alive, and you discover yourself to be a greater person by far than you ever dreamed yourself to be (Patanjali, founder of Yoga in ancient India, as translated by Edmond Bordeaux Szekely in *Creative Work*, from *Money-Love*, p. 60).

Summary Chart of the Twelve Powers

Power	Purpose	Color	Body Location
Faith	Trust absolutely; spiritually know; believe with confidence and conviction	Royal Blue	Pineal Gland (Center of brain)
Strength	Endure; be resilient; stay the course; persist; persevere; and be mentally tough	Spring Green	Small of the back
Love	Harmonize, unify, unconditionally attract, feel affection.	Pink	Back of the heart
Imagination	Visualize; conceptualize; envision; think outside the box	Light Blue	Between the eyes
Power	Command authority of thoughts, feelings, and beliefs; claim mastery; express prerogatives and proficiencies	Purple	Throat, back of tongue, larynx
Understanding	Comprehend knowledge; interpret and make cognitive connections	Gold	Front forebrain
Wisdom	Intuitively discern and make heart connections; practically apply what is known	Yellow	Pit of stomach
Will	Choose; decide; direct; dictate; determine	Silver	Front forebrain
Order	Align; organize; sequence; arrange	Olive Green	Navel
Release	Discard; let go; remove; liberate; dismiss; eliminate	Russet Brown	Lower abdominal region
Zeal	Be enthusiastic and passionate; inspire self and others; motivate; excite	Orange	Medulla Oblongata (brain stem; back of neck)
Life	Maintain vitality and sustain energy; make whole; enliven and quicken	Red	The generative organs, external reproductive organs

Index

A

ABCDE Method 135-136
Abhayananda 113
Abrams 109
Achenaum 104
affirmations 16, 23, 24, 53, 67, 74, 75, 78, 82, 84, 140, 170, 171, 180, 183, 188, 189, 190, 193, 195
Amabile 60
American Psychological Association 5, 38, 87
Anderson 63
anger 47, 121, 144, 147, 148, 153, 154, 168, 169, 180
Annett 179
Arandjelovic 180
Atlee 106
attraction 43, 44, 45, 46, 67
Authentic Self 4, 8, 19, 20, 35, 50, 63, 76, 93, 107, 124, 138, 153, 165, 169, 180

B

Bach 184
Baltes 103, 104
Baryshnikov 139
Battenwhich 18
Beauregard 49
Begley 4, 15, 175
Besant 142
behavior 30, 50, 63, 73, 95, 126, 154, 166, 177, 178
belief system 5, 7, 14, 64, 149, 150
Benson 45
Beversdorf 62
Bhagavad-Gita 21
Bhasin 45
bias for action 165, 166
Big Bang 162, 163, 164, 166
Biology 6, 47, 90, 164, 198
Blake 47
Blavatsky 113
Blind FAITH 16, 18, 19
Boodoo 87
Bouchard 87
Bourne 178
Boykin 87
brain 4, 6, 13, 14, 15, 30, 31, 45, 47, 48, 49, 57, 58, 61, 62, 63, 73, 74, 79, 92, 136, 138, 150, 152, 153, 161, 175, 176, 179, 180, 195
Buddha 98, 107, 157, 164, 172

Brassen 15
Brett 180
Brody 87, 100
Buchel 15
Buddha 98, 157, 164, 172
Butterworth 20, 25, 82, 84, 95, 129, 131, 149

C

Cady 15, 17, 84, 88, 95
Cameron 32, 172
Campbell 172
Cantor 184
Case Example 7, 185, 187, 189
Cave Allegory 64
Ceci 87
cereal aisle 107
Chadwick 59
Charney 38
Charron 138
children 18, 19, 50, 51, 58, 61, 65, 72, 121, 122, 138
Chinmoy 159
Choice Map 126-128
choices 6, 7, 21, 22, 77, 101, 117-126, 128, 129, 139, 186, 190
Clark 113
Color 5, 13, 29, 43, 57, 71, 87, 99, 117, 133, 145, 161, 175, 184, 193, 194, 195
Conscious Belief 187, 188, 190
Conscious FAITH 19
Conscious IMAGINATION 63
Conscious LIFE 180
Conscious LOVE 50
Conscious ORDER 137, 138
Conscious POWER 76
Conscious RELEASE 152, 153
Conscious STRENGTH 35
Conscious UNDERSTANDING 92, 93
Conscious WILL 123, 124
Conscious WISDOM 106, 107
Conscious ZEAL 169
Consciousness 4, 5, 8, 19, 20, 21, 24, 34, 35, 40, 47, 48, 49, 50, 54, 59, 60, 62, 64, 66, 72, 74, 75, 76, 77, 79, 80, 81, 82, 83, 92, 103, 106, 112, 113, 118, 120, 121, 122, 123, 124, 126, 137, 142, 145, 147, 148, 149, 152, 153, 155, 164, 168, 169, 172, 174, 178, 179, 180, 181, 185, 188, 190, 195
Cooper 194
Core Self 4

Courtemanche 49
Craig-Purcell 172
Creagan 147
creative voice 61
creativity 44, 58, 60, 61, 62, 63, 64, 177
Cripps 179
crises 31, 34, 38
Csikszentmihalyi 3
Curie 40, 95
Curtis 40, 129
Cyrulnik 38

D

D'Aquili 178
Dalai Lama 40
Davidson 31
Davies 105, 162
Day 77
de Chardin 54
de Montaigne 95
Dead Poets' Society 125
Deci 125
decision-making 30, 100, 126
Decker 95
Deeper Self 4, 7, 20, 21, 75, 178
Definitely Maybe 121
denials 23, 24, 74, 149, 188, 189
Dijksterhuis 120
DiMaggio 72
discern 33, 99, 100, 101, 102, 104, 105, 106, 112, 113, 118, 153, 186, 187, 189, 190
Disney 55
Divine Ideas 8, 19, 20, 35, 50, 63, 66, 71, 72, 76, 83, 92, 93, 101, 106, 107, 122, 123, 124, 138, 140, 142, 153, 169, 180, 195
Divine Ideas, Laws, and Principles 8, 19, 35, 50, 63, 76, 93, 106, 107, 122, 124, 138, 153, 169, 180
Divine Mind 44, 54, 122, 151, 195
Divine Nature 8, 21, 43, 88, 106, 190
Divine Order 134, 135, 140, 189
DNA 109, 111, 162, 197
Dobbs 109
dogma 64
Dr. Oz 168
Dr. Seuss 58
Dusek 45
Dyer 129

E

echo 79, 88, 101
Egocentric FAITH 13
Egocentric IMAGINATION 57
Egocentric LIFE 175, 178, 179
Egocentric LOVE 43
Egocentric ORDER 6, 133
Egocentric POWER 71, 151
Egocentric RELEASE 145, 151
Egocentric STRENGTH 29
Egocentric UNDERSTANDING 87
egocentric voice 31
Egocentric WILL 117
Egocentric WISDOM 99, 104
Egocentric ZEAL 161, 167
Einstein 16, 58, 64, 67, 86
elevated consciousness 6, 13, 29, 43, 57, 71, 87, 99, 117, 120, 133, 145, 161, 175, 181
Elias 52
Ellington 181
Emerson 78
Emotion 31, 44, 47, 49, 74, 75, 168
emotional hijacking 30
emotions 4, 29, 31, 44, 46, 47, 48, 49, 77, 78, 146, 156
Erhard 72
Extraordinary Self 20, 35, 124, 181
Extraordinary You 5, 4, 20, 155

F

Fahey 169
FAITH 3, 11-25, 29, 31, 35, 95, 118, 126, 160, 170, 183, 186, 187, 188, 190, 196
FAITH Condo 15-16
false beliefs 154
fear 8, 13, 18, 30, 31, 33, 57, 60, 73, 74, 76, 108, 121, 124, 148, 150, 152, 153
Ferrucci 40
Fillmore 3, 21, 25, 40, 48, 54, 67, 81, 95, 113, 115, 129, 132, 142, 157, 160, 164, 170, 172, 174, 193, 194, 195
Fillmore Challenge 81
fishbowl 148, 149
Fitterling 38
Flaherty 62
Ford 78

Index

forgiveness 76, 100, 101, 139
Fox 69, 113
Frank 16
Fredrickson 29, 34, 46, 47
Freeman 84, 172

G

Gamer 15
Gandhi 25, 54, 116
Gardner 63, 90
Gatlin 129
Gawain 184
Gibran 172
Gifford 153
goals 23, 38, 65, 66, 74, 75, 94, 103, 136, 147, 155, 156, 176
God 2, 4, 12, 16, 18, 19, 25, 44, 45, 52, 54, 67, 76, 84, 95, 105, 106, 109, 117, 119, 120, 122, 123, 129, 134, 147, 149, 151, 156, 162, 163, 172, 174, 178
God's Will 4, 119, 120
Goldberg 5
Goldsmith 113
Goleman 30, 75
Goswami 181
Gottfredson 90
Graham, K. 41
Graham, M. 173
gratitude 46, 47
Greenberg 74
Greene 163
Griswold 193
Grossmann 49
Gusnard 30

H

H.E.A.T. Formula 164
Haisch 18, 106
Hales 5
Hall 97
Hallowell 178
Halpern 87
Hamblin 67
Hanh 54, 144, 157
harmony 44, 46, 48, 49, 54, 132, 133
Harrington 194

Harvard 5, 50, 60, 72, 101, 102
Hasbrouck 67, 142
Hasselbeck 3, 4, 45, 46, 134, 198
Hausmann 2, 25, 84
He 47
Headquarters 20, 140
health 3, 5, 32, 48, 52, 74, 77, 84, 88, 92, 104, 111, 139, 147, 149, 153, 156, 165, 169, 172, 177, 178, 179, 180, 188
Heilman 62, 63
highest level of consciousness 8, 24, 81, 126, 190
Highest Self 182
Hirsch 63
Holton v, 3, 4, 45, 46, 134, 136, 197
hope 15, 16, 37, 46, 47, 108, 117, 142, 149, 197
Hopkins 193
Horney 184
Hospice 176
Houston 40, 151
Howard Bros Circus Model 167
Hudson 134
human personality 7, 19, 35, 50, 63, 76, 79, 93, 106, 124, 137, 148, 153, 169, 180

I

Ibn 149
IMAGINATION 3, 21, 55-67, 118, 134, 186, 187, 189, 190
inner peace 1, 2, 3, 20, 79, 111, 147, 149, 181
Intellectual UNDERSTANDING 88, 89
intentions 21, 78, 122, 126, 175
Isaiah 28
Ivry 180
Iyengar 126

J

Jafolla 129
Jensen 72
Jesus 14, 24, 52, 75, 100, 147, 157, 164
Jiang 47
Jinnah 141
Jobs 124
Joseph 45
Jordan 37
joy 2, 3, 20, 40, 44, 46, 47, 54, 88, 101, 108, 121, 149, 172, 181

judgment 72, 100, 101, 102, 103, 104, 113, 126, 155, 172, 194
Jung 67
Junk-o-logic 100

K

Kahnerman 119
Kaminski 93
Kasser 103
Keller 184
Kemeny 169
Kemp 129
Khoshaba 32
King 54, 117
Kirk 153
Kiss 48, 51
Kitselman 184
Koechlin 138
Koestler 46, 47, 61
Krishna 21, 164
Krishnamurti 142
Krskova 48

L

lack 25, 33, 38, 95, 121, 152, 153, 154, 167, 177
Law of Attraction 45
Law of Mind Action 45, 78
Lawrence 184
LeDoux 150
Lelly 129
Lennon 81
Lerner 153, 169
Libermann 45
life 173
LIFE 118, 167, 175-183, 186, 187, 189, 190, 196
Light 4, 15, 16, 18, 54, 57, 64, 65, 66, 95, 99, 103, 109, 113, 142, 162, 172, 176
Lipton 164
Loehlin 87
Lombardo 103
loss 5, 32, 38, 184, 189
LOVE 41-54, 72, 78, 87, 99, 117, 118, 133, 186, 187, 188, 190, 195, 196
Lynch 67, 84, 95
Lyubomirsky 177

M

Macaskill 77
MacLeod 30
Maddi 32
Maltby 77
Mandela 172
Marden 25
Mariechild 42
mastery 71, 72, 73, 84, 195
Mazarin 152
mental shift 81
metaphysical 147, 152, 197, 198
Militz 193
Miller 12
Millman 25, 113
Misic 180
Mladenovic 180
Morgenstern 136
Mother Teresa 54
Muir 62
multiverse 162, 163
mynah bird 153
Myss 84

N

Nadeau 62
Neff 179
Neisser 87
neurobiology 61
neurocircuitry 179
neuroplasticity 4, 15, 57, 58, 79
neuroscience 3, 4, 6, 31, 33, 47, 58, 62, 73, 78, 100, 176, 179, 197
neurotheology 3, 5, 7, 14, 18
Newberg 4, 5, 7, 13, 14, 18, 57, 178
Nietzsche 172
Nin 157
NO Strategy 155

Obstacles 37
O'Murchu 25
Oneness 20, 76, 88, 140, 149, 151

Index

optical delusions 64, 65
ORDER 6, 118, 131-142, 186, 187, 189, 190, 196
ordinary consciousness 7, 13, 19, 29, 35, 43, 50, 57, 63, 71, 76, 87, 93, 99, 106, 117, 120, 124, 133, 137, 145, 153, 161, 169, 175, 180
Out 45
Ozbay 38

P

Page 193
Palmer 172
panic attacks 178
Paquette 49
Parker-Pope 179
Patanjali 195
performance 30, 32, 126
Perloff 87
Perls 184
Phelps 31
physical body 37, 93, 176, 190, 195
Pike Syndrome 79
pineal gland 13
Planck 103
Plato 64
Ponder 67, 95, 101, 129, 157
Positive Psychology 2, 3, 5, 37, 46, 50, 79, 100, 197
Positivity 15, 16, 46, 47, 63
Pounders 142
Powell 95
POWER 71-84, 118, 162, 163, 167, 186, 187, 189, 190, 195, 196
Power of Choice 117, 119
Powers 30
practice 8, 14, 21, 22, 23, 31, 38, 40, 52, 65, 75, 76, 82, 91, 93, 105, 111, 127, 138, 141, 142, 145, 149, 151, 155, 170, 177, 180, 182, 198
prefrontal cortex 31, 74, 136
Primack 109
productivity 30, 177, 178
psycho-spatial processing 58

Q

quantum physics 3, 4, 163
Quirk 150

R

Raichle 30
Raio 31
Ratey 178
relationships 38, 50, 63, 73, 145, 150, 177, 184, 194
RELEASE 118, 143-157, 165, 166, 169, 186, 187, 189, 190, 196
Repa 150
resilience 32, 33, 37, 38, 47, 102
Riccardi 31
Ringling Brothers Circus museum 167
Rinpoche 113
Rosch 178
Rosemergy 95, 142, 201
Roth 184
Rowe 63
Rowland 54, 84
Ruegg 64

S

Saphire-Bernstein 73
Sark 184
Schroeder 157
Schultz 184
Schwartz 4
Segerstrom 169
self-confidence 38
self-doubt 148, 154
Seligman 3, 5, 79
Shakespeare 146
Sharot 31
Shaw 56
Sheldon 103
Shepherd 11
Shumlan 30
Siegel 54
Sikking 84
Silence 88, 101, 123, 139, 140, 181, 182
six properties of wisdom: 104
Smith 91, 104
Smock 40, 142
Snyder 30
Southwick 38
Speigel 125
Spencer 180
Spiritual Alphabetical Order 139, 140

spiritual DNA 109, 162
spiritual growth 89, 122, 138, 140, 149, 181
Spiritual Laws 16, 17
Spiritual Nature 88, 149, 169
Spiritual UNDERSTANDING 88, 92, 95, 113, 162
St-Pierre 49
Staik 73
Stanojkovic 180
Staudinger 104
Steinberg 179
Steiner 40, 54
Sternberg 87, 90, 91
story 30, 35, 59, 74, 77, 91, 109, 110, 111, 120, 125, 146, 153, 154, 166, 184
STRENGTH 2, 27, 28-40, 72, 91, 116, 167, 183, 186, 187, 188, 190, 195, 196
stress 31, 37, 38, 45, 52, 73, 101, 169, 178, 180
stuff 32, 51, 146, 147, 148, 150, 156, 163
subconscious belief 35, 62, 123, 137, 152, 186
Suttle 135

T

Talarovicova 48
Tao Te Ching 157
Taylor 73, 169
Templeton Foundation 99
Ten Boom 25
Ten-Minute Jump Start 135, 136
Tew 157
Thoreau 157
3-P Formula of POWER 74
Tibbals 167
Tiedens 153, 169
Tolle 143
Tracy 136
Trimarchi 90
triumverate of Powers 89
Truth 15, 16, 17, 20, 23, 25, 40, 45, 46, 54, 78, 88, 92, 100, 101, 122, 123, 125, 139, 140, 147, 149, 151, 190, 193, 197, 198
Tsunami 91
Tugade 29
Turner 109, 113
Tversky 119

U

Ueland 67
Unconscious FAITH 19
Unconscious IMAGINATION 62
unconscious level 7, 62
Unconscious LIFE 179
Unconscious LOVE 49
Unconscious ORDER 137
Unconscious POWER 76
Unconscious RELEASE 152
Unconscious STRENGTH 35
Unconscious UNDERSTANDING 92
Unconscious WILL 123
Unconscious WISDOM 106
Unconscious ZEAL: 168
Underdeveloped FAITH 13
Underdeveloped IMAGINATION 57
Underdeveloped LIFE 175, 177, 178
Underdeveloped LOVE 43
Underdeveloped ORDER 6, 133
Underdeveloped POWER 6, 71, 137
Underdeveloped RELEASE 145, 150
Underdeveloped STRENGTH 29
Underdeveloped UNDERSTANDING 87
Underdeveloped WILL 117, 120
Underdeveloped WISDOM 99, 102, 104
Underdeveloped ZEAL 161, 167
UNDERSTANDING 43, 49, 72, 87-95, 99, 102, 105, 117, 118, 119, 127, 151, 186, 187, 189, 190, 195, 196
Understanding FAITH 16, 17, 18, 19
unforgiveness 148, 154

V

Vaillant 50
Vaish 49
Valvano 172
Van Dyke 177
Van Gogh 85
Verstynen 180
Viorst 27
visualizing 38, 57, 61, 189
Vivekananda 70
Vladejic 180

Index

W

Wager 33
Wallas 61
Wallas stage model 61
Walsch 157
Wang 179
Waugh 33
WAY acronym 123
West 67, 95
whine-ology 122
WILL 4, 6, 78, 89, 105, 117-129, 139, 167, 186, 187, 189, 190, 196
Williams 6, 125
Williamson 109
Wilson 40, 67
WISDOM 43, 49, 72, 87, 89, 92, 97-113, 117, 118, 119, 127, 148, 165, 166, 167, 186, 187, 189, 190, 196
Wisdom Research Network 99
Wohlhueter 45
Woodward 49
worry 33, 40, 46, 61, 110, 138, 148
Wright 101

Y

Yang 47
Yogananda 117

Z

Zald 47
ZEAL 118, 159-172, 177, 183, 186, 187, 189, 190, 196
Zerbini 45

Credits:

Book cover & interior design: Cher Holton
Editing: Bil Holton

Artwork/Photography (used with permission):

© 2013 Clipart.com: Pages 2, 12, 28, 42, 44, 49, 51, 56, 58, 70, 72, 86, 92, 98, 100, 116, 122, 132, 135, 136, 139, 144, 160, 167, 174, 179, 185

© 2013 Cher Holton: Pages 3, 9, 11, 15, 20, 27, 37, 41, 55, 62, 67, 69, 78, 81, 84, 85, 88, 89, 95, 97, 107, 108, 113, 115, 121, 124, 126, 129, 131, 137, 142, 143, 146, 154, 157, 159, 165, 168, 172, 173, 181, 184,

© 2013 Bil Holton: p. 151 photo; (poster C. Holton)

p. 14 (© alexmaher | stock.xchng
p. 30 (© mgerardi | stock.xchng
p. 34 (© Alexey Stiep | dreamstime.com
p. 37 poster background (© duchesssa | stockxchng)
p. 45 (© stock.xchng)
p. 46 (© filmfoto | dreamstime.com)
p. 63 (© Jeepce | dreamstime.com)
p. 64 (© Ben Earwicker | stock.xchng)
p. 74 (© Hubis | dreamstime.com)
p. 79 (© Lukyslukys | dreamstime.com)
p. 91 (© BCritchley | dreamstime.com)
p. 93 (© Photowitch | dreamstime.com)
p. 100 (© Skypixel | dreamstime.com)
p. 118 (© Yudesign | dreamstime.com)
p. 134 (© Tepic | dreamstime.com)
P. 148 (© Briangoff | dreamstime.com)
P. 161 (© Embe | dreamstime.com)
p. 176 (© Rudall30 | dreamstime.com)
p. 205 (© Gaillyn Photography)
p. 206 (© Paul Hasselbeck)

About the Authors

Revs. Drs. Bil and Cher Holton are ordained Unity ministers, and co-founders of The Holton Consulting Group, Inc. and The Center of Metaphysical Christianity. They work with both corporate and spiritual clients, with a mission of helping people connect to the "Extraordinary You" within ~ in business and in life. Their impressive client list includes Fortune 100 companies, healthcare facilities, universities, associations, government agencies, churches, and spiritual centers. They are prolific authors, publishing over 50 titles, including *The Manager's Short Course to a Long Career*, which was selected by SoundView Executive Summaries as one of their Top 30 Business Books, and *The New Metaphysical Versions of Matthew, Mark, Luke, and John*—the first ever verse-by-verse metaphysical interpretation of the four Gospels.

Rev. Dr. Bil Holton has a solid reputation for his strength of character, engaging personality, and creative yet practical application of neuroscience, Positive Psychology, and neurotheology to his work. His metaphysical teachings and his ability to bring spiritual Truth into such clarity that people are able to walk the spiritual path with practical feet put him in high demand as a teacher and spiritual coach. When he isn't involved in work and research, Bil enjoys golf, travel, jigsaw puzzles, the theatre, and landscaping.

Rev. Dr. Cher Holton claims her name is an acronym for her personal mission: Creating Hope, Enthusiasm, and Results ... and she brings her zest for living and her practical applications of Truth principles to everything she does. Her background includes being a "Preacher's Kid," a Certified Speaking Professional, and a Certified Management Consultant, which make her a much-sought-after facilitator, speaker, and coach. When she isn't involved in work and research, Cher enjoys a good mystery novel, crossword & logic puzzles, the theatre, travel, and design work.

On a personal note, the Holtons like to push the envelope and maintain their zest for life by taking what they call "Indiana Jones Adventures," such as white-water rafting, sky diving, and fire walking. American-style ballroom dancing is also in their DNA. Although they have retired their competitive dance shoes, Bil and Cher love to perform ballroom showcases and exhibitions. Their two sons, beautiful daughters-in-law, and three incredible grandchildren all live nearby. Their visits are always joyful.

***Rev. Dr. Paul Hasselbeck*** currently serves as Dean, Spiritual Education and Enrichment, for Unity Institute at Unity Village, MO. Paul hosts a weekly internet radio program, *Metaphysical Romp*, which airs live on Tuesdays at 2 p.m. Central Time on www.unity.fm. The thought provoking, mind-stretching programs are also available as downloadable podcasts.

Paul holds a Bachelor of Science in Biology from the University of Cincinnati, a Doctorate of Dental Surgery from the Ohio State University, and is an ordained Unity minister through Unity Institute. He was a Navy dentist prior to establishing a successful private practice in San Juan, Puerto Rico, where he learned to be functional in Spanish.

Paul discovered the Unity Movement in Puerto Rico while he was an avid student and facilitator of *A Course in Miracles*. Paul is one of the co-founders of the only English speaking Unity Church in Puerto Rico before he even knew much about the Unity movement. Prior to becoming Dean, Spiritual Education and Enrichment, he served at Unity Church of Overland Park, Kansas, as Minister of Prayer and Pastoral Care and as a Retreat Minister at Unity School of Christianity. Paul figures he has gone from preventing tooth decay to preventing truth decay, and recommends mental floss over dental floss and meditation over medication!

Rev. Dr. Paul Hasselbeck is the author of several books, including *Point of Power: Practical Metaphysics to Help You Transform Your Life and Realize Your Magnificence* (published in English and Spanish); and *Heart-centered Metaphysics: A Deeper Look at Unity Teachings*. He and the Holtons have worked together on several books, including *Get Over It! The Truth About What You Know That Just Ain't So!* (also tralnslated into Spanish)*; Get Over These, Too! More Truths About What You Know That Just Ain't So; PowerUP: The Twelve Powers Revisited as Accelerated Abilities; PowerUP Inspirational Card Set*; and *Applying Heart-Centered Metaphysics*.

Paul has a particular passion for using language in accurate and precise ways, bringing metaphysics fully into the 21st Century. He views language as an intrument of faith and as a spiritual practice. His presentations have taken him around the country, where he is known for his mind-stretching content supported by a variety of unusual props. Participants consistently applaud his ability to make the topics of metaphysics and spirituality practical and understandable.

Born and raised in Cincinnati, Ohio, Paul now resides in Overland Park, Kansas. Paul has been a bit of an eclectic collector over the years, collecting titles (Ensign, Lieutenant, Doctor, Reverend, and Dean); American Art Pottery from the early 1900s (Rookwood, Weller, Roseville, Van Briggle, Weller and Hull); exotic birds (from finches to macaws, at one point Paul had an aviary in his home housing over 100 birds); and dogs (two sweet Yorkshire Terriers now call Paul's home theirs!). In his "spare time," Paul enjoys fitness activities, estate sales, surfing the Internet, and reading.

Other Books by These Authors:

By Rev. Dr. Bil Holton, Rev. Dr. Cher Holton, or co-authored together:

The Gospel of Matthew, New Metaphysical Version
The Gospel of Mark, New Metaphysical Version
The Gospel of Luke, New Metaphysical Version
The Gospel of John, New Metaphysical Version
The Dance Between Science and Spirituality
The Gospels Revisited: Favorite Scriptures with their Metaphysical Interpretations
The Meta New Testament: Volumes I and II
Living at the Speed of Life: Staying in Control in a World Gone Bonkers!
Power Up Your Engagement! Extraordinary Leaders, Extraordinary Employees, Working Togther
The Manager's Short Course to a Long Career
Crackerjack Choices: 200 of the Best Choices You Will Ever Make
From Ballroom to Bottom Line ... in business and in life
Business Prayers for Millennium Managers
SUPPOSE . . . Questions to Turbo-Charge Your Business and Your Life

By Rev. Paul Hasselbeck:

Point of Power: Practical Metaphysics to Help You Transform Your Life and Realize Your Magnificence (published in English and Spanish)
Heart-centered Metaphysics: A Deeper Look at Unity Teachings

Co-authored by Rev. Paul Hasselbeck and Rev. Dr. Bil Holton:

Get Over It! The Truth About What You Know That Just Ain't So!
Get Over These, Too! More Truth About What You Know That Just Ain't So!

Co-authored by Rev. Paul Hasselbeck and Rev. Dr. Cher Holton:

PowerUP: The Twelve Powers Revisited as Accelerated Abilities
Applying Heart-Centered Metaphysics: A Workbook to Bring Metaphysics To Life in Your Life)

The authors also have many digital books available in a variety of formats through Smashwords.com/profile/view/bilholton and through Amazon and B&N

To order books or invite the authors to speak at your organization, spiritual center, or association, contact:

service@TheMetaphysicalWebsite.com or info@holtonconsulting.com

We invite you to visit their cutting-edge website, read their blog, and sign up for their newsletter at:
www.TheMetaphysicalWebsite.com *and* ***www.HoltonConsulting.com***

www.ingramcontent.com/pod-product-compliance
Ingram Content Group UK Ltd.
Pitfield, Milton Keynes, MK11 3LW, UK
UKHW051700240426
12048UKWH00046B/706